Dana's
TOP TEN TABLE

Dana's
TOP TEN TABLE

200
fresh takes
on
family-favorite
meals

DANA McCAULEY

HarperCollins*Publishers*Ltd

Dana's Top Ten Table
Text and photography © 2007 by Dana McCauley.
All rights reserved.

Published by HarperCollins Publishers Ltd

First Edition

HarperCollins books may be purchased for
educational, business, or sales promotional use
through our Special Markets Department.

HarperCollins Publishers Ltd
2 Bloor Street East, 20th Floor
Toronto, Ontario, Canada
M4W 1A8

www.harpercollins.ca

Library and Archives Canada Cataloguing in Publication

McCauley, Dana
Dana's top ten table : 200 fresh takes on family-
favorite meals / Dana McCauley.

ISBN-13: 978-0-00-200767-2
ISBN-10: 0-00-200767-3

1. Cookery. I. Title.

TX714.M29 2007   641.5   C2007-902803-9

HC 9 8 7 6 5 4 3 2 1

Printed and bound in the United States

Set in Helvetica
Design by Sharon Kish

Dedicated to the memories of two good cooks,
my grandmothers Vilda McCauley and Mary Badiuk.
Thanks for sharing your recipes and allowing me to lick the spoons!

ACKNOWLEDGMENTS

The efforts and talents of many people were needed to take these recipes from their origins as dirty dishes in my kitchen sink to the printed page. In particular I'm grateful to Kirsten Hanson, Noelle Zitzer, Gail Copeland, Tanya Trafford and Sharon Kish. Amy Snider, Sabrina Falone, Tracey Syvret, Charmaine Broughton, Martin Kouprie and Oliver Kouprie also helped *Dana's Top Ten Table* become a reality.

Contents

Introductory Notes

THE COMFORTS OF HOME

Our lifestyles have changed significantly in the last 50 years. While today most mothers work outside of the home and families spend as much time together in the car as they do around the dinner table, our culture still equates home with comfort and family. Evidence of this can be found all around us. From the expansive granite and stainless steel kitchens that are the centerpieces of designer homes, to the fact that although we spend more money at restaurants than ever before, many of the meals we purchase are delivered or taken home to be eaten in familiar surroundings. A recent study of Canadian eating behavior revealed that on average people are eating dinner at home 245 times per year. American figures reveal a similar pattern. Does this mean that North Americans are preparing home-cooked meals each night? No, it's just that more often than not, we'd rather eat at home.

Unfortunately, even on the days when we want to make a meal from scratch, many of us increasingly find that we don't have the cooking skills necessary to make a basic dinner with confidence. And so, when we try to recreate restaurant foods we've enjoyed at home and abroad, we discover that our ambitions are bigger than our culinary talents!

One reason that so many people lack basic cooking skills is that for the last two and half generations the rising number of working mothers has meant that many women don't have the time to teach their children how to cook (and let's face it, it's usually the woman of the house who does most of the cooking, even today). It shouldn't come as a surprise then to learn that 94 percent of children aged 10 to 17 can access the Internet but only 42 percent can cook a spaghetti dinner. This state of affairs isn't helped any by the removal of home economics programs from many school systems. When you add it all together, it's no wonder we're quickly becoming a society of people who are lost, and sometimes even nervous, in the kitchen.

The encouraging news is that many people still want to cook. Of the group of computer-savvy, kitchen-challenged kids mentioned above, 64 percent said they'd like to help more with cooking at home. Likewise, the proliferation of cooking schools, food-oriented websites and cookery shows on TV indicates that a desire to prepare tasty, home-cooked meals still abounds.

THE TRUTH ABOUT FOOD TRENDS

As a food trend expert it's my job to suss out the latest new flavors and analyze changes in eating patterns. While doing my research I'm often surprised not by how much things change in the food world, but by how much they stay the same. Although flavors and cuisines come and go, and panini makers, fondue pots and other appliances may alter our cooking habits for a short time, consumer research repeatedly reveals that people want dinnertime solutions that deliver inspiration for new and better ways to prepare their favorite foods. In fact, there are basically ten main meals that we make in various ways over and over. Although the percentages of what is more or less preferred change slightly each year, the top 10 foods North Americans say they eat regularly have remained the same since at least the early eighties. In alphabetical order our favorite entrées continue to be:

- burgers
- casseroles and one-dish meals
- chicken
- fish and seafood
- pasta
- pizza
- pork
- sandwiches
- soup
- steak

This insight about the top 10 favorite foods people eat most often provides the framework for *Dana's Top Ten Table.* Each chapter contains 20 recipes for the foods we love. Some are classic versions of foods that never go out of style such as macaroni and cheese, while others are adaptations of exciting restaurant flavor trends such as chimichurri steak that are written especially for home cooks who want to try something new.

This collection of recipes reflects the trends that are currently influencing restaurant menus, packaged product development and food writers. As a result, although this book delivers your food favorites, the recipes are stylish and "now." When the classics are presented, I've strived to make them the ultimate version of the original. And, in many cases, I've found faster, easier, and healthier ways to prepare them than before. The result is a collection of 200 recipes that are sure to please many palates.

Because our lives are so busy, cooking dinner often loses out to restaurant meals or a prepared frozen entrée. To help you budget your time, each recipe includes approximate preparation and cooking times so that you can choose recipes to fit your schedule. Many of the recipes also include tips for making and storing prepared food so that you can create your own homemade frozen entrées.

Finally, realizing that cooking can be intimidating for people with little experience, each recipe has been written with an eye for detail. Directions include not only what to do but how to do it and have been carefully tested by professional recipe testers. As a result, you should easily be able to match closely the samples we created in our test kitchen, regardless of your level of cooking experience.

MEAL PLANNING

Ask anyone what they had for dinner last night and more often than not the main course will be the food they mention. *Dana's Top Ten Table* contains recipes for entrées only since these are the cornerstones of the meal (and usually the first thing that comes to mind when many people think about what to make for dinner). I do offer a few side dish suggestions here and there to help you along, however, some of the most popular and best side dishes are so simple they don't require recipes: steamed green beans; lightly buttered, boiled new potatoes; steamed, fluffy long-grain rice.

HOW TO USE THIS BOOK

Although I'd be very pleased to come to your house and find the pages of this book splattered and torn at the edges from nightly use, I'd truly be gratified if the margins were crowded with your handwritten additions and changes. I hope that you'll view *Dana's Top Ten Table* as a resource designed to give you good, dependable recipes but also as a book of inspiring ideas that you can use as a launch pad for your own creativity. Feel free to customize these wonderful recipes and make them your family's very own!

A FEW LAST (IMPORTANT) WORDS BEFORE YOU BEGIN COOKING

Like other cookery writers, I always work using a set of assumptions about the ingredients and equipment that are to be used to prepare my recipes. Please take a moment to read the following list of guidelines before you prepare any of the delicious recipes from this book. Familiarizing yourself with these basic rules will ensure that the time you spend in the kitchen produces great results! That said, don't be afraid if you do have to make substitutions for any of the items listed. The results will still be good. I want you to enjoy cooking. My guidelines are meant to take the guesswork out of cooking and save you time and frustration so that you can prepare healthy and nutritious home-cooked meals for your family with confidence.

- Eggs are large.
- Milk is 2% unless otherwise stated.
- Butter is salted.
- Garlic is freshly minced.
- Vegetables and fruits are medium size unless otherwise stated.
- Meat and fish are trimmed of any visible fat or gristle.
- Cheese and other dairy products are full fat unless otherwise specified.
- Pepper is black and it is freshly and finely ground unless otherwise specified.
- All equipment used to prepare these recipes is household quality and strength. (If you have a commercial-quality stove, for instance, your stovetop cooking heat may need to be lowered slightly.)
- Citrus juices are freshly squeezed.
- Salt is table salt and iodized, unless otherwise specified.

- Ginger: Although I personally prefer to cook with freshly minced gingerroot, statistics prove that many people buy and use the bottled variety. Therefore, we used bottled minced ginger when testing these recipes to ensure that they would taste great in most people's homes. Bottled minced ginger loses its potency fairly quickly so if you don't finish a bottle within three weeks after opening it, you should replace it.
- All fresh produce such as lettuce, tomatoes, fruits, herbs, etc., are washed before use.

COOKING MEAT: SAFETY TIPS

To check the internal temperature of meat to ensure it is cooked thoroughly, use an instant-read thermometer. This thermometer is probably one of the most useful kitchen gadgets you can own since it takes the guesswork out of knowing if meat is sufficiently cooked. To use an instant-read thermometer correctly, place the probe into the meat, being sure not to make contact with bone or gristle. For thin pieces of meat such as burgers and fast-fry steaks and chops, insert the thermometer through the side of the meat so that you can assess the internal temperature accurately. The chart below indicates the recommended internal temperatures for cooking meat safely.

MEAT TEMPERATURE CHART

Food	Temperature
Fully cooked and ready-to-eat meats (e.g., ham, roast)	You can eat it cold or you can heat it.
Beef and veal steaks and roasts	63°C (145°F) medium-rare 71°C (160°F) medium 77°C (170°F) well done
Pork chops, ribs, roasts; ground beef, ground pork and ground veal, including burgers and sausages made with ground beef/pork/veal	71°C (160°F)
Stuffing and casseroles, hotdogs, leftovers, egg dishes; ground chicken and ground turkey, including burgers and sausages made with ground chicken/turkey	74°C (165°F)
Chicken and turkey breasts, legs, thighs and wings	74°C (165°F)
Chicken and turkey, whole bird	85°C (185°F)

Source: http://www.inspection.gc.ca/english/fssa/concen/tipcon/thermoe.shtml

In addition to ensuring that meat is properly cooked, it's important never to reuse dishes or utensils that have come in contact with raw meat without first washing them. Also, if you want to use leftover marinade or basting sauce on the finished dish, it must first be boiled for 1 minute.

And just one more thing about food safety: Always be sure to wash your hands thoroughly before starting to cook and after handling raw meat.

Burgers

American business icon Paul Getty famously claimed to be "an inveterate aficionado of such prosaic American foods as flapjacks and hamburgers." Apparently, Getty's fondness for good burgers is not uncommon. Foodservice industry statistics indicate that Americans eat more than five *billion* restaurant-made burgers each year. And they are such a favorite food that they continue to be a top 10 choice for home-cooked dinners, too. Grilled in abundance during the warm summer months and pan-fried or broiled frequently the rest of the year, the widespread appeal of burgers has elevated these humble patties from a mere food item to a cultural symbol.

There seem to be as many stories about how hamburgers originated as there are ways to prepare and garnish these succulent, ground-meat patties. The burger recipes in this chapter run the gamut from all-beef basic burgers such as Sirloin Burgers that will suit purists, to Gourmet Brie Burgers that take this tried-and-true food to new culinary heights. There are also several burgers in this collection that are inspired by other favorite foods. Turkey Parmigiana Burgers blend the convenience and appeal of hamburgers with the taste experience of an Italian comfort food classic to create a burger experience that is sure to be a winner on pasta night.

A note about cooking instructions for burgers

The cooking instructions for the recipes in this chapter are given for grilling on an indoor or outdoor grill. All of these burger recipes also can be cooked easily in the oven under the broiler. Position the upper oven rack in the top third of the oven and preheat the broiler. Place the burgers on the broiler pan (this pan can be purchased separately if you don't have the one that came with your oven). Cook the patties under the broiler for 10 minutes per side or until cooked through—the internal temperature on an instant-read thermometer should register 160°F (71°C). Follow any other instructions in the recipe for adding ingredients such as cheese or basting with sauce during cooking.

Likewise, all of these burger recipes can be prepared in a skillet set over medium-high heat. Cook the patties uncovered and turn them often, for 15 to 20 minutes or until cooked through—the internal temperature on an instant-read thermometer should register 160°F (71°C).

Many restaurant menus feature "100% beef" burgers yet most homemade burger recipes are filled with all kinds of ingredients that are included to either enhance flavor or improve texture. There are several reasons recipe writers add so many ingredients to their burger recipes. One is that a whole chapter full of burgers made with only meat, salt and pepper would make for a pretty small chapter. However, another more valid reason is that consumers routinely choose to buy lean and extra lean ground beef. These varieties of ground meat contain as much as 95 percent lean meat. Although better for our health, neither of these grades of beef makes a particularly good burger. It's the fat content in ground meat that contributes both juiciness and flavor, so when the meat used is low in fat, other ingredients need to be added to mimic these lost qualities.

For these reasons, my meaty Sirloin Burger recipe uses regular or medium ground beef, which contains about 80 percent lean meat. To make the burger delicious and crunchy on the outside and juicy and tender on the inside, this recipe also includes additional fat in the form of butter. The result: burgers so succulent and flavorful that each bite makes you want to take another!

Sirloin Burgers (Basic Beef Burgers)

PREP: 10 minutes | **COOK:** 12 minutes | **YIELD:** 6 burgers

2 lb (1 kg) regular (or medium) ground beef
½ tsp (2 mL) each salt and pepper
2 tbsp (30 mL) melted butter
1 clove garlic, minced

Crumble the beef into a large bowl. Sprinkle the salt and pepper evenly over the meat. Toss gently to combine.

Handling the meat as little as possible, use damp hands to shape it into 6 equal-size thick patties. Be careful not to compress the meat more than necessary. Preheat the grill to high.

Stir the butter with the garlic and brush evenly over the raw patties. Place the patties on the grate. Reduce the heat to medium-high. Grill the burgers, turning once or twice, for 6 minutes per side or until cooked all the way through. Test for doneness by inserting an instant-read thermometer through the side of each burger. The temperature should be 160°F (71°C).

A *lunch counter* and diner standard for decades, burgers topped with sautéed mushrooms and Swiss cheese always seem like a more satisfying meal to me than plain burgers with ketchup, mustard and the other typical burger toppings. For this particular recipe I find that lean ground beef is ideal since the juicy, buttery-flavored mushroom and onion topping makes up for the slightly drier patty.

Mushroom Swiss Burgers

PREP: 10 minutes | **COOK:** 30 minutes | **YIELD:** 4 burgers

TOPPING:
    4 tsp (20 mL) butter
    ½ onion, peeled and thinly sliced
    4 cups (1 L) sliced button mushrooms
    ¼ tsp (1 mL) each salt and pepper
BURGERS:
    ½ onion, peeled and finely grated
    1 tbsp (15 mL) Dijon mustard
    ½ tsp (2 mL) salt
    ¼ tsp (1 mL) pepper
    1 clove garlic, minced
    1 egg, beaten
    ¼ cup (50 mL) fresh regular or whole wheat bread crumbs
    1 lb (500 g) lean ground beef
    1 tbsp (15 mL) vegetable oil (approx)
    4 slices Swiss cheese
    4 hamburger buns (optional)

TOPPING: Melt the butter in a skillet set over medium heat. Add the onion and cook, stirring often, for 5 minutes. Increase the heat to medium-high and stir in the mushrooms, salt and pepper. Cook, stirring occasionally, for 5 minutes or until mushrooms are browned all over. Transfer the mushroom mixture to a bowl and keep warm.

BURGERS: Combine the onion, mustard, salt, pepper, garlic and egg. Stir until well combined. Stir in the bread crumbs. Crumble in the ground beef and toss gently until evenly combined. Shape into 4 equal-size patties.

Return the skillet to the stovetop and set over medium heat. Add enough of the oil to prevent the patties from sticking. Add the patties. Cook, turning once or twice, for 15 to 20 minutes or until cooked through. Test for doneness using an instant-read thermometer if unsure. The internal temperature should be 160°F (71°C). Top each patty with a slice of cheese, and cover the pan for 45 seconds. To serve the burgers as an entrée, place each one on a plate and top with some of the warm mushrooms and onions. To serve as a sandwich, place patties on buns and top each one with an equal amount of the mushroom mixture.

This super-size burger is fun to make for kids' parties or for when the family gathers for a casual backyard supper. Although the creamy Caesar, tomato and onion topping is almost always a hit with kids, it might not be to everyone's liking. You can leave it off and serve separately along with a selection of other toppings and condiments so that everyone can customize their portion of the burger.

Although transferring the patty to and from the grate can be tricky to master at first, there is a foolproof way you can ensure it stays together. Shape the patty on piece of perforated, nonstick grill foil or greased heavy-duty foil that has been pierced all over to allow drainage. Then, slide the raw meat mixture—still on the foil—onto the grate and cook until the bottom of the patty is set and firm enough to turn as directed.

Shallow-rimmed pizza pans or rimless baking sheets work best for moving the patty to and from the grate.

Grande Family Burger

PREP: 10 minutes | **COOK:** 20 minutes | **YIELD:** 6 to 8 servings

3 eggs, beaten
1 cup (250 mL) fresh bread crumbs
¼ cup (50 mL) each grated onion and ketchup or barbecue sauce
1 tbsp (15 mL) Dijon mustard
1 clove garlic, minced
1 tsp (5 mL) dried thyme leaves
½ tsp (2 mL) each salt and pepper
2 lb (1 kg) lean ground beef
1 round 10-inch (25 cm) Calabrese or sourdough loaf
¼ cup (50 mL) creamy Caesar-style salad dressing
1 each tomato and small red onion, thinly sliced

Preheat the grill to medium. Stir the eggs with the bread crumbs, onion, ketchup, mustard, garlic, thyme, salt and pepper. Crumble in the beef; mix gently but well. Turn the meat mixture out onto a baking sheet; form into one 9-inch (23 cm) patty.

Grease the grate well. Slide the patty onto the grate, using a long, flexible metal spatula to assist the transfer from tray to grate. Cover and grill for 12 minutes. Slide the patty onto a baking sheet, turn it over carefully, and slide it back onto the grate. Cook for 5 to 8 minutes longer or until an instant-read thermometer registers 160°F (71°C) when inserted into the center of the patty. Slide cooked patty off the grate onto a clean baking sheet.

Cut the Calabrese loaf into three layers so that there is a bottom, a middle and a top; reserve the middle layer for another use (such as fresh bread crumbs or homemade croutons). Place the patty on the bottom slice of bread. Spread with salad dressing and top with the sliced tomato and onion. Top with remaining bread. Cut into wedges and serve.

Adding the savory flavors of chili con carne to ground beef patties and serving them on a halved, toasted bun makes for a tasty combination of two longtime family favorites. These patties are also good used as a topper for an iceberg lettuce and tomato salad when a lighter meal is what you're craving. If you've never cooked with salsa before, be sure you choose a mild variety (you can always add more spice at the table!).

Chili and Bean Burgers

PREP: 10 minutes | **COOK:** 30 minutes | **YIELD:** 6 burgers

2 slices whole wheat or other bread, torn
¼ cup (50 mL) chopped green onion
1 egg
2 tsp (10 mL) each chili powder and dried oregano leaves
½ tsp (2 mL) each salt and pepper
1 can (19 oz/540 mL) kidney beans, drained and rinsed
1 lb (500 g) ground beef
¼ cup (50 mL) corn kernels, fresh or frozen
⅓ cup (75 mL) salsa
8 hamburger buns
Sour cream (optional)
Shredded Cheddar cheese (optional)

Preheat the oven to 350°F (180°C). Pulse the bread in a food processor just until crumbly. Add the green onion, egg, chili powder, oregano, salt and pepper. Pulse the motor until the ingredients are combined. Add the beans and pulse until well combined but still chunky. Transfer the mixture to a bowl. Crumble in the beef and sprinkle in the corn; using your hands, gently blend the meat and corn with the bean mixture.

Form the mixture into 6 patties. Set the patties on a foil-lined baking sheet. Bake for 25 to 30 minutes, or until cooked through. Top with salsa. Serve on toasted rolls with sour cream and cheese (if using).

You're sure to receive applause from your dinner party guests when you serve these super-thick patties filled with delectable melted cheese! Superbly decadent and wonderfully impressive looking, these glossy burgers are in the same league as filet mignon—but much less expensive.

Brie is a soft, mild cheese with a downy, edible rind. When it heats up as the burgers cook, it becomes runny and saucy . . . mmmm! These burgers are as exciting to look at as they are to eat.

SEE PHOTO INSERT

Gourmet Brie Burgers

PREP: 15 minutes | **COOK:** 20 to 25 minutes | **YIELD:** 6 burgers

1 egg, beaten
2 tbsp (30 mL) ketchup
1 tbsp (15 mL) honey
2 tsp (10 mL) dried thyme leaves
1 clove garlic, minced
¾ tsp (4 mL) each salt and pepper
½ cup (125 mL) butter, melted
2 lb (1 kg) ground sirloin
¼ lb (125 g) cold Brie or Camembert cheese, cut into 6 equal-size cubes
½ cup (125 mL) barbecue sauce

Preheat the grill to medium-high. Whisk the egg with the ketchup, honey, thyme, garlic, salt and pepper. Whisk in the butter until completely combined. Crumble the meat into a large bowl using your fingers. Pour in the egg mixture and gently blend into meat until just combined.

Line a baking sheet with perforated, nonstick grill foil or greased heavy-duty foil that has been pierced all over to allow drainage. Divide the meat mixture into 12 portions. Gently pat one portion of meat into a 1 cup (250 mL) dry measuring cup. Add a piece of the cheese and another portion of meat. Pat firmly to compress the mixture so that the cup is filled to about ¾ full, making a very thick patty with the cheese sealed inside. Run a knife around the edge of the measuring cup and turn each patty out onto the foil-lined tray. Repeat with remaining meat and cheese.

Transfer the burger-topped baking sheet to the grill. Slide the foil together with the burgers onto the grate. Cook the burgers for 6 minutes. Turn and reduce the heat to medium. Cook, turning at least once more and basting often with barbecue sauce, for about 15 minutes longer or until an instant-read thermometer inserted into the center of each patty registers 170°F (85°C). Serve patties on buns with traditional burger condiments or with a vegetable side dish such as roasted potatoes or baked sweet potatoes.

Variation

BACON-WRAPPED BRIE BURGERS: Wrap 2 slices of bacon around the circumference of each raw patty. Tie a piece of butcher's twine around each patty until snug but not tight. Proceed as directed above.

Chipotle peppers, a smoked version of the popular green jalapeños, seem to be all over restaurant menus and grocery store shelves these days. From barbecued ribs to submarine sandwiches and salad dressings, the trendy chipotle pepper is among the most popular flavors launched recently.

The canned version of these peppers is super convenient to use at home since each can is not too big (about 7 oz/ 215 g) and the leftover peppers can be stored in the refrigerator in a tightly covered container for several weeks. If canned chipotles prove difficult to find, substitute chipotle-flavored hot pepper sauce; add it ¼ tsp (1 mL) at a time to the barbecue sauce until the desired heat and smoky intensity is achieved.

Santa Fe Cheeseburgers

PREP: 15 minutes | **COOK:** 20 minutes | **YIELD:** 4 burgers

GLAZE:
  ¼ cup (50 mL) barbecue sauce
  1 chipotle pepper in adobo sauce, minced

BURGERS:
  3 tbsp (45 mL) steak or barbecue sauce
  1 tbsp (15 mL) Dijon mustard
  2 tsp (10 mL) hot pepper sauce
  1 egg, beaten
  ¼ cup (50 mL) dry bread crumbs
  1 tbsp (15 mL) chopped fresh parsley
  1 clove garlic, minced
  1 lb (500 g) medium or lean ground beef
  6 Cheddar cheese slices
  4 toasted kaiser rolls
  ¼ cup (50 mL) mayonnaise
  Pickles, lettuce, tomatoes and other traditional burger condiments

GLAZE: Stir the barbecue sauce with the chipotle pepper. Reserve.

BURGERS: Preheat the grill to medium-high. Stir the steak or barbecue sauce with the mustard, hot pepper sauce, egg, bread crumbs, parsley and garlic. Crumble in the ground beef and gently combine. Halve 2 cheese slices, then fold in half again to make 4 small squares. Gently shape one-quarter of the beef mixture around each cheese square to make the patties.

Grease the grate and add the patties. Cook the burgers for 10 minutes. Turn the burgers over and brush the tops with the reserved glaze. Grill for 10 minutes more or until cooked through. Top with remaining 4 cheese slices; cover and grill for 30 seconds.

Spread the mayonnaise over the toasted rolls. Top with patties, pickles, lettuce, tomatoes and any other traditional burger condiments you enjoy.

In the late 1890s diner-style restaurants operating in retired railway cars began to open in cities such as New York, Boston and Philadelphia. Hamburgers, which by some accounts were first served a few years earlier at the Outagamie County Fair in Wisconsin, and grilled cheese sandwiches were a part of the diner menu from day one. Although references to the origins of patty melts are difficult to find, it's easy to imagine how one day a customer who couldn't decide whether to order the burger or the grilled cheese and was asked if he might not like a slice of cheese atop his burger to solve his dilemma.

Kids will love the novelty of patty melts as a fast supper while older eaters will enjoy taking their taste buds on a trip down memory lane. For a total diner experience, serve these toasty sandwiches with coleslaw and finish the meal with a slice of pie and a cup of coffee!

Prepare this recipe in an electric sandwich maker for an even crispier exterior.

Diner-style Patty Melts

PREP: 10 minutes | **COOK:** 20 to 25 minutes | **YIELD:** 4 burgers

2 tsp (10 mL) vegetable oil
4 frozen packaged hamburger patties
1 onion, peeled and thinly sliced
½ tsp (2 mL) each salt and pepper
½ tsp (2 mL) dried thyme leaves
3 tbsp (45 mL) ketchup
½ tsp (2 mL) Worcestershire sauce
1 small clove garlic, minced
8 slices sourdough or rye bread
4 slices processed or Cheddar cheese
2 tbsp (30 mL) butter

Heat the oil in a large, nonstick skillet set over medium-high heat. Add the frozen patties, leaving an open space in the middle. Arrange the onion, salt, pepper and thyme in the open area in the center of the pan. Cover the pan and cook, stirring the onions often and turning the patties as needed, for 10 to 15 minutes or until the meat is cooked through and the onions are very soft. Remove the patties from the pan and place on a paper towel-lined plate. Stir the ketchup, Worcestershire and garlic into the pan and cook the onions for 2 minutes longer. Remove the onion mixture from the pan and reserve.

Wipe the pan out with a paper towel. Place each patty on a piece of bread. Top with an equal amount of the onion mixture and a slice of cheese. Top with remaining bread slices and butter the outside of each sandwich evenly.

Set the skillet over medium heat. Cook the patty melts in batches for 1 to 2 minutes per side or until the cheese is melted and the bread is golden.

This burger recipe offers an easy way to make an interesting and tasty ground beef entrée that also has broad family appeal. With an allure similar to meatballs but the ease of preparation that makes burgers a winner for weeknight suppers, these cheese-topped patties are a quick meal served with spaghetti tossed in tomato sauce and a simple side dish of sautéed green peppers. Or serve them on Italian-style buns with extra tomato sauce, like a meatball sandwich.

Italian Cheeseburgers

PREP: 10 minutes | **COOK:** 12 minutes | **YIELD:** 6 burgers

2 eggs
¼ cup (50 mL) pizza sauce or ketchup
1 cup (250 mL) fresh bread crumbs
1 cup (250 mL) grated Parmesan cheese
1 tbsp (15 mL) chopped fresh oregano (or 1 tsp/5 mL dried oregano leaves)
1 tbsp (15 mL) yellow mustard
½ tsp (2 mL) each salt and pepper
1 lb (500 g) lean ground beef
3 slices mozzarella cheese, about 3 oz (90 g), halved

Beat the eggs. Stir the eggs with the pizza sauce, bread crumbs, Parmesan cheese, oregano, mustard, salt and pepper. Crumble in the beef and mix well. Shape the beef mixture into 6 patties, each about ¾ inches (2 cm) thick.

Preheat the barbecue to medium-high. Lightly grease the grate and place burgers on the grill. Reduce the heat to medium and cook burgers, covered, for 5 minutes. Turn and cook for 5 minutes longer. Top each burger with mozzarella cheese and cook for 1 to 2 minutes longer or until burgers are no longer pink in the center and cheese is melted.

Veal, turkey or chicken parmigiana cutlets are a classic Italian restaurant entrée in North America. Making classic parmigiana cutlets at home first requires time-consuming pounding and breading of the meat. Because the cutlets are small, you need to make a large batch to feed an entire family. Making a big batch requires using lots of cooking oil, which not only makes the cutlets messy to prepare but is quite high in calories, too.

I love the classic version, and I often treat myself to the take-out veal parmigiana dinner from my local Italian restaurant when I've had a hard day and need some comfort food. On other nights when I'm craving the same flavors and I feel like cooking, I make these burgers, which deliver similar flavors but are a little leaner and faster to prepare than breaded cutlets.

If your nonstick skillet has a plastic handle, wrap it in foil to protect it from the heat of the oven.

Turkey Parmigiana Burgers

PREP: 10 minutes | **COOK:** 20 minutes | **YIELD:** 6 burgers

⅓ cup (75 mL) tomato sauce
¼ cup (50 mL) ketchup
¾ cup (175 mL) grated Parmesan cheese
1 tbsp (15 mL) tomato paste
1½ tsp (7 mL) each dried basil and oregano leaves
1 small onion, peeled and coarsely grated
3 cloves garlic, minced
½ tsp (2 mL) salt
¼ tsp (1 mL) pepper
1 egg, beaten
½ cup (125 mL) fresh bread crumbs
1½ lb (750 g) lean ground turkey or chicken
1 tbsp (15 mL) vegetable oil
3 slices mozzarella cheese
6 Calabrese rolls (optional)

Stir the tomato sauce with the ketchup, Parmesan cheese, tomato paste, basil and oregano. Divide the tomato sauce mixture in half. Place half of the mixture in a microwaveable bowl or measuring cup; microwave at High for 30 to 90 seconds until boiling. Reserve.

Combine the remaining half of tomato sauce mixture with the onion, garlic, salt, pepper and egg. Stir in the bread crumbs. Crumble the meat into the same bowl and toss gently until evenly combined. Preheat the oven to 350°F (180°C).

Shape equal amounts of the meat mixture into 6 patties. Heat the oil in an ovenproof, nonstick skillet set over medium-high heat. Brown the patties for 2 minutes on each side. Transfer to a baking sheet.

Spoon the reserved cooked sauce mixture evenly over each patty and place the baking sheet in the oven. Bake for 15 minutes or until cooked through. Cut each piece of mozzarella cheese on a diagonal to make two triangles. Top each burger with a triangle of cheese. Serve on rolls (if using).

As an experienced food trend tracker, I can tell you that many ingredient and flavor trends trickle down from fine dining restaurant menus to the consumer level. One of the foods positioned to become mainstream is the bison burger. Over the last two years bison and buffalo burgers turned up on numerous menu audits and began appearing on cooking shows and as newly launched private label products at upscale grocers. What's the attraction? Besides being delicious and lean, bison is a meat unique to North America, which makes it a stellar ingredient choice for chefs who want to cook using regional foods.

Moreover, in flavor bison is quite similar to beef. As a result, bison is a good alternative choice for chefs and consumers who are concerned about health scares that have plagued the beef industry in recent years. With bison, they can still enjoy much of the flavor and experience of eating a beef burger.

To highlight its wild roots, try serving these burgers on toasted buns with sautéed wild mushrooms and onions. Or, if cheese is a must on your burger, try topping these patties with thinly sliced Oka cheese. As it melts, this cheese will become a scrumptious, creamy, mild topping. Or top the burgers with apple rings that have been brushed with maple syrup and grilled until golden and you'll have a mouth-watering gourmet burger that will wow your friends!

SEE PHOTO INSERT

Butter-basted Bison Burgers

PREP: 10 minutes | **COOK:** 10 minutes | **YIELD:** 4 burgers

BASTING BUTTER:
⅓ cup (75 mL) melted butter
1 large clove garlic, minced
1 tsp (5 mL) chopped fresh thyme
½ tsp (2 mL) salt
¾ tsp (4 mL) pepper

BURGERS:
1 egg, beaten
1 lb (500 g) medium ground bison or buffalo
½ cup (125 mL) fresh bread crumbs

BASTING BUTTER: Combine the butter, garlic, thyme, salt and pepper. Reserve. Preheat the grill to medium-high.

BURGERS: Beat the egg in a large bowl. Crumble in the meat and sprinkle the bread crumbs evenly over top. Drizzle 2 tbsp (30 mL) of the basting butter into the meat mixture and gently combine the ingredients. Using damp hands, divide the meat mixture into 4 equal portions. Gently compress each portion into a square patty of even thickness.

Divide the remaining basting butter in half. Brush the patties on one side with some of the butter. Place the patties on the grate, brushed side down. Reduce the heat to medium immediately and brush the other side of each patty with more basting mixture. Cook the patties, turning once, for 5 minutes per side or until cooked through. Brush with remaining basting butter as the patties come off the grill. Serve on toasted buns with your choice of toppings.

GOURMET BRIE BURGERS

page 7

BUTTER-BASTED BISON BURGERS
page 12

GRILLED SWEET MUSTARD SALMON BURGERS
page 19

TERIYAKI BEEF SHORT RIBS WITH RAINBOW PEPPERS
page 32

ZESTY HERBED TOMATO LASAGNA
page 34

CLAM-STUFFED BAKED POTATOES
page 39

OVEN-FRIED CHICKEN WITH BUTTERMILK GRAVY

page 48

CLUBHOUSE GRILLED CHICKEN SALAD
page 55

A study in contrasts, these burgers are a great dinner option when you feel like eating something a little out of the ordinary but don't want to spend time experimenting with something completely new.

I like to use the pre-peeled and cored golden pineapples sold in the produce section since they are not only easy to work with but also have a terrific flavor when grilled. There are many different brands of maple-flavored barbecue sauce available. If your local grocery store doesn't carry one, just add a tablespoon or two of pure maple syrup to any basic barbecue sauce.

Sweet and Spicy Maple Chicken Burgers

PREP: 10 minutes | **COOK:** 20 minutes | **YIELD:** 6 burgers

½ cup (125 mL) maple-flavored barbecue sauce
1 tbsp (15 mL) hot pepper sauce
¼ cup (50 mL) chopped green onion
½ cup (125 mL) dry bread crumbs
1 tbsp (15 mL) Dijon mustard
1 clove garlic, minced
1 egg, beaten
½ tsp (2 mL) each salt and pepper
1 lb (500 g) ground chicken or pork
6 thin pineapple rings
6 slices mozzarella cheese
6 toasted sesame rolls
Sliced red onion and lettuce leaves

Stir the barbecue sauce with the hot pepper sauce. Divide in half. Set aside one half and stir the other half of the sauce mixture with the green onion, bread crumbs, mustard, garlic, egg, salt and pepper. Add the ground chicken and mix gently, until well combined. Shape into 6 patties, each about ¾ inch (2 cm) thick. Chill patties for 30 minutes. Brush the pineapple rings with some of the reserved sauce.

Preheat the grill to medium-high and line the grate with perforated, nonstick grill foil. Add the patties to the grate and reduce the heat to medium. Cook for 6 minutes. Turn patties and brush with reserved sauce mixture. Cook the patties for 6 to 8 minutes more or until the internal temperature registers 165°F (74°C) on an instant-read thermometer. Top each patty with a slice of cheese and remove from the grate. Meanwhile, grill the pineapple rings for 2 to 3 minutes per side or until well marked. Serve the patties on toasted rolls garnished with grilled pineapple rings, red onion and lettuce.

Saucy, smoky and cheesy, these wonderfully satisfying juicy burgers have a robust taste that just doesn't quit. Using ground chicken instead of ground beef helps to temper some of the richness of the cheese and bacon so that the burgers aren't too filling.

One of my pet peeves with ground chicken is that some processors virtually purée the meat so that they can incorporate more of the sinew and connective tissue. This is basically like adding filler, and it makes the meat difficult to shape into uniform patties. So, when buying ground chicken choose meat that is *minced.* The color of the mince should be mostly pink with just a few little white flecks (the flecks will be made up of fat, sinew and soft bits of cartilage). If quality ground chicken isn't available, make this recipe with ground turkey instead.

Coleslaw-topped Chicken Burgers

PREP: 15 minutes | **COOK:** 22 minutes | **YIELD:** 8 burgers

¾ cup (175 mL) mesquite or other smoky flavored barbecue sauce
1 small onion, peeled and grated
1 clove garlic, minced
1 egg, beaten
¼ tsp (1 mL) each salt and pepper
½ cup (125 mL) fresh bread crumbs
2 lb (1 kg) ground chicken
16 slices crisp, cooked bacon
8 slices Cheddar or Swiss cheese
8 kaiser rolls or other crusty, round rolls
2 cups (500 mL) deli-made coleslaw

Preheat the grill to medium-high. Stir ⅓ cup (75 mL) of the barbecue sauce with the onion, garlic, egg, salt and pepper. Add the bread crumbs and the chicken. Gently toss until the ingredients are well combined. Divide the meat equally and shape into 8 burgers.

Grill the burgers, turning and basting as needed with remaining barbecue sauce, for 18 to 20 minutes or until cooked through. Top each burger with 2 slices of bacon and 1 slice of cheese; close the grill lid for 15 seconds. Transfer cheese-and-bacon-topped patties to the buns. Garnish with coleslaw.

With a fresh, bright flavor that is reminiscent of the much-loved fillings used for making Asian pot sticker-style dumplings, these patties are likely to become a family favorite.

I like to serve these patties as an entrée with fried or steamed rice and broccoli spears. They also can be served on a bun with wasabi mayonnaise, tomato and lettuce if you're in the mood for an upscale, internationally inspired burger.

If serving these patties on a bun, garnish with wasabi mayonnaise. To make wasabi mayonnaise, blend ½ cup (125 mL) of mayonnaise (light or regular) with ½ tsp (2 mL) of wasabi paste. Taste and add a little more of either the mayonnaise or wasabi paste as desired.

Ginger Scallion Patties

PREP: 10 minutes | **COOK:** 15 to 20 minutes | **YIELD:** 4 patties

½ cup (125 mL) finely chopped scallions or green onion
3 tbsp (45 mL) soy sauce
1 tbsp (15 mL) minced fresh ginger
1 clove garlic, minced
¼ tsp (1 mL) each salt and pepper
1 egg, beaten
½ cup (125 mL) fresh bread crumbs
1 lb (500 g) lean ground pork or beef
2 tbsp (30 mL) vegetable oil

Combine the onion, soy sauce, ginger, garlic, salt, pepper and egg. Stir until well combined. Stir in the bread crumbs. Crumble in the ground meat and toss gently until evenly combined. Shape the meat mixture into 4 equal-size patties, each about ¾ inch (2 cm) thick.

Heat the oil in a large skillet or grill pan set over medium-high heat. Add the patties and reduce the heat to medium. Cook, turning once or twice as needed, for 15 to 20 minutes or until cooked through. Lift out of the pan using a slotted metal spatula and blot on a paper towel-lined plate before serving.

The refreshing combination of lemon and dill make these burgers appealing to eat during warm weather and more delicate tasting than a regular beef burger. In springtime, serve these patties without a bun, accompanied by steamed asparagus or snow peas and roasted baby new potatoes. When served on a bun, choose mild-flavored condiments such as mayonnaise and avoid strong garnishes such as dill pickles or sliced raw onion, which will overpower the other flavors. You can substitute ground chicken or turkey for the ground veal if preferred.

Lemon Dill Veal Burgers

PREP: 10 minutes | **COOK:** 15 to 20 minutes | **YIELD:** 4 patties

4 tsp (20 mL) finely grated onion
2 tbsp (30 mL) finely chopped fresh dill or 2 tsp (10 mL) dried dillweed
2 tsp (10 mL) finely grated lemon zest
½ tsp (2 mL) salt
¼ tsp (1 mL) pepper
1 clove garlic, minced
1 egg, beaten
½ cup (125 mL) fresh bread crumbs
1 lb (500 g) lean ground veal
2 tbsp (30 mL) vegetable oil
4 slices Swiss cheese (optional)

Combine the onion, dill, lemon zest, salt, pepper, garlic, and egg. Stir until well combined. Stir in the bread crumbs. Crumble in the ground veal and toss gently until evenly combined. Shape into 4 equal-size patties.

STOVETOP INSTRUCTIONS: Heat the oil in a large skillet or grill pan set over medium heat. Add the patties. Cook, turning once or twice, for 15 to 20 minutes or until cooked through; top the patties with cheese slices (if using) and cover pan for 15 seconds. Lift out of the pan using a slotted metal spatula and blot on a paper towel-lined plate before serving.

GRILLING INSTRUCTIONS: Preheat the grill to medium-high. Grease the grate and add the patties. Reduce the heat to medium. Grill the burgers for 8 to 10 minutes per side or until cooked through. Top each burger with a slice of cheese (if using); cover and grill for 30 seconds or just until the cheese is melted.

These tasty patties have a full, rich taste that elevates the familiar burger from a dependable comfort food to an extraordinary entrée. Serve these flavorful lamb disks with asparagus and boiled new potatoes for a traditional dinner or with a couscous or lentil salad for a more exotic mealtime experience.

Fresh mint is usually easy to find year round and is the perfect herb to complement the lamb. If you can't find fresh mint, substitute fresh coriander. Cranberry sauce is available in both whole-berry and jellied varieties. The whole-berry kind makes for an especially attractive presentation over the hot burgers.

Mint Cranberry Lamb Patty Melts

PREP: 10 minutes | **COOK:** 15 to 18 minutes | **YIELD:** 8 patties

1 tsp (5 mL) each ground cinnamon and salt
½ tsp (2 mL) pepper
2 eggs, beaten
½ cup (125 mL) fresh bread crumbs
2 tbsp (30 mL) chopped fresh mint
2 lb (1 kg) lean ground lamb or pork
2 tbsp (30 mL) vegetable oil
1 cup (250 mL) shredded mozzarella cheese (optional)
½ cup (125 mL) cranberry sauce

Whisk the cinnamon, salt and pepper into the eggs. Stir in the bread crumbs and mint. Crumble the meat into a bowl and toss gently with the mint mixture until evenly combined.

Divide the meat into 8 portions and form into evenly shaped patties. Heat the oil in a large, heavy skillet set over medium-high heat. Add the patties to the pan. Cook the patties, turning as needed to prevent scorching, for 15 to 18 minutes or until cooked through (internal temperature should register 71°C/160°F on an instant-read thermometer).

Remove the skillet from the heat. Sprinkle each patty evenly with cheese (if using) and cover the skillet for 1 minute. Serve patties topped with a generous spoonful of cranberry sauce.

Ground lamb is used in many North African and Middle Eastern cuisines as a basis for koftas, which are spiced (although not necessarily *spicy*) meat- or vegetable-based balls. Experts on language say that the word *kofta* is derived from the Persian word *koofteh*, which translates into "pounded meat." These burgers borrow a lot from authentic koftas, but they're easier to shape and faster to cook.

For a lighter Mediterranean-style meal, you can omit the pita and tzatziki and serve these burgers with a tabouleh salad.

Moroccan Lamb Burgers

PREP: 10 minutes | **COOK:** 20 minutes | **YIELD:** 4 burgers

1 small onion, peeled and finely grated
1 tbsp (15 mL) finely chopped fresh mint
1 tbsp (15 mL) lemon juice
½ tsp (2 mL) ground cinnamon
½ tsp (2 mL) hot pepper sauce
½ tsp (2 mL) salt
¼ tsp (1 mL) pepper
1 egg, beaten
1 clove garlic, minced
½ cup (125 mL) fresh bread crumbs
1 lb (500 g) lean ground lamb
2 tbsp (30 mL) vegetable oil
2 pitas, halved
Coarsely shredded lettuce, chopped tomato and tzatziki sauce

Combine the onion, mint, lemon juice, cinnamon, hot pepper sauce, salt, pepper, egg and garlic. Stir until well combined. Stir in the bread crumbs. Crumble in the ground lamb and toss gently until evenly combined. Shape the meat mixture into 4 equal-size patties.

STOVETOP INSTRUCTIONS: Heat the oil in a large skillet or grill pan set over medium heat. Add the patties. Cover and cook, turning once or twice, for 15 to 20 minutes or until cooked through. Lift patties out of the pan using a slotted spatula and blot briefly on a paper towel-lined plate before serving. Place burgers in halved pitas and stuff pitas with coarsely shredded lettuce and chopped tomato; serve drizzled with tzatziki.

GRILLING INSTRUCTIONS: Preheat the grill to medium-high. Grease the grate and add the burgers. Grill burgers for 7 to 8 minutes per side or until cooked through. Serve in halved pitas as above.

Salmon has a bold flavor that is well suited to both grilling and being paired with strongly flavored ingredients such as pickles and mustard. Cook salmon patties until well set and golden around the edges, but still slightly coral-colored in the center. Although fresh salmon is recommended for this recipe, thawed frozen fish will work well, too.

To make your own tartar sauce, combine mayonnaise with a small amount of green relish, chopped capers and lemon juice to taste.

SEE PHOTO INSERT

Grilled Sweet Mustard Salmon Burgers

PREP: 10 minutes | **COOK:** 20 minutes | **YIELD:** 4 burgers

1 lb (500 g) skinless, boneless fresh salmon
⅓ cup (75 mL) coarse, fresh bread crumbs
¼ cup (50 mL) finely chopped bread and butter pickles or green relish
¼ cup (50 mL) finely chopped green onion
1 tbsp (15 mL) Dijon mustard
1 egg, beaten
½ tsp (2 mL) each salt and pepper
4 slices mozzarella cheese (optional)
¼ cup (50 mL) tartar sauce, store-bought or homemade
4 toasted kaiser rolls
Leaf lettuce

Preheat the grill to medium-high. Line a baking sheet with perforated, nonstick grill foil or lightly greased heavy-duty foil that has been pierced to make drainage holes.

Flake the raw salmon into chunks using two forks. Place these pieces into a large bowl. Mix the salmon gently with the bread crumbs, pickles, green onion, mustard, egg, salt and pepper. Form into 4 large patties and place on the prepared baking sheet.

Slide the foil with the patties onto the grate. Grill the patties for 8 to 10 minutes per side or until browned on the outside but coral-colored in the very center. Top with mozzarella slices (if using) for the last few seconds before removing patties from the grate.

Spread some of the tartar sauce on each roll and top with lettuce and a salmon burger.

A *light cornmeal coating* gives these patties a crunchy crust on the outside that contrasts nicely with the softer texture of the potato-and-salmon inside. Although these patties can be served on a soft bun with lettuce and tomato, they are lovely served on their own. Top them off with additional honey mustard whether you serve them as an entrée or on a bun.

Dilly Fresh Salmon Patties

PREP: 10 minutes | **COOK:** 16 minutes | **YIELD:** 6 patties

1 medium potato, about 6 oz (175 g)
1 lb (500 g) skinless, boneless salmon fillets
1 egg
1 tbsp (15 mL) honey mustard
2 tbsp (30 mL) chopped fresh dill
1 green onion, sliced
1 tsp (5 mL) salt
¼ tsp (1 mL) pepper
¼ cup (50 mL) cornmeal
1 tbsp (15 mL) vegetable oil

Scrub the potato and pierce in a few places with a sharp knife. Microwave at High for 3 minutes or until tender. Let stand until cool enough to handle. Peel and mash the potato roughly with a fork.

Cut the salmon into chunks and place in the food processor. Using the pulse button, chop the salmon into smaller but still chunky pieces. Add the mashed potato, egg, mustard, dill, green onion, salt and pepper. Process until combined but not smooth (the mixture should be the same texture or coarser than ground meat; if you overprocess it, it will become too wet).

Sprinkle the cornmeal on a piece of waxed paper. Form the salmon mixture into 6 equal-size patties and coat in cornmeal until evenly covered on both sides.

Heat the oil in a large nonstick skillet set over medium-high heat. Add 3 patties to the pan and reduce the heat to medium. Cook for 4 minutes per side or until firm, golden brown and just slightly coral-colored on the inside. Remove the patties from the skillet and repeat with remaining 3 patties.

Niçoise is a French culinary term that has become a shorthand way of saying that a recipe contains tuna, black olives, tomatoes and anchovies—common pantry items in the kitchens of Nice, France. Though this recipe is not among the traditional Niçoise dishes, it is a fast and inexpensive tasty main course featuring many of the flavors of Nice.

In my experience, the more expensive solid light albacore tuna is overrated. Although very lean and mild tasting, this type of tuna can have a dry texture and lack flavor. Instead, I find that water- or broth-packed chunk light tuna has a more appealing taste and is more successfully incorporated into other ingredients when cooking.

Niçoise Burgers

PREP: 5 minutes | **COOK:** 10 minutes | **YIELD:** 4 burgers

2 eggs
⅓ cup (75 mL) dry bread crumbs
1 tbsp (15 mL) mayonnaise
1 tsp (5 mL) Dijon mustard
1 clove garlic, minced
¼ cup (50 mL) finely chopped, pitted black olives
¼ tsp (1 mL) pepper
¼ tsp (1 mL) anchovy paste
2 cans (6 oz/170 g each) water-packed tuna
1 tomato, seeded and finely chopped
1 tbsp (15 mL) vegetable oil
4 whole wheat kaisers or hamburger buns
Alfalfa sprouts or lettuce (optional)
Mayonnaise (optional)

Beat the eggs lightly and mix in the bread crumbs, mayonnaise, mustard, garlic, olives, pepper and anchovy paste. Drain the tuna and transfer it to a bowl; break into pieces using a fork. Stir the tuna and tomatoes into the bread crumb mixture until well combined. Shape equal amounts of the tuna mixture into 4 patties, each about ½ inch (1 cm) thick.

Heat a nonstick skillet over medium heat. Add the oil and cook the patties, turning once, for 10 minutes or until golden brown. Place on buns and top with sprouts or lettuce (if using). Serve with extra mayonnaise on the side, if you like. These burgers can also be served without buns, accompanied by a green bean and potato salad.

Fresh tuna steaks can be quite expensive; however, if you buy your fresh tuna at a store where they clean and cut the fish themselves, you may be able to purchase the less costly trimmings. To ensure that the tuna doesn't become fishy smelling as it heats up whirling around in the food processor, make sure that the fish is well chilled before adding it to the bowl. It also helps to place the bowl and the blade in the freezer for a few minutes before using.

Although fresh tuna steaks are best cooked and served rare, these burgers should be cooked until opaque or only slightly pale pink in the center so that they hold together. They can be served a couple of ways. They are very delicious as a light supper served atop salad greens tossed with miso dressing. Or you can serve them on buns garnished with wasabi mayonnaise (page 15), tomatoes and cucumbers.

Teriyaki Tuna Burgers

PREP: 10 minutes | **COOK:** 6 minutes | **YIELD:** 8 burgers

2 lb (1 kg) fresh tuna steaks
3 tbsp (45 mL) teriyaki sauce
2 tbsp (30 mL) chopped green onion
2 tsp (10 mL) toasted sesame oil
2 tsp (10 mL) freshly grated ginger
1 tsp (5 mL) Dijon mustard
½ tsp (2 mL) hot pepper sauce
2 cloves garlic, minced

Cut the tuna into small pieces and place in a food processor fitted with a metal blade. Pulse until the tuna is chopped but still chunky. Add the teriyaki sauce, green onion, sesame oil, ginger, mustard, hot pepper sauce and garlic. Pulse just until the ingredients are combined.

Shape the tuna mixture into 8 equal-size patties. Preheat the outdoor or indoor grill, or a skillet to medium-high. Grease well. Add the patties and cook, turning gently, for 2 to 3 minutes per side.

Casseroles & One-Dish Meals

Casseroles have a long legacy that extends at least as far back as Ancient Greece. However, it was during the 1940s and 1950s that casseroles as we know them really came into their own. During the war years, with the men away in the military, family incomes were tight. Casseroles offered home cooks ways to economize by using meat as a flavoring or garnish instead of as a main ingredient. Casseroles were also economical time-wise. When women worked in factories to support the war effort, they needed simple, nutritious dishes like tuna casserole that were fast and easy to prepare for their families. Packaged food companies understood this consumer need and were there with the recipes and convenience products that made casseroles a regular weeknight meal.

After the war, family life didn't go back to the way it was but continued to change. The appearance of time-saving appliances made more time available for activities other than household chores. Casseroles and one-dish meals were a perfect fit for the busy post-war family.

Today, the economic and time-saving appeal of casseroles and one-dish meals remains popular. Because many casserole recipes are not only quick to prepare, but also easily made ahead, they're ideal for busy nights when cooking would otherwise be impossible. And when there is a bit of time to cook, skillet and other one-dish meals are much loved as weeknight dinners because they're fast and easy to make, easy to serve and often involve less cleanup than a meal that requires several pots and pans to prepare.

In this chapter you'll find easy solutions for every mealtime dilemma. There are tried-and-true classics such as Homestyle Beef Stew and exciting new meal ideas such as Clam-stuffed Baked Potatoes. Just because a meal is quick to make doesn't mean it has to be boring!

For today's busy home cooks, homey, humble foods such as soups and stews have a special status. They bring back memories of a time when we weren't all so rushed, plus they have the advantage that they can be prepared in advance to be reheated and eaten another day. A simmering soup or stew will fill your home with mouth-watering aromas. If you don't have time to tend to a pot of stew, a slow cooker can be a handy device. Just prepare the ingredients, put them in the pot, turn it on and walk away.

This traditional stew is a great recipe to make on the weekend to serve for dinner later in the week. Whether it's simmered on the stovetop or in a slow cooker, this classic retro stew is guaranteed to become a well-loved addition to your repertoire.

Pre-cut rutabaga and squash are available in most produce sections and are a great time saver.

Homestyle Beef Stew

PREP: 25 minutes | **COOK:** 4 hours | **YIELD:** 8 servings

2 tbsp (30 mL) vegetable oil (approx)
2 slices bacon, chopped
¼ cup (60 mL) all-purpose flour
1 tsp (5 mL) pepper
2 lb (1 kg) cubed stewing beef, trimmed
1 pouch (1½ oz/38 g) onion soup mix
1 tsp (5 mL) each dried rosemary and thyme leaves
1 tsp (5 mL) minced garlic
3 tbsp (45 mL) tomato paste
2½ cups (625 mL) water
½ cup (125 mL) red wine or additional water
3 cups (750 mL) cubed, peeled potatoes
2 cups (500 mL) cubed, peeled rutabaga or butternut squash
1 cup (250 mL) each baby carrots and fresh or frozen peas

Heat 1 tbsp (15 mL) of the oil in a Dutch oven set over medium-high heat. Add the bacon and cook, stirring occasionally, for 5 minutes. Meanwhile, in a large bowl, stir together the flour and pepper. Toss the beef cubes with the flour mixture. Remove bacon and set aside. Working in batches, brown the beef cubes on all sides, using the remaining oil if necessary. Return browned beef cubes and reserved bacon to the pot. Stir in any remaining flour mixture from the bowl, the soup mix, rosemary, thyme, garlic, tomato paste, water and red wine. Bring to a boil. Reduce the heat to low and simmer, stirring occasionally for 2 hours.

Stir in the potatoes, rutabaga and carrots. Cook for 1 to 1½ hours or until vegetables are tender and stew is thickened, stirring occasionally. Stir in the peas and cook for 5 minutes before serving.

SLOW COOKER METHOD: Brown the meat as directed and transfer to the slow cooker. Add the seasonings and cooking liquids and cook on High for 1 hour. Add the vegetables and cook for 3 to 3½ hours or reduce the heat to Low and cook for 7 hours.

This comfort food classic never goes out of style! Originally named for a nineteenth-century Russian diplomat named Count Paul Stroganoff, this recipe is basically an upscale version of beef stew, dressed up by adding sour cream to the gravy. Serve this fast and easy to make stew over noodles (traditional), with mashed potatoes or in a bread bowl. Regardless, this thick and creamy meat concoction is wonderfully soothing after a long, difficult day.

You can make a double batch of this stew and freeze the extra portions in single-serve containers that can be heated for a quick dinner or a heat-and-eat lunch at school or work. If you are going to do this, it is important that you reserve the sour cream and add it only after the stew has been thawed and reheated.

Chop the onion, carrot and celery in a food processor to save time.

Beef Stroganoff

PREP: 20 minutes | **COOK:** 1 hour | **YIELD:** 6 servings

2 tbsp (30 mL) butter
2 strips bacon, finely chopped, or ¼ cup (50 mL) finely chopped ham
1 onion, peeled and finely chopped
1 each carrot and celery stalk, finely chopped
1 bay leaf
2 tsp (10 mL) dried thyme leaves
½ tsp (2 mL) each salt and pepper
2 lb (1 kg) sirloin steak cut into thin strips
¼ cup (50 mL) all-purpose flour
1 tbsp (15 mL) vegetable oil (approx)
½ cup (125 mL) red wine (optional)
2½ cups (500 mL) beef or chicken broth
8 oz (250 g) small mushroom caps
½ cup (125 mL) sour cream
2 tbsp (30 mL) chopped fresh parsley
Hot buttered pappardelle or egg noodles

Melt the butter in a Dutch oven set over medium heat. Stir in the bacon and cook, stirring often, for 5 minutes or until browned. Stir in the onion, carrot, celery, bay leaf, thyme, salt and pepper. Cook the vegetable mixture, stirring often, for 5 minutes or until the onion is softened. Transfer the vegetable mixture to a bowl and reserve.

Pat the beef dry with a paper towel and toss with the flour in a bag or large bowl until evenly coated. Increase the heat under the pan to medium-high. Brown the beef, in the oil, in 3 or 4 batches. Add additional oil to the pan if needed. Once browned, remove the beef strips and reserve in the same bowl as the vegetables.

Add the wine (if using) to the pan and cook for 1 minute, stirring to scrape up any cooked-on bits. Add the reserved vegetables, browned beef and the broth to the pan and bring to a boil. Stir in the mushrooms. Reduce the heat to low and simmer, partially covered, for 30 minutes. Remove the lid and simmer for 30 minutes more or until sauce is thickened.

Stir in sour cream and parsley. Reheat but do not boil. Taste and adjust salt and pepper if necessary. Remove bay leaf before serving over noodles.

One of the reasons I love being a professional cook is that no matter how long you've been in the business and regardless of how many places you've visited, there is always something new to learn about food.

When I first began to learn about festive Jewish cookery, I was absolutely inspired by the taste of a classic Sephardic Jewish dish called tsimmes. Like this stew, it contained beef, fruit and root vegetables. The combination was absolutely irresistible. Rich and sweet yet savory, it was completely different from the plain brown gravy based stews that I grew up eating.

Sephardic culture is rooted in the Iberian Peninsula where Sephardic Judaism originated. Throughout the centuries Sephardic Jews, in an effort to preserve their culture and beliefs, migrated from Spain to North Africa, Turkey and as far as India. Along the way they integrated elements of these exotic cuisines into their Spanish and Portuguese family recipes. As a result, Sephardic cooking is, like this stew, evocatively spiced and often contains dried fruit and legumes.

Choose Medjoule dates for best results. Packaged blocks of dates tend to be dry and lack flavor.

Sephardic Beef Stew

PREP: 20 minutes | **COOK:** 3 hours | **YIELD:** 6 servings

1 tbsp (15 mL) olive oil (approx)
1 each onion and celery stalk, finely chopped
½ tsp (2 mL) each salt, pepper and cayenne
1 lb (500 g) trimmed sirloin steak or stewing beef
2 tbsp (30 mL) cornstarch
½ cup (125 mL) white wine
2 cloves garlic, minced
1 tbsp (15 mL) minced ginger
2½ cups (625 mL) chicken broth
2 cups (500 mL) each chopped parsnips and carrots
1 large potato, peeled and chopped
1 cup (250 mL) whole, pitted dried dates
¼ cup (50 mL) whole dried apricots

Preheat the oven to 350°F (180°C). Heat the oil in a large, deep saucepan or Dutch oven set over medium heat. Add the onion, celery, salt, pepper and cayenne. Cook, partially covered, for 7 minutes. Meanwhile, trim any visible fat or gristle from the meat and dice into 1-inch (2.5 cm) cubes. Toss with cornstarch until evenly coated.

Increase the heat under the pan to medium-high. Add the meat to the pan and cook until the meat is lightly browned and the bottom of the pan is golden. Add extra oil if necessary to prevent scorching. Add the wine and stir to scrape up any cooked-on bits. Stir in the garlic, ginger and broth. Bring to a boil. Cover tightly and transfer the covered pan to the oven. Braise for 60 minutes.

Add the parsnips, carrots, potato, dates and apricots. Cover and return the pan to oven for 45 minutes. Remove cover; stir well and then cook for 60 minutes longer or until beef and vegetables are fork tender.

Enjoy a taste of the South Pacific with this easy version of a popular take-out dish. Green curry is frequently used in Thai cooking. It has a flavor totally unlike Indian-style curry mixtures. Green curry is a blend of many ingredients, including green chilies, lemongrass and lime. It is difficult to mix at home but can usually be found in the Asian section of grocery stores, sold in jars or pouches. Look for kaffir lime leaves in the freezer section if they aren't offered fresh in the produce area.

Thai Coconut Beef and Green Curry

PREP: 15 minutes | **COOK:** 2¾ hours | **YIELD:** 4 to 6 servings

2 lb (1 kg) lean stewing beef, cut into 1-inch (2.5 cm) chunks
2 tbsp (30 mL) all-purpose flour
½ tsp (2 mL) each salt and pepper
2 tbsp (30 mL) vegetable oil
1 onion, chopped
2 cloves garlic, minced
1 can (398 mL) coconut milk
⅓ cup (75 mL) lime juice
3 tbsp (45 mL) brown sugar
2 tbsp (30 mL) tomato paste
1 tbsp (15 mL) minced ginger
2 tsp (10 mL) Thai green curry paste
2 kaffir lime leaves (optional)
¼ cup (50 mL) chopped fresh coriander
3 cups (750 mL) cooked rice noodles or white rice
1 red pepper, very thinly sliced
1 cup (250 mL) mung bean sprouts, well rinsed
¼ cup (50 mL) chopped unsalted peanuts

Toss the beef with the flour, salt and pepper in a large bowl. Heat 1 tbsp (15 mL) of the oil in a Dutch oven set over medium-high heat. Brown the beef in batches; transfer to a platter as browned. Reserve. Reduce the heat under the Dutch oven to medium. Add the remaining oil, onion and garlic to the pan. Sauté until golden. Return the meat to the pan.

Whisk the coconut milk with the lime juice, brown sugar, tomato paste, ginger and green curry paste. Stir this mixture into the Dutch oven. Add the lime leaves (if using). Bring to a boil. Reduce the heat to low and simmer, stirring occasionally, for 2½ hours. Stir in the coriander just before serving. Ladle the curry over rice noodles or rice; garnish with red pepper strips, bean sprouts and peanuts.

SLOW COOKER METHOD: Brown the beef and onion mixture as directed, then transfer to a slow cooker. Add the coconut milk mixture and cook on High for 4 hours or on Low for 8 hours. Garnish as directed.

Cook once, eat twice: Prepare a double batch of the curry without adding the coriander. Freeze the extra to serve another night. Reheat, stirring often, in the microwave or in a covered saucepan over medium heat.

Simple enough for a beginner cook to make without stress, this quick and easy dinner is a crowd-pleaser with kids (and adults!) who have a taste for Mexican flavors.

Although TVP (textured vegetable protein) meatballs can be used instead of beef meatballs, the fat in the meat that adds richness and helps to give the sauce a smooth, satisfying texture will be missed.

Meatball Chili Con Carne

PREP: 10 minutes | **COOK:** 30 minutes | **YIELD:** 4 servings

2 tbsp (30 mL) vegetable oil

1 onion, peeled and chopped

1 tbsp (15 mL) chili powder

1 tsp (5 mL) dried oregano leaves

½ tsp each cumin, salt and pepper

2½ cups (625 mL) canned diced tomatoes

2 tbsp (30 mL) ketchup

2 cloves garlic, minced

1 green pepper, chopped

1 lb (500 g) frozen meatballs, about 1 box

1 can (19 oz/540 mL) kidney or black beans, drained and rinsed

2 tbsp (30 mL) sour cream

1 green onion, chopped

Heat the oil in a large saucepan or Dutch oven set over medium heat. Add the onion, chili powder, oregano, cumin, salt and pepper. Cook, stirring often, for 5 minutes.

Stir in the tomatoes, ketchup, garlic and green pepper and bring to a boil. Add the meatballs and stir until well combined. Reduce the heat to low. Partially cover the pan and simmer, stirring the mixture occasionally, for 15 minutes.

Add the kidney beans to the tomato mixture. Cook, stirring often, for 5 minutes. Garnish each serving with sour cream and green onion.

Chipotle (chip-oat-lay) peppers are smoked, dried jalapeño peppers. Their flavor has taken firm hold on fast-food menus the last couple of years, flavoring sauces and condiments for everything from subs to ribs. Bringing the chipotle trend home is super easy now that chipotle-flavored sauce (available in the condiment section of most grocery stores) is widely available. The rich, red-brown colored hot sauce adds a deep, spicy flavor to this dish and makes it a weeknight wonder that you'll make again and again!

Serve this skillet casserole with warm corn tortillas or boiled potatoes to create a fast, zesty-tasting meal.

Chipotle Chicken Skillet Casserole

PREP: 10 minutes | **COOK:** 25 minutes | **YIELD:** 4 servings

1 oil-packed sun-dried tomato
¼ cup (50 mL) loosely packed fresh coriander leaves
2 tbsp (30 mL) cayenne chipotle sauce or 1 tbsp (15 mL) each barbecue sauce and hot pepper sauce
1 tsp (5 mL) chili powder
1 tsp (5 mL) finely grated lime zest
1 tsp (5 mL) vegetable oil
2 lb (1 kg) skinless, boneless chicken thighs, about 16
½ tsp (2 mL) each salt and pepper
1 large onion, peeled and sliced thinly
1 green pepper, chopped

Blot the sun-dried tomato on a paper towel to remove excess oil. Combine the tomato, coriander leaves, chipotle sauce, chili powder and lime zest in a blender or mini chopper. Blend, adding up to ¼ cup (50 mL) of water, until mixture is smooth. Reserve.

Heat the oil in a nonstick skillet set over medium-high heat. Pat the chicken thighs dry with paper towel and sprinkle evenly with salt and pepper. Add the chicken pieces to the pan and brown for about 3 minutes per side. Transfer the chicken to a plate and add the onion to the skillet. Reduce the heat to medium. Cook, stirring occasionally, for 5 minutes. Add the green pepper and mix to combine with onion.

Return the chicken and any accumulated meat juices to the pan; arrange the meat on top of the vegetables. Spread the chipotle mixture over chicken using the back of a spoon. Cover the skillet tightly and simmer for about 15 minutes or until chicken is no longer pink in the center.

This recipe uses fresh sausages (which contain raw meat and must be cooked before eating). Fresh sausages made their appearance on the food scene as early as 424 BC and they're still popular. They are one of the best shortcut ingredients a busy cook can buy. Since quality fresh sausage meat is already seasoned by a professional cook, adding pieces of sausage or splitting the casings open and using sausage meat as the base for a recipe is a great way to prepare dinner quickly and add flavor easily.

If you like, you can vary the kind of sausages and the type of cheese you use in this recipe. For instance, bratwurst with Swiss cheese is a winning combo as is pork-and-apple sausage with aged Cheddar. No matter what combination proves to be a favorite on your dinner table, you'll love this fast and simple skillet supper that has all the comfort of a slowly baked casserole.

Sausage and Potato Skillet Supper

PREP: 10 minutes | **COOK:** 30 minutes | **YIELD:** 6 servings

1 tbsp (15 mL) vegetable oil
1 onion, peeled and chopped
2 Italian sausages, casings removed
2 large potatoes, well scrubbed and cut into ½-inch (1 cm) cubes
3 cups (750 mL) baby spinach
2 cups (500 mL) canned diced tomatoes with juices
2 cups (500 mL) Italian-style shredded cheese blend

Preheat the oven to 350°F (180°C). Heat the oil in an ovenproof skillet set over medium-high heat. Add the onion and cook for 2 minutes. Add the sausage meat to the pan, breaking it up finely with the edges of a wooden spoon. Add the potatoes and cook, stirring often, until lightly browned, about 5 minutes.

Stir in the spinach and tomatoes and bring to a boil. Sprinkle the cheese evenly over the pan and transfer to the oven. Bake for 20 minutes or until pan juices are bubbly and potatoes are tender.

On our first trip to France, my mother fell in love with the French comfort food classic cassoulet. This seductive dish of beans, duck and sausage from France's Languedoc region is a true test of a cook's patience as it takes about two days to complete. Duck legs that have been poached in goose fat are combined with sausage, white beans and chicken broth, topped with buttered bread crumbs and minced garlic, then cooked very slowly in a tall crock until the beans are tender and the crumbs have formed a toasty, golden crust.

As delicious as it is, cassoulet is also very high in calories. So, as a tribute to my busy, health-conscious mom, I developed this hearty, much simplified (and leaner) version of cassoulet. I've even opted for whole wheat bread crumbs, which are not only tasty but also higher in fiber than crumbs made from the traditional white baguette.

White Bean and Sausage Casserole

PREP: 15 minutes | **COOK:** 20 minutes | **YIELD:** 4 servings

1 tsp (5 mL) vegetable oil

2 precooked, hot sausages, halved and sliced

2 carrots, peeled and chopped

1 onion, peeled and chopped

3 tbsp (45 mL) chopped fresh parsley

1 tsp (5 mL) each crumbled dried rosemary and dried thyme or sage leaves

2 cloves garlic, minced

1 cup (250 mL) canned diced tomatoes, drained

¾ cup (175 mL) sodium-reduced chicken or vegetable broth

1 can (19 oz/540 mL) white pea (navy) or white kidney beans, drained and rinsed

¼ tsp (1 mL) each salt and pepper

½ cup (125 mL) fresh whole wheat bread crumbs

2 tbsp (30 mL) shredded or grated Parmesan cheese

2 tbsp (30 mL) melted butter

Heat the oil in a nonstick skillet set over medium-high heat. Add the sausage and sauté until browned. Remove from pan using a slotted spoon and blot on paper towels; reserve.

Reduce the heat to medium and add the carrots, onion, parsley, rosemary and thyme or sage. Cook for 5 minutes, stirring often. Add the garlic, tomatoes and broth. Bring to a boil.

Use a fork to mash about one-quarter of the beans. Stir all the beans, the reserved sausage, salt and pepper into the vegetables. Reduce the heat and simmer gently, uncovered, until the vegetables are tender and the mixture is thickened, about 10 minutes.

Meanwhile, preheat the broiler to high. Combine the bread crumbs and Parmesan cheese. Drizzle in the butter and stir to combine. Transfer the bean mixture to a 9-inch (2.5 L) square or round baking dish and sprinkle evenly with the bread crumb mixture. Broil for 2 to 3 minutes or until well browned. Serve with crisp salad greens tossed with a light dressing.

Casseroles & One-Dish Meals

Slow cooking in a yummy, citrus-accented teriyaki sauce makes these short ribs truly extraordinary. The slow cooking does take time, but it's well worth the wait. When they're done, these ribs are succulent and tender. This economical yet robustly flavored cut of meat is ideal for a family supper or for casual entertaining. To complete this meal, serve with steamed rice. White rice works best to soak up the sauce, but you can use brown rice if you prefer.

Mirin is a low-alcohol, sweet rice wine that is often used in Japanese cooking to add flavor to sauces and glazes. It is also often labeled simply rice wine or cooking sake.

Sweet peppers—red, green, yellow, or orange (or even purple!)—not only add color and flavor to recipes, they're also packed with vitamins C and A, and contain antioxidants, healthful compounds that help our bodies fight off many diseases.

SEE PHOTO INSERT

Teriyaki Beef Short Ribs with Rainbow Peppers

PREP: 15 minutes | **COOK:** 4 hours | **YIELD:** 6 servings

1 tbsp (15 mL) vegetable oil
1 tsp (5 mL) toasted sesame oil
3½ lb (1.75 kg) thinly sliced beef short ribs
¾ cup (175 mL) teriyaki sauce
⅔ cup (150 mL) lemon juice
½ cup (125 mL) brown sugar, loosely packed
3 tbsp (45 mL) cornstarch
2 tbsp (30 mL) mirin or sherry
1 tbsp (15 mL) each minced fresh ginger and hot pepper sauce
1 clove garlic, minced
1 each red, yellow and orange pepper, thinly sliced
Cooked rice
2 green onions, sliced
1 tbsp (15 mL) toasted sesame seeds

Preheat the oven to 325°F (160°C). Heat the vegetable and sesame oils in a large Dutch oven set over medium-high heat. Brown the ribs on all sides, adding them to the pan in batches. Reserve the browned ribs on a platter. When all the ribs are browned, combine them and any accumulated juices in the Dutch oven.

Whisk the teriyaki sauce with the lemon juice, brown sugar, cornstarch, mirin, ginger, hot pepper sauce and garlic until smooth. Pour this mixture over the ribs. Bring to a boil. Transfer the dish straight to the oven and cook, covered, for 3 hours. Add the peppers and cook, uncovered, for 45 minutes longer or until the ribs are so tender that the meat is almost (but not quite!) falling from the bone. For an elegant presentation, transfer the ribs and peppers to a rice-lined platter. Sprinkle with green onion and sesame seeds. Or serve on individual plates, over rice, and sprinkle with the green onion and sesame seeds.

SLOW COOKER METHOD: Transfer the browned ribs to the slow cooker. Add the teriyaki sauce, lemon juice, brown sugar, cornstarch, mirin, ginger, hot pepper sauce and garlic. Cook on High for 4 hours or on Low for 7½ hours. Add the peppers and cook for 20 to 30 minutes or until the ribs are so tender that the meat is almost falling from the bone. Garnish and serve as above.

Steaming-hot pot pies, consisting of a meaty chicken stew covered by a flaky, golden crust, are a hearty indulgence. Many people of British heritage grew up eating pot pies on Monday and Tuesday evenings when Mum recycled the Sunday roast leftovers into another meal.

Today, few people take the time to make pot pies from scratch since they are easy to find in the frozen food section of grocery stores and appear on pub menus the world over. My simplified version features flavors and ingredients that aren't usually found in the commercial varieties. And to eliminate the fear factor for people who find pastry too messy or too difficult to make themselves, this recipe uses prepared refrigerated pastry—which also allows you to get dinner on the table faster! To speed things up even more, you can use leftover cooked chicken or buy a deli-cooked rotisserie bird to make the base for this warming dinner.

Springtime Chicken and Asparagus Pot Pie

PREP: 10 minutes | **COOK:** 25 minutes | **YIELD:** 6 servings

1 tbsp (15 mL) butter

2 cups (500 mL) sliced shiitake, button or other mushrooms

¼ cup (50 mL) finely chopped green onion

1 tbsp (15 mL) chopped fresh tarragon or 1 tsp (5 mL) dried tarragon leaves

½ tsp (2 mL) each salt and pepper

2 tbsp (30 mL) lemon juice

1 tbsp (15 mL) cornstarch

1½ cups (375 mL) milk

2 cups (500 mL) cubed, cooked chicken

2 cups (500 mL) blanched asparagus tips or green beans

1 pkg (8 oz /250 g) refrigerated multigrain or regular crescent roll dough, or frozen puff pastry, thawed

1 egg, beaten

Preheat the oven to 375°F (190°C). Melt the butter in a deep skillet set over medium heat. Add the mushrooms, green onion, tarragon, salt and pepper. Cook, stirring often, for 5 minutes, or until softened. Stir in the lemon juice. Whisk the cornstarch with the milk; gradually stir this mixture into the mushroom mixture. Bring to a boil, stirring until thickened. Stir in the chicken and asparagus tips and remove the pan from the heat.

Divide the filling mixture between 6 buttered, 1-cup (250 mL) ramekins or individual foil pot pie tins. Unroll the crescent roll dough and seal the perforations using your fingertips. Cut into 6 squares. (If using puff pastry, roll out and cut into 6 squares.) Gently stretch each square of dough until it is large enough so that it not only covers each ramekin, but also hangs over the edges of the dish. Brush the pastry with beaten egg. Bake for about 15 minutes or until the top is golden and the filling is warmed through.

This satisfying, sky-high meatless lasagna is the perfect size for one meal. Every time I make it, at least one of my guests asks for the recipe. Because this dish uses shredded Parmesan (rather than grated), you don't miss the meat. As the cheese strands melt, some of the fat combines with the tomato sauce to produce a finished dish with a wonderfully satisfying mouth feel that is very similar to a meat-filled lasagna.

If the fresh lagana noodles available at your local store aren't easily cut to fit a loaf pan, you can always improvise. All that matters is that you cut two noodles that will fit the pan as closely as possible and use them for the top and bottom layers, to provide the "structural support." Then it won't matter if the other layers are made up of less perfectly fitted noodles.

SEE PHOTO INSERT

Zesty Herbed Tomato Lasagna

PREP: 20 minutes | **COOK:** 55 minutes | **YIELD:** 4 to 6 servings

3 tbsp (45 mL) olive oil
2 onions, finely chopped
3 cloves garlic, minced
2 tbsp (30 mL) finely chopped fresh oregano
2 tsp (10 mL) finely chopped fresh thyme
½ tsp (2 mL) each salt and pepper
3 cups (750 mL) tomato sauce
½ tsp (2 mL) granulated sugar (approx)
2 tbsp (30 mL) each chopped fresh parsley and basil (or 2 tsp dried, crumbled basil leaves)
1¼ cups (300 mL) coarsely shredded Parmesan cheese
8 fresh lasagna noodles, trimmed to fit a 5- by 9-inch (2 L) loaf pan
1 cup (250 mL) shredded mozzarella cheese

Heat the oil in a wide saucepan set over medium-low heat. Add the onions, garlic, oregano, thyme, salt and pepper. Partially cover the pan and cook, stirring often, for 10 minutes or until onions are translucent.

Stir in the tomato sauce and increase the heat to medium. Bring the sauce to a boil. Simmer, partially covered and stirring occasionally, for 15 minutes. Taste and gradually add up to ½ tsp (2 mL) sugar if the sauce tastes too tangy. Stir in the parsley, basil and 1 cup (250 mL) of the shredded Parmesan cheese.

Oil a 5- by 9-inch (2 L) glass or metal loaf pan. Preheat the oven to 350°F (180°C). Spoon a little sauce into the bottom of the pan. Top with a noodle. Repeat layers, ending with sauce, until pan is filled and all the sauce has been used. Cover with nonstick foil and bake the lasagna for 35 to 45 minutes or until bubbly. Remove the foil and sprinkle mozzarella cheese and remaining ¼ cup Parmesan cheese evenly over the top of the lasagna. Broil for 3 minutes or until the cheese is browned and bubbling.

Cook once, eat twice: Double this recipe and freeze one batch before baking. Bake from frozen for 60 minutes or until hot and and bubbly. Top with cheese and broil as directed.

I am almost never without onions or the flavoring ingredients that make them so irresistible when slowly caramelized in a skillet. In fact, caramelized onions are my secret culinary weapon. I often use this unassuming condiment to transform a ho-hum meal into something special. Whether it is simply topping a grilled steak with a tangle of these yummy strands or sprinkling a generous handful atop a cheese pizza, the effect is always transcendent and easy to accomplish. In this hearty and satisfying lasagna, the caramelized onions and mushrooms are so stupendous, no one will even notice there isn't any meat!

I depend on a recipe like this one when a good dinner is required but there isn't much time to shop. Almost all of the ingredients are pantry staples, with just a few items you'll need to pick up on the way home.

Caramelized Onion and Mushroom Lasagna

PREP: 20 minutes | **COOK:** 1 hour 20 minutes | **YIELD:** 8 servings

- **1 tbsp (15 mL) each butter and vegetable oil**
- **2 large onions, peeled and thinly sliced**
- **1 clove garlic, minced**
- **1 tsp (5 mL) dried thyme leaves**
- **½ tsp (2 mL) each salt and freshly ground pepper**
- **2 tbsp (30 mL) granulated sugar**
- **¼ cup (50 mL) dry sherry, white wine or chicken broth**
- **1 tsp (5 mL) Worcestershire sauce**
- **3 cups (750 mL) sliced mixed mushrooms such as button, shiitake or oyster**
- **3 cups (750 mL) tomato or pasta sauce**
- **12 fresh lasagna noodles, trimmed to fit a 13- by 9-inch (3 L) lasagna pan**
- **1 cup (250 mL) grated Parmesan cheese**
- **1¼ cups (300 mL) shredded Gruyère or other Swiss cheese**

Preheat the oven to 350°F (180°C). In a skillet set over medium heat, melt half the butter with half the oil. Add the onions, garlic, thyme, salt and pepper. Cook this mixture, stirring often, for 10 minutes or until the onions are translucent. Increase the heat to medium-high and cook, stirring often, for 5 minutes or until the onions are just beginning to brown.

Sprinkle in the sugar and continue to cook, stirring the mixture often, until all the ingredients are very brown but not scorched. Pour in the sherry and Worcestershire sauce. Stir to scrape up any cooked-on bits that cling to the bottom of the pan. Remove this mixture from pan and reserve. Add the remaining butter and oil to the pan; add the mushrooms and sauté for 2 minutes or until browned. Add to the reserved onions and toss to combine. Reserve.

Spread approximately ½ cup (125 mL) of the sauce in the bottom of a 13- by 9-inch (3 L) lasagna or oblong dish. Arrange 3 noodles over the sauce. Spoon one-quarter of the remaining sauce over this layer and sprinkle with one-third of the onion-mushroom mixture. Repeat layers twice, ending on the top with the last three noodles. Spread the remaining sauce evenly over the top noodles. Sprinkle evenly with cheeses. Cover casserole with nonstick foil and bake for 45 to 55 minutes. Remove the foil and broil for 2 to 3 minutes or until golden. Let stand for 10 minutes before serving.

Combining two family favorites in one dish ensures that this zesty entrée will be a hit with everyone at the dinner table. I often make this lasagna after dinner on the same night I make fajitas so that I can create two meals at once. First, I prepare double the amount of the seasoned meat and vegetable mixture. After reserving half of this mixture, I serve the other half with tortillas and the traditional fajita accompaniments. After we've eaten, I combine the remaining meat and vegetable mixture with the pasta sauce, salsa, noodles and cheese as directed to make the lasagna to bake in a day or two. One mess, two meals—you have to love that idea when you're busy!

Fajita Lasagna

PREP: 25 minutes | **COOK:** 60 minutes | **YIELD:** 8 servings

2 tbsp (30 mL) vegetable oil
1 onion, peeled and sliced
1 lb (500 g) skinless, boneless chicken breast, cubed
1 each red and green peppers, thinly sliced
1 tbsp (15 mL) chili powder
½ tsp (2 mL) each salt, pepper, ground cumin and dried oregano leaves
1 minced chipotle pepper in adobo sauce (optional)
2 cloves garlic, minced
2½ cups (625 mL) pasta sauce
1½ cups (375 mL) salsa
12 oven-ready lasagna noodles
2 cups (500 mL) shredded Mexican cheese blend or Cheddar

Preheat the oven to 350°F (180°C). Heat the oil in a nonstick skillet set over medium heat. Add the onion and cook, stirring often, for 5 minutes.

Increase the heat to medium-high and add the chicken. Cook, stirring often, for 2 minutes. Add the peppers and continue to cook, stirring often, for 3 to 5 minutes or until the meat and vegetables are browned. Stir in the chili powder, salt and pepper, cumin, oregano, chipotle pepper (if using) and garlic.

Stir the pasta sauce with the salsa. Stir 2 cups (500 mL) of this mixture into the meat mixture. Spread approximately half of the remaining sauce mixture (approx 1 cup/250 mL) over the bottom of a 13- by 9-inch (3 L) lasagna or oblong baking dish. Arrange 3 noodles over the sauce. Spoon over one-third of the meat mixture. Repeat layers twice, ending with a top layer that uses the last 3 noodles. Spread remaining sauce evenly over the top noodles. Sprinkle with cheese. Cover with nonstick foil and bake for 45 to 55 minutes. Remove the foil and broil for 2 to 3 minutes or until golden. Let stand for 10 minutes before serving.

Freezer version: Substitute cooked, regular lasagna noodles for the oven-ready noodles. Freeze the lasagna unbaked. Bake from frozen, covered, in a 400°F (200°C) oven for 60 to 70 minutes.

CHILI LEMON CHICKEN
page 61

ROSEMARY-ORANGE SEARED TUNA AND GREENS

page 84

EASY SHRIMP AND CORN STIR-FRY
page 86

SHRIMP "RAVIOLI" WITH ASPARAGUS AND SHIITAKE MUSHROOMS
page 87

CHILI LAGER STEAMED MUSSELS
page 88

BROCCOLI CHEDDAR STUFFED SHELLS
page 91

CLASSIC BAKED ZITI WITH SUN-DRIED TOMATO SAUCE

page 92

SUPER PIZZA SPREAD
page 119

This gently curried beef casserole hails from Africa, where it has a long history and has been made and eaten in the Cape of Good Hope region since the seventeenth century. The name *bobotie* comes from an Indonesian word, *Bobotok,* which isn't surprising since employees of the Dutch East India Company often visited countries such as Indonesia as they traveled the spice route and are responsible for bringing the recipe to settlers' communities in Kenya, Botswana, Zimbabwe and Zambia.

This classic version is made with lean ground beef; however, ground lamb and ground pork are also commonly used to make this dish and can be substituted if you like. Because bobotie is so easy to make and serve, this casserole is perfect for potlucks and buffets. And since it is different from the regular potluck fare, it's sure to be a conversation starter, too.

Bobotie

PREP: 20 minutes | **COOK:** 40 minutes | **YIELD:** 8 servings

2 tbsp (30 mL) butter
2 lb (1 kg) lean ground beef
1 onion, peeled and chopped
1 bay leaf
¼ tsp (1 mL) salt
2 cloves garlic, minced
4 tsp (20 mL) mild Indian curry paste
2 tsp (10 mL) finely grated lemon zest
3 tbsp (45 mL) lemon juice
¾ cup (175 mL) chopped dried apricots or sultana raisins
½ cup (125 mL) blanched slivered almonds
5 eggs
1 cup (250 mL) milk
1 cup (250 mL) fresh bread crumbs
¾ cup (175 mL) 35% whipping cream
Mango chutney

Preheat the oven to 325°F (160°C). Melt the butter in a skillet set over medium heat. Add the beef, onion, bay leaf and salt. Cook, stirring often, for 7 minutes or until all the ingredients are browned. Add the garlic, curry paste, lemon zest and lemon juice. Cook for 1 minute. Stir in the apricots and almonds. Whisk 1 of the eggs with the milk. Stir in the bread crumbs and then stir this mixture into the meat mixture. Transfer to a well-greased 13- by 9-inch (3 L) baking dish.

Whisk the remaining 4 eggs with the cream and pour over top of meat mixture. Bake in the preheated oven for about 40 minutes or until golden and custard topping is set but still soft. Serve with chutney on the side.

Traditional shepherd's pies were made from saucy mixtures consisting of minced lamb or mutton topped with whipped potatoes. Today this dish has become so universal that it's possible to find recipes for it that use every kind of meat for the base and vegetables such as squash, rutabaga and sweet potato for the mashed topping.

My Mexican-inspired version adds a fresh twist by turning this filling meal on its head—the potatoes are used as a cushiony nest on the bottom for the meat mixture on the top! Since children are sometimes reluctant to try new foods, I garnish the top of the casserole with cheese and green onions to remind them of other dishes they love such as tacos and chili.

Frozen corn kernels can be used if you don't have fresh or canned. To use them straight from the freezer, measure them out, place them in a colander and run under hot water for a few seconds until defrosted.

Canned beans are a quick and easy-to-use ingredient, but you might not always need the whole can. Leftovers can be put in freezer bags and frozen for use later. You might want to measure them out in ½-cup (125 mL) or 1-cup (250 mL) portions so you'll have a premeasured quantity all ready to go for another recipe.

Upside-down Mexican Shepherd's Pie

PREP: 10 minutes | **COOK:** 30 minutes | **YIELD:** 4 servings

GRAVY:
  2 tbsp (30 mL) butter
  2 tbsp (30 mL) all-purpose flour
  1 cup (250 mL) beef or chicken broth

SHEPHERD'S PIE:
  1 tsp (5 mL) vegetable oil
  ¾ lb (375 g) lean ground beef
  1 tsp (5 mL) each chili powder and ground cumin
  ¾ cup (175 mL) salsa
  ½ cup (125 mL) each drained and rinsed canned black beans and corn
    kernels
  3 cups (750 mL) hot cooked potatoes
  ¼ cup (50 mL) milk
  ¼ tsp (1 mL) each salt and pepper
  1 cup (250 mL) shredded Cheddar cheese, divided
  2 green onions, chopped

GRAVY: Melt the butter in a saucepan set over medium-low heat. Add the flour and stir until lightly browned. Whisk in a little of the broth until smooth. Once well combined, gradually whisk in the rest of the broth. Increase the heat to medium-high; bring the gravy to a boil and cook, stirring often, for 2 minutes or until thickened. Reserve.

SHEPHERD'S PIE: Preheat the oven to 350°F (180°C). Meanwhile, heat the vegetable oil in a nonstick skillet set over medium heat. Add the beef, chili powder and cumin. Cook, stirring, until the mixture is browned all over. Drain off the fat. Stir in the salsa, black beans, corn and reserved gravy.

Mash the potatoes with the milk, salt and pepper until fluffy. Stir half of the cheese and the green onions into the potatoes. Spread the potato mixture over the bottom and up the sides of a greased 9-inch (2.5 L) square baking dish. Spoon the meat mixture into the potato-lined dish and top with the remaining cheese and onions. Bake for 15 to 20 minutes or until the cheese is melted.

Using the simple flavors that have made clam chowder one of the world's most popular seafood soups, this one-dish meal is comforting and clever at the same time. In fact, this recipe has what I call the "watercooler quality." That means that if you make it for dinner guests, the next day they'll be likely to tell others about the interesting, great-tasting meal you served.

This recipe uses canned clams for convenience. You can easily use fresh baby clams as long as they are cooked before being added to the potato mixture.

SEE PHOTO INSERT

Clam-stuffed Baked Potatoes

PREP: 15 minutes | **COOK:** 30 minutes | **YIELD:** 6 servings

6 Russet potatoes, baked
½ cup (125 mL) milk
¼ cup (50 mL) softened butter
2 tbsp (30 mL) honey mustard
1 cup (250 mL) shredded old Cheddar cheese (approx)
2 green onions, chopped
1 tomato, seeded and finely diced
¼ cup (50 mL) thawed frozen corn kernels
¼ cup (50 mL) crumbled cooked bacon
1 can (5 oz/142 g) baby clams, drained
2 tbsp (30 mL) finely chopped fresh parsley

Using a sharp knife, cut a thin, lengthwise slice off the top of each potato. Discard these lids, or reserve for another purpose (such as making stuffed potato skin appetizers). Scoop the cooked potato out of each potato skin, leaving about ¼ inch (1 mm) of potato next to the skin. Mash the scooped potatoes with the milk, butter and mustard in a large bowl. Preheat the oven to 375°F (190°C).

Add the cheese, onions, tomato, corn, bacon, clams and parsley to the mashed potatoes. Blend gently to combine. Divide the filling evenly between the hollowed potato skins, mounding to fill. Bake for 20 to 30 minutes or until piping hot in the center. If you're a cheese lover, sprinkle with a little extra cheese during the last minute of cooking.

Featuring white, moist chunks of fish and cubed potatoes in a creamy, cheesy sauce capped with a crunchy, golden almond and bread-crumb layer, this casserole is warming and welcome on even the coldest winter day.

If you need something for a potluck or to serve at a casual dinner party, this easy dish is a good bet. All you need to add to make a complete meal is a crisp green salad or a steamed green vegetable on the side.

Creamy Fish Chowder Casserole

PREP: 15 minutes | **COOK:** 30 minutes | **YIELD:** 6 servings

CASEROLE:
- ¼ cup (50 mL) butter
- 2 cups (500 mL) each sliced mushrooms and cooked, cubed potatoes
- 1 each large onion, garlic clove and celery stalk, finely chopped
- 3 tbsp (45 mL) all-purpose flour
- ¼ cup (50 mL) dry sherry or vermouth (optional)
- 1½ cups (375 mL) milk
- 1½ cups (375 mL) shredded Gruyère or other Swiss cheese
- 1 tsp (5 mL) each salt, pepper and nutmeg
- 1 lb (500 g) fresh or thawed, frozen haddock or pollock fillets

TOPPING:
- ½ cup (125 mL) fresh bread crumbs
- ¼ cup (50 mL) slivered almonds
- 2 tbsp (30 mL) melted butter

CASEROLE: Melt half the butter in a large nonstick skillet set over medium–high heat. Add the mushrooms, potato, onion, garlic and celery. Cook, stirring often, for 5 minutes or until potatoes are brown. Remove mixture from the pan. Reserve.

Melt the remaining butter in a saucepan and stir in the flour. Cook for 1 minute. Whisk in the sherry (if using). Whisk in the milk until very smooth. Remove the pan from the heat and stir in the cheese, salt, pepper and nutmeg. Preheat the oven to 350°F (180°C). Cut the fish into bite-size chunks. Fold the fish and reserved vegetables into the sauce. Transfer the mixture to a greased 7- by 11-inch (2 L) baking dish or 9-inch (2.5 L) square baking dish.

TOPPING: Toss bread crumbs with almonds, drizzle with butter and combine. Sprinkle the almond mixture evenly down the length of the casserole to make a 3-inch (7.5 cm) band. (If using a square baking pan, sprinkle topping down the center of the casserole; you may have some leftover topping.) Bake the casserole for 30 minutes or until hot and bubbly.

There's nothing like a hearty, home-cooked meal shared with family and friends to make life's little problems fade away. But who has time to make a holiday roast turkey with all the trimmings these days? And besides, unless you have a really big, hungry crowd, you always seem to find yourself with leftovers that just don't seem to end.

The great news is that if you love the flavors of festive holiday dinners but not all the work involved and the days (and days!) of turkey sandwiches, you can make this casserole instead. Made with chicken instead of turkey, this dish is homey, comforting and easy to assemble.

Since double, skinless, boneless chicken breasts are usually available only in stores that have an on-site butcher, you may find it easier to make this recipe using single chicken breasts. Simply adjust the number to 4 and proceed as directed. Single breasts cook faster than doubles, so you should check for doneness at the 40-minute mark.

Potato Pecan Holiday Chicken Casserole

PREP: 15 minutes | **COOK:** 60 minutes | **YIELD:** 6 servings

- **1 tbsp (15 mL) vegetable oil (approx)**
- **1 onion, chopped**
- **1 clove garlic, minced**
- **¼ cup (50 mL) dried cranberries**
- **1 cup (250 mL) chopped cremini or button mushrooms**
- **2 cups (500 mL) shredded mozzarella cheese**
- **2 large potatoes, peeled, cooked and mashed**
- **¼ cup (50 mL) chopped, toasted pecans**
- **2 double, skinless, boneless chicken breasts, about 1 lb (500 g) each**
- **½ tsp (2 mL) each salt and pepper**
- **½ cup (125 mL) cranberry jelly, melted**
- **2 tbsp (30 mL) chopped fresh sage leaves (or 1 tsp/5 mL crumbled dried sage leaves)**
- **1 tbsp (15 mL) each water and balsamic vinegar**

Heat the oil in a nonstick skillet set over medium-high heat. Add the onion, garlic, dried cranberries and mushrooms; cook for 7 to 10 minutes until the vegetables are tender and golden. Cool slightly. Blend this mixture with the cheese, potatoes and half of the pecans. (Can be made to this point up to 1 day ahead then covered and refrigerated. Bring mixture to room temperature for 30 minutes before proceeding.)

Preheat the oven to 350°F (180°C). Grease a 7- by 11-inch (2 L) casserole dish with additional oil. Spoon in the potato mixture and spread evenly. Sprinkle the chicken breasts evenly with salt and pepper. Place the chicken on top of the potato mixture with the narrow ends of each breast meeting in the center of the dish.

Stir the melted cranberry jelly with the sage, water and balsamic vinegar. Brush half of this mixture over the chicken. Roast, basting occasionally with the remaining jelly mixture, for 45 to 60 minutes or until an instant-read thermometer inserted into the thickest part of the chicken registers 165°F (74°C). Sprinkle with remaining nuts. Rest the casserole for 5 to 10 minutes before slicing and serving.

Unlike the stodgy rice-and-ground-meat stuffed green peppers that were popular in the 1970s when I was growing up, these colorful stuffed veggies have a fresh, light flavor that is very sophisticated and, in my opinion, much more appealing.

I like to serve this light entrée hot or at room temperature. Although these stuffed pepper halves can be a complete meal by themselves, each half can also be paired with a chicken or beef kabob or a crisp salad if you want a little something more.

Lebanese couscous is considerably larger than the couscous many of us may be more familiar with. It is a baby pea-size orb that, unlike Israeli and North African couscous (which needs only to be covered in boiling water to cook through), must be simmered in boiling, salted water for several minutes and then drained in a colander. If Lebanese couscous isn't available, choose a small round-shaped Italian pastina (tiny pasta) such as acini di pepe instead.

Mediterranean Stuffed Peppers with Nutless Basil Pesto

PREP: 20 minutes | **COOK:** 20 minutes | **YIELD:** 8 servings

3 cups (750 mL) cooked Lebanese couscous or round pastina
½ cup (125 mL) crumbled, crisp cooked bacon pieces or finely chopped sun-dried tomatoes
3 tbsp (45 mL) Nutless Basil Pesto (page 43) or deli-made fresh pesto
1 tsp (5 mL) finely grated lemon zest
1 each red, yellow, orange and green pepper
½ cup (125 mL) crumbled feta cheese

Preheat the oven to 350°F (180°C) or the grill to medium. Fluff the couscous or pasta with a fork. Toss with the bacon, pesto and lemon zest until well blended. Halve each pepper lengthwise and remove the white membranes and seeds but leave the stems intact.

Using two pepper halves at a time, microwave at High for 1 minute. Fill each pepper with an equal amount of the couscous mixture.

Bake or grill all of the peppers at once for 15 minutes or until the peppers are softened but not limp. Sprinkle each filled, baked pepper evenly with feta cheese; cook for 2 minutes longer.

Although it would sometimes be easier—especially on a weeknight—to use bought pesto, I almost always make my own. I'd love to tell you that my choice is the result of culinary purity, but that isn't the case. In fact, there's a gourmet grocery store near my house that sells excellent pesto in their deli; I'd have no qualms about buying this time-saving product if it weren't for the fact that my husband is allergic to pine nuts, one of the main ingredients in classic pesto recipes.

With or without nuts, pesto is a wonderful shortcut ingredient. I infuse bottled salad dressings with freshness by stirring in a spoonful of pesto and use it as a topping for bowls of plain pasta with tomato sauce. Likewise, a spoonful of pesto blended with mayonnaise can enliven an ordinary ham or chicken salad sandwich.

Nutless Basil Pesto

YIELD: 1½ cups (375 mL)

2½ cups (625 mL) packed fresh basil
1 cup (250 mL) packed fresh parsley
½ cup (125 mL) grated Parmesan cheese
2 tbsp (30 mL) lemon juice
½ tsp (2 mL) salt
4 cloves garlic, minced
¾ cup (175 mL) extra virgin olive oil

Chop the basil, parsley, Parmesan, lemon juice, salt and garlic finely in a food processor. With the motor running, drizzle in the olive oil and blend until smooth. Place the pesto in a clean, dry container; cover tightly and keep refrigerated or frozen until needed.

Roasting at high heat caramelizes the outside of meat and potatoes and adds flavor that you just can't duplicate with other cooking methods. But roasting large pieces of meat such as a whole chicken takes a lot of time, something few people have on most weeknights. Cutting the vegetables in this recipe into bite-size pieces and using individual portions of chicken speeds up the cooking. Although you have to invest a bit of time in chopping, the payoff is that you'll be able to enjoy the satisfying roasted flavors of this simple dish that much sooner.

Choose a roasting pan that is deep enough to allow you to easily toss the ingredients during cooking but that isn't so deep that the ingredients braise in their own juices. I find a metal lasagna pan works well.

One-pan Indian Roasted Chicken with Potatoes

PREP: 10 minutes | **COOK:** 45 minutes | **YIELD:** 4 servings

- 1 tbsp (15 mL) mild Indian curry paste
- 1 tbsp (15 mL) lime juice
- 2 lb (1 kg) chicken breasts and legs
- 3 cups (750 mL) halved baby new potatoes
- 1 bunch green onions
- 2 tbsp (30 mL) vegetable oil
- ½ tsp (2 mL) each salt and pepper

Preheat the oven to 400°F (200°C). Blend the curry paste with the lime juice until well combined. Add the chicken and potatoes and toss to coat. Remove the roots from the bulb of each green onion. Trim the green onions so that you have a tail of about 1 inch (5 cm) of the green part extending from the bulb. Add bulb ends to the chicken mixture. Thinly slice ¼ cup (50 mL) of the remaining green part of the onions and reserve.

Pour the oil into the roasting pan and place in the oven until very hot, about 5 minutes. Spread the chicken mixture out evenly in the preheated pan. Sprinkle with salt and pepper. Return the pan to the oven. Cook, stirring occasionally, for 45 to 50 minutes or until an instant-read thermometer inserted into the largest piece of chicken registers 165°F (74°C). Stir in the reserved sliced green onions before serving.

Chicken

If King Henry IV were alive today, he'd be very pleased to see that his wish to find a chicken in everyone's cooking pot once a week has been more than granted. In fact, chicken has become one of the most popular foods in North America. In the United States the average annual consumption per person is about 88 pounds; in Canada, it's over 66 pounds.

Chicken is found in many different cuisines from around the world. One of the attractions of chicken as an ingredient is that it is so versatile. It can be used to make something as simple and comforting as a soup or stew, or baked, roasted, barbecued, stir-fried, tossed in a salad, used for burgers and meatloaf (chicken loaf actually!) and more. Its delicate flavor pairs nicely with a variety of sauces and seasonings. Chicken is also fast to cook—especially when using boneless meat cut into pieces—so it's a wonderful dinnertime choice for busy people.

In this chapter there are comfort food stalwarts aplenty, including Oven-fried Chicken with Buttermilk Gravy and Classic Chicken Cacciatore. There are also many recipes that feature exotic, international flavors, such as Indian Butter Chicken and Chicken Satays with Spicy Peanut Mopping Sauce. With so many wonderful chicken choices, I doubt any of us will be eating less of it anytime soon!

In my updated version of coq au vin (literally *chicken in wine*) I've made this classic 1960s dinner party favorite faster to prepare by starting with boneless chicken that is cooked on the stovetop rather than slowly braised in the oven for a long time. And rather than have you peel lots of tiny pearl onions (a tedious, time-consuming task), I've substituted thickly sliced cooking onions. Despite these revisions, the heart of this dish remains unchanged, so when you serve this retro classic you'll still feel like a modern-day Julia Child!

I like to use boneless chicken thighs for recipes like this one because they are always succulent, tender and flavorful. Cubed, skinless, boneless chicken breasts can be used, too, if you prefer. They'll just have a more delicate flavor. Regardless of what part of the chicken you choose, remember that it is customary to serve the finished dish with the same wine that was used in the recipe. Although the cognac is an optional ingredient, it adds a wonderful dimension and fullness to the sauce, so if you have some on hand, be sure to add it.

Stovetop Coq au Vin

PREP: 25 minutes | **COOK:** 35 minutes | **YIELD:** 6 servings

3 tbsp (45 mL) vegetable oil, divided
½ cup (125 mL) coarsely chopped bacon
2 onions, peeled and thickly sliced
1 tsp (5 mL) each dried thyme leaves and rosemary leaves
¼ cup (50 mL) all-purpose flour
1 tsp (5 mL) each salt and pepper
2 lb (1 kg) boneless chicken thighs, quartered
2 tbsp (30 mL) cognac or brandy (optional)
1 cup (250 mL) chicken broth
2 tbsp (30 mL) tomato paste
2 cloves garlic, minced
2 cups (500 mL) red wine such as Bourdeaux, merlot, Rioja or Chianti
1 bay leaf
3 cups (750 mL) small button mushrooms

Heat 1 tbsp (15 mL) of the oil in a Dutch oven set over medium heat. Add the bacon and cook for 5 minutes or until lightly browned. Add the onion, thyme and rosemary and sauté for 2 minutes. Meanwhile, combine the flour with the salt and pepper in a plastic bag or large bowl. Add the chicken thighs and shake or toss to coat evenly with the seasoned flour.

Scrape the onion mixture from the pot into a bowl. Reserve. Increase the heat under the Dutch oven to medium-high. Brown the chicken in batches, adding extra oil to the pan as needed. Dust the browned chicken with any flour mixture remaining in the bowl. Return all of the browned chicken and the onion mixture to the Dutch oven. Make a well in the center of the browned ingredients and add the cognac (if using). Cook until evaporated, for about 1 minute, scraping up the browned bits on the bottom of the pot.

Stir the broth with the tomato paste and garlic. Add this mixture to the Dutch oven. Pour in the wine and add the bay leaf. Bring to a boil. Reduce the heat to medium. Add the mushrooms and simmer for 30 minutes or until the sauce is thickened. Taste and add more salt and pepper if necessary. Remove and discard the bay leaf before serving.

This Italian-American dish is redolent of wine, tomatoes and complex, slowly simmered flavors. Cacciatore translates from Italian as "huntsman's style" so it isn't surprising that this rustic dish proves supremely satisfying on a crisp, fall evening. My version uses only chicken drumsticks since I find that they are the most flavorful and visually appealing of all the chicken parts.

On weekends when I have time to linger in the kitchen preparing supper, I serve this mushroom-studded chicken stew with polenta or a simple buttered pasta. The result is a trattoria-style dinner that is elegant enough for company but broadly appealing so that it can satisfy a family, too. When time is short or when I don't want to dirty another saucepan, I just ladle this stew over thick slices of toasted Italian bread.

Classic Chicken Cacciatore

PREP: 25 minutes | **COOK:** 60 minutes | **YIELD:** 4 servings

3 tbsp (45 mL) all-purpose flour
1 tsp (5 mL) each salt and pepper
2 lb (1 kg) chicken drumsticks, with skin
3 tbsp (45 mL) vegetable oil, divided (approx)
½ cup (125 mL) red wine or low-sodium chicken broth
1 large onion, peeled and sliced
1½ tsp (7 mL) each dried thyme and oregano leaves
2 cups (500 mL) sliced mushrooms, about 4 oz (125 g)
1 can (28 oz/796 mL) diced tomatoes, with juices
3 tbsp (45 mL) tomato paste
1 tbsp (15 mL) balsamic vinegar
1 green pepper, cored and chopped
2 cloves garlic, minced

Mix the flour with the salt and pepper in a plastic bag or large bowl. Add the chicken drumsticks and shake or toss to coat evenly with the seasoned flour. Heat half the oil in a large, deep skillet or Dutch oven set over medium-high heat. Brown the chicken all over, working in batches. Add up to 1 tbsp (15 mL) more oil if needed. Transfer browned pieces to a bowl. Reserve.

Stir the wine into the pan and bring to a boil. Stir to scrape up the cooked-on bits. When the volume of wine is reduced, add the remaining oil and reduce the heat to medium. Add the onion, thyme and oregano. Cook, stirring often, for 5 minutes or until softened. Add the mushrooms and cook for 5 to 8 minutes longer. Add a small amount of the diced tomatoes and stir to scrape up all the cooked-on bits. Then, add the remaining tomatoes, tomato paste, balsamic vinegar, green pepper, and garlic.

Bring the mixture to a boil, stirring often with a wooden spoon. Nestle the browned chicken pieces down into the tomato mixture and reduce the heat to low. Simmer, stirring and turning the meat occasionally, for 45 to 50 minutes or until the chicken is cooked through and the pan juices are thickened.

If you long for the crunch and flavor of fried chicken but dread the mess left behind from the preparation, then this recipe is for you! Based on the classic 1950s diner-style fried chicken that was traditionally served with dumplings, grits or mashed potatoes (my personal favorite!) and gravy on the side, this comforting entrée is easy enough to make even on a busy weeknight. It's sure to be a hit with kids and adults alike.

Buttermilk in the marinade keeps the chicken tender and juicy and in the gravy it cuts the richness nicely. If you don't have buttermilk or yogurt on hand, substitute ½ cup (125 mL) sour cream blended with ¼ cup (50 mL) milk in the marinade and 1 tbsp (15 mL) sour cream in the gravy.

This recipe doubles easily, so don't hesitate to make extra chicken to serve later in the week or to pack in lunchboxes.

SEE PHOTO INSERT

Oven-fried Chicken with Buttermilk Gravy

PREP: 15 minutes | **MARINATE:** 30 minutes or up to 2 days
COOK: 45 minutes | **YIELD:** 4 servings

MARINADE:
 ¾ cup (175 mL) buttermilk or plain yogurt
 2 tbsp (30 mL) Dijon mustard
 1 tbsp (15 mL) minced green onion
 1 tbsp (15 mL) vegetable oil
 1 clove garlic, minced
 1 tsp (5 mL) pepper
 8 chicken drumsticks or 4 bone-in chicken breasts, about 1¾ lb (875 g)
COATING:
 2 cups (500 mL) cornflake-style cereal, crushed (about ⅔ cup [150 mL])
 1 cup (250 mL) grated Parmesan cheese
GRAVY:
 1 tbsp (15 mL) butter
 ¼ cup (50 mL) finely chopped onion
 ¼ tsp (1 mL) pepper
 2 tbsp (30 mL) all-purpose flour
 1½ cups (375 mL) low-sodium chicken broth
 ¼ cup (50 mL) buttermilk

MARINADE: Whisk the buttermilk with the mustard, green onion, vegetable oil, garlic and pepper. Add the drumsticks and toss to combine. Cover and marinate for at least 30 minutes at room temperature or in the refrigerator for up to 2 days.

COATING: Preheat the oven to 375°F (190°C). Place the crumbs and cheese in a plastic bag; shake to combine. Remove the chicken from the marinade. Coat in the crumb mixture. Arrange on a foil-lined baking sheet that has been sprayed with cooking spray. Discard any unused crumbs. Bake for 40 to 45 minutes or until coating is golden and chicken is cooked through.

GRAVY: Melt the butter in a saucepan set over medium heat. Add the onions and pepper. Cook, stirring often, for 5 minutes or until the onions are translucent. Blend in the flour. Add the broth gradually, stirring constantly. Bring to a boil. Reduce the heat and simmer for 5 minutes or until thickened. Stir in the buttermilk.

Increasingly often, versions of butter chicken are turning up on mainstream restaurant menus and in the frozen section of grocery stores as North Americans discover the delicious, richly spiced flavors of India. Cardamom is the key ingredient that gives butter chicken its lingering and satisfying taste. A member of the ginger family, this spice is normally found in ground form in the spice section of grocery stores.

My Indian Butter Chicken recipe uses just a small amount of cardamom. But cardamom is also a great spice to add to desserts that use ground cinnamon and ginger; so, after you buy some for this recipe you'll have many opportunities to experiment with cardamom when baking, too. Cardamom is also one of the spices added to black tea and milk to make the hugely popular Masala chai tea drinks that coffee shops sell, as Chai Lattes.

Indian Butter Chicken

PREP: 25 minutes | **COOK:** 40 minutes | **YIELD:** 6 servings

> 2 lb (1 kg) skinless, boneless chicken breasts, about 4
> ½ tsp (2 mL) each salt and pepper
> ¼ cup (50 mL) butter
> 2 tbsp (30 mL) vegetable oil
> 2 onions, peeled and sliced
> 3 cloves garlic, minced
> 1 tbsp (15 mL) tomato paste
> 4 tsp (20 mL) mild Indian curry paste
> 2 tsp (10 mL) minced fresh ginger
> 1 tsp (5 mL) ground cinnamon
> ¼ tsp (1 mL) cardamom
> 1 can (28 oz/796 mL) diced tomatoes, with juices
> ⅓ cup (75 mL) 35% whipping cream or sour cream
> 2 tsp (10 mL) lime juice
> ¼ cup (50 mL) chopped fresh coriander leaves
> Salt
> Steamed rice or naan bread
> Lime wedges

Cut each chicken breast in half across its width. Sprinkle the chicken with salt and pepper. Melt half the butter with the oil in a Dutch oven set over medium-high heat. Add the chicken to the pan in batches and cook, turning as necessary, until browned. Transfer the chicken pieces to a plate as they brown and reserve.

Reduce the heat under the pan to medium. Add the onions, garlic and tomato paste; cook, stirring occasionally, for 2 minutes. Stir in the curry paste, ginger, cinnamon and cardamom. Cook, stirring, for 30 seconds. Add the tomatoes, including their juices, the remaining butter and the browned chicken and any accumulated meat juices to the pan and bring to a boil.

Reduce the heat and simmer gently, covered, for 25 minutes or until the chicken is cooked through. Stir in the cream, lime juice and coriander. Heat until the mixture is very hot but not boiling. Season the sauce with salt to taste. Serve butter chicken with rice or naan bread. Garnish with lime wedges.

Besides being deliciously aromatic and spicy, Indian foods are growing in popularity because of the health benefits that many of the ingredients used in Indian cooking have to offer.

Dal is one of the foods infused with healthful benefits. Although dal is the Hindi word for a variety of pulses, on Indian restaurant menus in Britain and North America this word usually refers to a saucy lentil mixture that has been cooked with spices. Lentils are high in fiber and contain other nutrients such as iron and folate. Some of the best known Indian dal dishes are side dishes such as *channa dal,* which is made with yellow split peas, and *massor dal,* which is made with orange lentils. In this chicken and lentil recipe, side dish meets main course since chicken is added to the lentil mixture to create a one-dish meal. To limit the mess and the preparation time, I use precooked canned green or brown lentils. Both of these lentil varieties are easy to find in grocery stores so this meal can be made quickly any night of the week.

Curried Chicken and Dal

PREP: 10 minutes | **COOK:** 25 minutes | **YIELD:** 4 servings

2 tbsp (30 mL) vegetable oil
4 tsp (20 mL) mild Indian curry paste
2 skinless, boneless chicken breasts, about 1 lb (500 g)
1 onion, finely peeled and chopped
2 large tomatoes, seeded and chopped
2 cans (19 oz/540 mL each) cooked green or brown lentils
3 tbsp (45 mL) chopped fresh coriander
½ tsp (2 mL) salt
¼ tsp (1 mL) pepper

Preheat the oven to 350°F (180°C). Blend together half of each the oil and the curry paste. Brush this mixture all over the chicken and set aside. Heat the remaining oil in a skillet set over medium heat. Add the onion and cook, stirring occasionally, for 5 minutes. Increase the heat to medium-high. Add the chicken and cook, turning as needed, for 5 minutes or until golden.

Leaving the onions in the skillet, transfer only the chicken to a baking pan and cook in the preheated oven for 15 minutes or until cooked through.

Meanwhile, stir the remaining curry paste and the tomatoes into the onion mixture still in the skillet. Cook for 2 minutes. Drain the lentils, rinse well and add them to the skillet. Stir until the ingredients are well combined. Reduce the heat to low. Cook, stirring often, until the lentils are heated through. Stir in the coriander and salt and pepper to taste. Slice the chicken and fan over lentils to serve.

This satisfying, quick-to-fix chicken stew is the perfect size for smaller families. Raisins and a spice blend of ground coriander, cumin, cinnamon and just a pinch of cayenne give this entrée an exotic taste reminiscent of North African cooking. Unlike fresh coriander (also called cilantro), which has a very strong, distinctive flavor, the ground coriander seed used here is sweet and slightly nutty tasting. It partners naturally with the cumin and cinnamon and as the stew cooks, the spices combine to release a complex, slow-simmered gourmet flavor after only a short amount of cooking time.

Serve this aromatic stew with hot, cooked rice or warm flatbread; with a refreshing green lettuce and cucumber salad; or simply on its own.

Caravan Chicken and Lentil Stew

PREP: 15 minutes | **COOK:** 25 minutes | **YIELD:** 3 to 4 servings

¾ lb (375 g) skinless, boneless chicken thighs or breasts
2 tbsp (30 mL) vegetable oil
½ onion, peeled and chopped
1 clove garlic, minced
½ tsp (2 mL) each ground coriander seed and salt
¼ tsp (1 mL) each ground cumin and cinnamon
Pinch cayenne
1 tbsp (15 mL) tomato paste
1 small potato, cooked and mashed
1 cup (250 mL) cooked, canned brown or green lentils
2 tbsp (30 mL) golden raisins
1 cup (250 mL) chicken or vegetable broth
2 tbsp (30 mL) chopped fresh coriander leaves or parsley
1 tsp (5 mL) toasted slivered or sliced almonds

Cut the chicken into bite-size pieces. Heat half the oil in a medium-size nonstick skillet set over medium-high heat; brown the chicken on all sides and remove from the pan. Reserve.

Reduce the heat to medium. Add the remaining oil to the pan and cook the onion and garlic for 5 minutes, stirring often. Stir in the coriander, salt, cumin, cinnamon and cayenne; cook, stirring, for 1 minute.

Meanwhile, blend the tomato paste with the potato and add to the pan. Rinse the lentils in a sieve under cold, running water and drain well. Add the lentils, reserved chicken and raisins to the pan and stir until well combined.

Add the broth and bring to a boil. Reduce the heat to medium and simmer gently, uncovered, until the mixture becomes thick, about 10 minutes. Sprinkle with fresh coriander and almonds before serving.

Cook once, eat twice: Make a double (or triple!) batch of this stew and freeze for another time.

Hoisin sauce is often called Peking sauce since it is the mixture served as a dip with the classic Chinese, crispy-skinned Peking Duck. Made from a mixture of soybean paste, garlic, mild chilies and spices, hoisin is a wonderfully versatile Chinese ingredient that can be used to glaze spareribs and add body and flavor to stir-fry sauces. Here it is used as the base for a sticky marinade and glaze.

Juicy, tender chicken thighs are especially good in this recipe because they have a wonderful flavor that can stand up to assertive ingredients such as hoisin, lime and ginger. The end result is a complex, exotic flavor that is unmistakably meaty and rich. Chicken breasts are also delicious in this recipe but you'll find that the meat's more delicate flavor gets lost in the sauce so that the dish isn't quite as interesting.

Use this marinade on duck breasts for an easy, elegant meal. Sear duck in a hot skillet and then finish in the oven.

Peking Grilled Chicken

PREP: 5 minutes | **COOK:** 20 minutes | **YIELD:** 6 servings

⅓ cup (75 mL) lime juice
2 tbsp (30 mL) hoisin sauce
1 tsp (5 mL) hot pepper sauce
1 tbsp (15 mL) brown sugar
2 tbsp (30 mL) minced fresh ginger
½ tsp (2 mL) each salt and pepper
1 green onion, thinly sliced
1½ lb (750 g) skinless, boneless chicken thighs or chicken breasts

Stir the lime juice with the hoisin sauce, hot pepper sauce, brown sugar, ginger, salt, pepper and green onion. Toss the chicken with the lime juice mixture. Marinate for 15 minutes at room temperature or refrigerate, covered, for up to 4 hours.

Preheat the grill to medium-high. Grease the grate well. Remove chicken from marinade and place on the grate, reserving marinade. Cook the chicken, turning and basting as needed with reserved marinade, for 14 to 20 minutes or until cooked through.

Cooking with chestnuts used to be a time-consuming, nail-splitting chore; however, the widespread availability of cooked, vacuum-packed chestnuts has changed that situation forever! Chestnuts are a sweet tasting, edible nutmeat that is deliciously mild. The flavor of chestnuts pairs nicely with foods such as chicken, game meats, tart apples, sage, thyme and other sweet herbs. Be careful not to buy sweetened, cooked chestnuts for this recipe. The sweetened product is often labeled as *marrons glacés* and is only suitable for baking.

Chicken Stew with Chestnuts and Apples

PREP: 10 minutes | **COOK:** 45 minutes | **YIELD:** 4 servings

1 tbsp (15 mL) all-purpose flour
1½ lb (750 g) skinless, boneless chicken thighs, about 8
2 tbsp (30 mL) vegetable oil
1 small onion, finely chopped
¼ cup (50 mL) each finely diced carrot, celery and dried apple
1 tbsp (15 mL) dried thyme leaves
1 bay leaf
½ tsp (2 mL) each salt and pepper
2 tbsp (30 mL) tomato paste
¼ cup (50 mL) ruby port or Madeira
2 cups (500 mL) chicken broth
1 cup (250 mL) peeled chestnuts, halved if large
1½ cups (375 mL) small button mushroom caps
2 tbsp (30 mL) finely chopped parsley
Thinly sliced apple

Place the flour in a plastic bag or large bowl. Add the chicken and shake or toss to coat. Set aside.

Heat half of the oil in a Dutch oven set over medium heat. Add the onion, carrot, celery, dried apple, thyme, bay leaf, salt and pepper. Partially cover and simmer, stirring occasionally, for 5 minutes. Stir in the tomato paste.

Push the vegetables to the edges of the pan and drizzle the remaining oil into the center. Increase the heat to medium-high. Brown the reserved chicken in the hot oil, pushing the brownest pieces of meat to the edges of the pan. Pour in the port and stir to scrape up any cooked-on bits. (If port evaporates quickly, add a small amount of the broth, if necessary.) Blend the pan ingredients together and cook, stirring, until the pan is almost dry.

Stirring, gradually add the broth, chestnuts and mushrooms to the Dutch oven. Bring the mixture to a boil and reduce the heat to low. Simmer for 30 minutes. Stir occasionally. Taste and adjust seasonings if necessary. Serve sprinkled with parsley and garnished with apple slices.

Despite its rich sounding name, buttermilk is actually one of the leanest of all milk products. Originally it was the liquid that dairy maids would pour off the cream as it was turned into butter. Today's buttermilk is made by adding bacteria cultures to non-fat milk so that the milk develops a slightly thickened texture and a tangy flavor.

When used in poultry marinades, buttermilk creates tender, juicy meat that is flavorful through and through and almost snow white inside. Although this garlicky flavored chicken is wonderfully delicious hot, this recipe is the one I most often use when making chicken breasts to be used cold in sandwiches or in salads since the buttermilk and herb mixture delivers such a nice, moist result.

If you have a grill press, place it on the grill at the same time as you light the burners. Spray the flat surface of the press lightly with cooking oil and place it on top of the chicken as it cooks. Grill for 14 to 16 minutes or until juices run clear, then glaze as directed.

Buttermilk Herb Marinated Chicken

PREP: 10 minutes | **MARINATE:** 30 minutes
COOK: 15 minutes | **YIELD:** 6 servings

MARINADE:
   ½ cup (125 mL) each buttermilk and light mayonnaise
   1 tbsp (15 mL) minced onion
   1 tsp (5 mL) each finely grated lemon zest and Dijon mustard
   1 tbsp (15 mL) olive oil
   1 small clove garlic, minced
   1 tbsp (15 mL) each chopped fresh chives, thyme and basil

CHICKEN:
   6 skinless, boneless chicken breasts, about 3 lb (1.5 kg)
   ¾ tsp (4 mL) each salt and pepper
   1 tbsp (15 mL) each honey and olive oil

MARINADE: Whisk the buttermilk with the mayonnaise, onion, lemon zest, mustard and vegetable oil. Stir in the garlic, chives, thyme and basil. (Mixture can be made ahead, covered tightly and refrigerated for up to 3 days. Shake well before using. Makes 1¼ cups.)

CHICKEN: Place the chicken in a shallow bowl or casserole. Add the marinade and toss to combine. Cover and refrigerate for at least 30 minutes at room temperature or in the refrigerator for up to 24 hours.

Preheat the grill to medium-high. Remove the chicken from the marinade, shaking off and discarding excess juices. Sprinkle the chicken all over with salt and pepper. Blend the honey with the vegetable oil. Reserve.

Lightly grease the grate. Grill the chicken, turning once or twice, for 10 minutes. Brush all over with the honey mixture. Grill, turning often, for another 5 minutes or until no longer pink in the center.

The most popular theory about the origin of the triple-decker club sandwich is that it was created in Saratoga Springs, New York, at the end of the nineteenth century by a chef at the Saratoga Springs gaming house frequented by an exclusive—and apparently hungry—clientele. By the time I was a kid, this concoction of chicken (or turkey), bacon, lettuce, tomato and mayo on toasted white bread had become a ubiquitous item on lunch counter and diner menus.

In my lighter twist on this traditional fare, some of the elegance that may have accompanied the original clubhouse is regained by wrapping the chicken in bacon and serving it warm on a skewer. The bacon adds a smoky, delicious flavor to the juicy skewers of chicken. Be sure to choose a barbecue sauce that isn't too strongly smoke flavored. Some of the more assertive smoke-flavored sauces on the market will overpower the delicate flavor of the chicken.

If you really have a hankering for the bread that came with the traditional club sandwich, you can add crusty sourdough croutons to the finished salad.

SEE PHOTO INSERT

Clubhouse Grilled Chicken Salad

PREP: 15 minutes | **COOK:** 12 minutes | **YIELD:** 4 servings

2 lb (500 g) skinless, boneless chicken breasts, about 4
½ cup (125 mL) barbecue sauce
12 slices of bacon
¼ cup (50 mL) mayonnaise
2 tbsp (30 mL) milk
1 tbsp (15 mL) very finely chopped fresh chives or green onion
Romaine or leafy green lettuce
Sliced tomatoes

Preheat the grill to medium. Cut the chicken breasts into 1-inch (2.5 cm) cubes and toss with the barbecue sauce. Chop each slice of bacon into thirds. Wrap each cube of chicken in a piece of bacon. Thread four bacon-wrapped pieces of chicken onto each skewer.

Lightly grease the grate. Grill the chicken skewers, turning as needed, for 12 to 15 minutes or until the chicken is cooked through and the bacon is crisp.

Meanwhile, blend the mayonnaise with the milk and chives. Reserve.

Place skewers over a bed of lettuce and tomato slices and drizzle with mayonnaise mixture.

Balsamic vinegar is now a common pantry item in many kitchens; however, until about 15 years ago, it was a specialty item. Better quality (and correspondingly more expensive) balsamic vinegars are fairly low acid and mellow tasting. For this recipe, you might want to splurge on a better quality bottle as it will make the glaze all the more exquisite.

Although cooking chicken breasts with the bone in has become less common over the past decade and a half, there's no doubt that the finished dish is more flavorful and juicy with bone-in chicken. If you are concerned about calories from fat, remove the skin before marinating the chicken breasts. Or, if you're in the mood to indulge, leave the skin on. The flavor of the glaze on the skin will be sensational! This is the recipe pictured on the front cover.

For truly superb results, you can also make this recipe using a whole chicken rotisserie-roasted on the barbecue following the manufacturer's directions.

Orange Balsamic Glazed Baked Chicken Breasts

PREP: 10 minutes | **MARINATE:** 15 minutes
COOK: 30 minutes | **YIELD:** 4 servings

¼ cup (50 mL) honey mustard
½ cup (125 mL) orange juice
1 tbsp (15 mL) chopped fresh rosemary or 4 tsp (20 mL) dried rosemary leaves
1 tbsp (15 mL) balsamic vinegar
½ tsp (2 mL) each salt and pepper
4 bone-in chicken breasts

Stir the mustard with the orange juice, rosemary, balsamic vinegar, salt and pepper. Place half of this mixture in a zip-top bag or a large bowl. Add the chicken and turn to coat in the marinade. Let stand at room temperature for at least 15 minutes or overnight in the refrigerator. Place the other half of the orange juice mixture in a microwaveable bowl and microwave at High for 30 to 60 seconds until boiling. Continue to microwave at High for about 1 minute or until slightly thickened.

Preheat the oven to 375°F (190°C). Place the chicken on a lightly greased rack over a baking sheet or broiling pan. Bake for 20 minutes. Baste all over with reserved sauce. Bake for 10 to 15 minutes longer or until an instant-read thermometer registers 165°F (74°C) when inserted into the thickest part of the chicken breast.

With its fresh, bright Mediterranean flavors, this marinated grilled chicken is likely to become a family favorite. If you prefer white meat, you can replace the chicken thighs with breasts; cook for 8 to 10 minutes per side or until juices run clear.

Be sure to use dried oregano, rosemary and thyme leaves and not the ground versions of these herbs. I find that the ground varieties of dried herbs tend to have an unpleasant flavor (and they also lose their potency quickly).

If you use the shorter 30-minute marinating time, you may want to soften the dried rosemary leaves in 2 tsp (10 mL) of boiling water before adding them—and their soaking water (it will be infused with flavor from the herb)—to the other marinade ingredients.

Lemon Grove Grilled Chicken

PREP: 10 minutes | **MARINATE:** 30 minutes
COOK: 15 minutes | **YIELD:** 4 servings

3 tbsp (45 mL) olive oil
⅓ cup (75 mL) lemon juice
1 tbsp (15 mL) honey mustard
1 tsp (5 mL) each dried oregano, rosemary and thyme leaves
2 cloves garlic, minced
1 tbsp (15 mL) chopped shallots or onions
1 tbsp (15 mL) drained, chopped capers
8 skinless, boneless chicken thighs, about 1 lb (500 g)
½ tsp (2 mL) each salt and pepper

Combine the oil with the lemon juice, mustard, oregano, rosemary, thyme, garlic, shallots and capers. Pour this mixture over the chicken, turning to coat the meat well. Cover the chicken tightly and marinate for at least 30 minutes at room temperature or for up to 24 hours in the refrigerator.

Preheat the grill to medium-high; grease the grate. Season the marinated chicken with salt and pepper. Arrange the meat on the grate. Cover and grill for about 8 minutes per side or until cooked through.

Cranberry and orange juice blended in equal parts is one of my favorite thirst-quenching drinks and it inspired this recipe for a fast weeknight entrée. I added fresh ginger and fresh coriander to give the mixture some zing. The result is a pleasant flavor that lingers in your mouth long after the last bite.

This entrée can be served so many ways. You can slice the chicken thinly over a salad or serve a whole breast with rice and stir-fried veggies.

Ginger Cranberry Chicken Breasts

PREP: 5 minutes | **COOK:** 40 minutes | **YIELD:** 6 servings

6 skinless, boneless chicken breasts, about 3 lb (1.5 kg)
½ tsp (2 mL) each salt and pepper
1 cup (250 mL) jellied cranberry sauce
¼ cup (50 mL) orange juice
2 tbsp (30 mL) minced fresh ginger
2 cloves garlic, minced
1 tbsp (15 mL) finely chopped fresh coriander

Preheat the oven to 450°F (230°C). Arrange the chicken breasts on a rack in a shallow roasting pan or casserole dish. Sprinkle each portion evenly with salt and pepper. Bake for 10 minutes.

Meanwhile, combine the cranberry sauce and orange juice in a microwaveable bowl. Microwave at High for 1½ to 2½ minutes until boiling, stirring occasionally until smooth. Stir in the ginger, garlic and coriander. Brush some of the sauce mixture over the chicken; cook the sauce-covered chicken for 5 minutes longer.

Reduce the oven temperature to 350°F (180°C). Bake, basting chicken often with remaining sauce mixture, for 20 to 25 minutes longer or until the chicken is well glazed and cooked through.

Variation

To add holiday flavor, substitute 1 tsp (5 mL) dried crumbled sage or rosemary for the coriander.

A pleasing blend of sweetness, spice and savory herbal flavors is the secret combination that will make your family think you hired a personal chef to prepare dinner! The last minute garnish of thinly sliced cheese and green onion transforms the finished dish from a plain, everyday chicken entrée into something special to look at, too.

Although other mustards such as yellow ballpark mustard or honey mustard can be substituted, classic Dijon mustard is the ideal choice for this recipe. The sharpness of this classic French condiment nicely cuts the sweetness of the apricot jelly.

Fruity Mustard Glazed Chicken

PREP: 15 minutes | **COOK:** 25 minutes | **YIELD:** 6 servings

½ cup (125 mL) apricot or cranberry jelly
3 tbsp (45 mL) Dijon mustard
1 tbsp (15 mL) lemon juice
1½ tsp (7 mL) chipotle-flavored or regular hot pepper sauce
2 tsp (10 mL) each minced fresh ginger and finely chopped fresh rosemary
1 clove garlic, minced
6 skinless, boneless chicken breasts, about 3 lb (1.5 kg)
1 tsp (5 mL) each salt and pepper
6 slices mozzarella cheese
2 tbsp (30 mL) finely chopped green onion

Melt the apricot jelly in a saucepan set over medium heat. Stir in the mustard, lemon juice, hot pepper sauce, ginger, rosemary and garlic. Simmer the mixture gently, stirring constantly, for 2 minutes or until smooth. Cool to room temperature. Divide in half.

GRILLING INSTRUCTIONS: Preheat the grill to medium-high and line the grate with perforated, nonstick grill foil. (If you don't have grill foil, grease the grate before placing the chicken on the grill.) Sprinkle the chicken breasts with salt and pepper. Brush half of the glaze over the raw chicken. Grill the glazed chicken for 8 minutes on one side. Turn and brush with some of the reserved glaze. Grill for 8 to 10 minutes longer, turning the chicken and basting it with the remaining glaze as necessary until cooked through.

Top each piece of glazed chicken with a slice of cheese. Cook, covered, for about 1 minute. Sprinkle with chopped green onion just before serving.

OVEN INSTRUCTIONS: Preheat the oven to 375°F (190°C). Arrange the chicken on a rack in a shallow roasting pan or casserole dish. Brush with some of the glaze as directed in the grilling method. Bake in the oven for 15 minutes. Turn the chicken and brush with remaining glaze, then continue to bake for 10 more minutes or until cooked through. Garnish as directed.

Cooking for a family can be a challenge when you have to accommodate the tastes of different age groups. Parents often compromise their own desire for sophisticated and different foods in order to serve a dinner that will please the kids. Or, if a parent does make a meal with adult appeal, they find they also have to make something separate to please the kids. This recipe appeals to all ages. Children love these chicken drumsticks that introduce them to new but not overly powerful flavors such as cardamom and ground coriander in a saucy, fun, hand-held format, while adults love the complex and interesting flavor.

Here's some great news: the marinade from this recipe is also terrific on pork chops, pork tenderloin and pork butt roasts. So, if this meal proves to be a hit at your table, go ahead and use the marinade on these pork cuts when you want something a little out of the ordinary but that is still sure to be a crowd pleaser.

Spice Market Chicken Drumsticks

PREP: 10 minutes | **MARINATE:** 4 hours
COOK: 30 minutes | **YIELD:** 6 servings

1 small onion, peeled and grated
¼ cup (50 mL) orange juice
2 tbsp (30 mL) brown sugar
½ tsp (2 mL) finely grated lime zest
1 tbsp (15 mL) lime juice
1 large clove garlic, minced
1 tbsp (15 mL) minced ginger
1 tsp (5 mL) each ground cinnamon and dried oregano leaves
½ tsp (2 mL) ground coriander
¼ tsp (1 mL) ground cardamom
¼ tsp (1 mL) each salt and pepper
2 lb (1 kg) chicken drumsticks, about 8

Stir the onion with the orange juice, brown sugar, lime zest, lime juice, garlic, ginger, cinnamon, oregano, coriander, cardamom, salt and pepper. Place the drumsticks in a zip-top bag. Pour in the orange juice mixture and seal tightly. Shake the bag, turning the chicken to coat all over. Marinate in the refrigerator for at least 4 hours for or up to 2 days.

Preheat the oven to 425°F (220°C). Bring the chicken to room temperature for 30 minutes; drain marinade into a bowl and reserve. Arrange the drumsticks on a rack set in a rimmed baking sheet. Roast in the oven for 15 minutes, turning and basting once or twice with reserved marinade. Discard any unused marinade.

Continue to roast the chicken, without basting, for 15 to 20 minutes longer or until an instant-read thermometer inserted into the meatiest part of one leg reads 165°F (74°C).

Cook once, eat twice: Double this recipe, freezing one half of the raw chicken in the marinade. Before cooking, thaw in the refrigerator completely. Drain marinade into a bowl and reserve. Cook as directed.

This quick, simple grilled chicken recipe delivers authentic southwestern flavors that are robust but still light. The secret is in the tart, smoky lemon marinade. If you're short on time, you can toss the chicken with the marinade in a zip-top bag and then put it in the freezer. Transfer the bag to the refrigerator the night before you intend to cook the chicken; thaw completely and then proceed with cooking as directed.

If you have a rotisserie attachment for your barbecue, this marinade is also a wonderful choice for a whole chicken that is to be slowly cooked on the spit (you'll really feel like you're out on the range!). If using on a whole chicken, marinate overnight and glaze with a few tablespoons of honey during the last 15 minutes of cooking. Refer to the manufacturer's instructions for cooking times.

SEE PHOTO INSERT

Chili Lemon Chicken

PREP: 10 minutes | **MARINATE:** 30 minutes
COOK: 10 to 20 minutes | **YIELD:** 4 to 6 servings

⅓ cup (75 mL) lemon juice
¼ cup (50 mL) barbecue sauce
1 tsp (5 mL) chipotle pepper or other hot sauce
¼ cup (50 mL) minced green onion
1 tbsp (15 mL) each chili powder and chopped fresh oregano
1 tsp (5 mL) ground cumin
½ tsp (2 mL) each salt and pepper
2 lb (1 kg) skinless, boneless chicken breasts (about 4) and/or thighs (about 9)

Whisk the lemon juice with the barbecue sauce, chipotle pepper sauce, green onion, chili powder, oregano, cumin, salt and pepper until well combined. Toss the marinade with the chicken pieces and transfer the meat and all the liquid to a zip-top freezer bag; seal. Marinate in the refrigerator, turning the bag occasionally, for at least 30 minutes or overnight.

Preheat the grill to medium-high. Lightly grease the grate. Remove the chicken from the marinade and place on the barbecue. Grill the chicken, turning once, for about 10 minutes for thighs and for about 20 minutes for breasts or until cooked through.

Since the natural sweetness of grape juice can be quite cloying, this recipe includes savory ingredients such as rosemary, Dijon mustard and balsamic vinegar. And to create a satisfying, lingering taste, I've used smoked paprika, which adds an appealing piquancy.

Vineland Glazed Roast Chicken

PREP: 30 minutes | **COOK:** 45 minutes | **YIELD:** 6 servings

GLAZE:

2 cups (500 mL) Concord grape juice
2 tbsp (30 mL) brown sugar
2 tbsp (30 mL) balsamic vinegar
2 cloves garlic, minced
1 tbsp (15 mL) finely chopped fresh rosemary
1 tbsp (15 mL) Dijon mustard
½ tsp (1 mL) smoked or regular paprika
3 lb (1.5 kg) bone-in chicken pieces
2 tbsp (30 mL) melted butter
1 tsp (5 mL) each salt and coarsely ground pepper

GLAZE: Place the grape juice, brown sugar, balsamic vinegar, garlic, rosemary, mustard and paprika in a saucepan. Bring to a boil. Reduce the heat to medium-low and simmer the mixture gently for 25 minutes or until the mixture is reduced and syrupy. Reserve.

Preheat the oven to 400°F (200°C). Coat the chicken evenly all over with the melted butter. Sprinkle each portion evenly with salt and pepper. Place the chicken pieces on a rack set in a rimmed baking sheet or shallow roasting pan. Transfer to the oven and roast for 20 minutes.

Roast the chicken, brushing liberally with the reserved glaze every 10 minutes, for 25 to 35 minutes longer or until an instant-read thermometer inserted into the fleshiest areas of the meat registers 165°F (74°C). Skim the fat from the roasting pan and discard. Strain the pan juices into any remaining glaze to make a sauce. Transfer the sauce mixture to a microwaveable bowl or sauceboat. Microwave at High for about 2 minutes or until boiling. Serve the chicken with the sauce on the side.

The flavor of this glaze is almost the same as that of the grape juice version but it may not provide the same health benefits. Because it is faster to prepare, use this shorcut version on busy nights, as a glaze for finishing grilled chicken breasts or on deli-cooked rotisserie roasted chickens that you reheat in your own oven for dinner.

Shortcut Glaze

PREP: 5 minutes | **YIELD:** Enough to coat 3 lb (1.5 kg) of chicken parts

¼ cup (50 mL) grape jelly, melted
1 tsp (5 mL) Dijon mustard
1 tsp (5 mL) balsamic vinegar
½ tsp (2 mL) chopped fresh rosemary leaves
½ tsp (2 mL) minced garlic
Pinch smoked paprika

Stir the melted jelly with the mustard, balsamic vinegar, rosemary, garlic and paprika. Glaze meat as directed on opposite page.

63

Using the same mixture for both the meat marinade and the salad dressing simplifies the preparation for this restaurant-style grilled chicken salad. Tamari is a mellow tasting, soy bean-based sauce that is quite similar to soy sauce. Tamari has a slightly thicker texture, so that it clings better to the chicken. The only other slightly exotic ingredient in this recipe is the Napa cabbage, sometimes also called Chinese cabbage. Napa cabbage has crinkly, thickly veined leaves that are very light green at the tips and fade to white near the base. Its flavor is delicate and mild, which gives all the tangy flavors from the dressing a chance to truly sing.

For a preparation shortcut, substitute 4 cups (1 L) bagged coleslaw mix for the Napa cabbage and carrot.

Tangy Thai Coleslaw with Grilled Chicken

PREP: 25 minutes | **COOK:** 20 minutes | **YIELD:** 4 servings

¼ cup (50 mL) orange juice
3 tbsp (45 mL) tamari or light soy sauce
3 tbsp (45 mL) rice wine vinegar
1 tbsp (15 mL) minced ginger
2 tsp (10 mL) granulated sugar
¾ tsp (4 mL) finely grated orange zest
¼ tsp (1 mL) hot pepper sauce
1 tbsp (15 mL) sesame oil
4 skinless, boneless chicken breasts, about 2 lb (1 kg)
¼ tsp (1 mL) each salt and pepper
4 cups (1 L) shredded Napa or Savoy cabbage
1 cup (250 mL) each coarsely shredded carrots, thinly sliced snow peas and finely diced mango
½ cup (125 mL) each mung bean sprouts, well rinsed, and thinly sliced red onion
¼ cup (50 mL) chopped fresh coriander leaves

In a small bowl combine the orange juice, tamari, rice wine vinegar, ginger, sugar, orange zest and hot pepper sauce; whisking constantly, drizzle in the sesame oil until well combined. Reserve.

Place the chicken breasts in a bowl. Add half of the dressing mixture and toss to combine. Heat the grill to medium-high. Sprinkle the chicken all over with salt and pepper. Grease the grate and grill the chicken for 8 to 10 minutes per side or until well marked and cooked through.

Place the cabbage, carrots, snow peas, mango, bean sprouts, red onion and coriander in a large bowl. Drizzle the remaining dressing over top and toss until well combined. Thinly slice the chicken and arrange an equal amount on 4 dinner plates. Top with coleslaw and serve.

Recipe variations for skewered chicken coated in sweet and spicy peanut sauce abound in Indonesian cuisine. In fact, this combination is so common in Indonesia that at many North American Indonesian restaurants peanut sauce is simply called satay sauce. My version of this classic is thickly and frequently slathered in sauce as it cooks; in fact, I almost literally apply the sauce with a mop so that these satays are super yummy and peanuty!

Although it may seem fussy to make satays on a weeknight, it's faster than making kabobs since there are fewer pieces of meat to thread onto each skewer. Plus the meat is so thin that it cooks very quickly. My favorite way to serve these saucy ribbons of chicken is over a salad of baby spinach, oranges, red onion and bean sprouts.

If time permits, soak wooden or bamboo skewers for 10 minutes (or longer) before using. This will prevent the skewers from becoming very charred and broken.

If life seems too short to thread chicken strips onto skewers, you can use whole, skinless, boneless chicken breasts in this recipe instead. Increase the grilling time to 17 to 20 minutes and mop the meat often with sauce as it cooks to keep it moist and delicious.

Chicken Satays with Spicy Peanut Mopping Sauce

PREP: 20 minutes | **COOK:** 10 minutes | **YIELD:** 6 servings

SAUCE:
   ½ cup (125 mL) each peanut butter, ketchup and orange juice
   2 tbsp (30 mL) teriyaki or soy sauce
   1 tbsp (15 mL) each Dijon mustard and honey
   2 tsp (10 mL) lemon juice
   2 green onions, chopped
   1 clove garlic
   1 tsp (5 mL) hot pepper sauce, or to taste

SATAYS:
   4 skinless, boneless chicken breasts, about 2 lb (1 kg)
   ¼ tsp (2 mL) each salt and pepper

SAUCE: Combine the peanut butter with the ketchup, orange juice, teriyaki sauce, mustard, honey, lemon juice, green onions and garlic in a blender or food processor. Blend until smooth. Add drops of hot pepper sauce to taste.

Transfer the sauce mixture to a saucepan and bring to a boil. Reduce the heat to low and simmer, stirring often, for 10 minutes. Cool to room temperature. (Sauce can be prepared to this point, chilled, covered and refrigerated for up to 5 days.) Divide sauce in half.

SATAYS: Preheat the grill to medium-high or the broiler to high. Slice the chicken breasts lengthwise into long, thin strips. Thread ribbons of chicken onto wooden skewers. Brush the meat evenly with half of the sauce. Season evenly with salt and pepper.

Lightly grease the grate. Arrange satays so that each one has room around it. Grill, turning as necessary, for 7 to 10 minutes or until cooked through. Serve satays with reserved sauce on the side for dipping.

Sometimes the classics need no updating whatsoever to be appealing! Such is the case with this silken-sauced chicken dish. This is one of those dishes that is always sophisticated and current. Given its long-standing appeal, this easy dish is an ideal entrée choice for occasions when you want to impress the people at your table with something that's simple yet special at the same time.

Any kind of mushroom will work well in this recipe, although morels, in season, will take this dish to an incredibly haute level. Shiitakes are my personal favorite since they lend a deep, satisfying flavor to the sauce. If using Portobello mushrooms, be sure to scoop out and discard the gills on the underside of the caps since they will cause the sauce to darken unattractively.

Chicken with Mushroom Cream Sauce

PREP: 10 minutes | **COOK:** 30 minutes | **YIELD:** 8 servings

1 tbsp (15 mL) vegetable oil
8 skinless, boneless chicken breasts, about 4 lb (2 kg)
¾ tsp (4 mL) salt
½ tsp (2 mL) black pepper
3 tbsp (45 mL) butter
1 small onion, peeled and very finely chopped
1 tbsp (15 mL) finely chopped fresh thyme
¼ tsp (1 mL) white pepper
2 cups (500 mL) sliced mushrooms
1¼ cups (300 mL) each low-sodium chicken broth and white wine
1 cup (250 mL) 35% whipping cream
Steamed spinach

Preheat the oven to 350°F (180°C). Heat the oil in a large, nonstick skillet set over medium-high heat. Sprinkle the chicken evenly with ½ tsp (2 mL) of the salt and the black pepper; add the meat to the pan. Brown the chicken on both sides. Transfer the chicken to a baking sheet; finish cooking it in the oven for 20 minutes longer or until cooked through.

Meanwhile, reduce the heat under the skillet to medium. Add the butter, onion, thyme, remaining salt and white pepper. Cook, stirring often, for 5 minutes. Increase the heat to high and add the mushrooms; sauté for 2 minutes or until golden. Stir in the broth and white wine; bring to a boil and cook for 10 to 12 minutes or until reduced to about 1 cup (250 mL) of liquid.

Stir the cream into the reduced wine mixture and bring to a boil. Cook for 7 to 8 minutes or until reduced and thickened. Arrange the chicken on a bed of steamed spinach. Spoon the sauce over the chicken before serving.

Fish & Seafood

Although fish and seafood have been chosen as a top 10 dinner choice by home cooks for at least two decades, our favorite items have shifted significantly in recent years. Where canned tuna used to hold the top spot in home pantries, today shrimp (most often frozen) is the most popular item from this category. One of the reasons for this shift is that the quality of fresh and frozen seafood has increased while prices have held steady and, in some cases, even dropped. Likewise, our culinary sophistication has increased so that foods like shrimp are no longer just for special occasions.

Eating fish more regularly is a trend that is connected closely to our society's increased interest in eating to promote and maintain wellness. In fact, fish and seafood consumption has been growing in tandem as nutritional information about the health benefits of omega fatty acids has emerged. Omega fatty acids are healthy compounds that have been linked with disease prevention; they are found in great-tasting familiar fish such as tuna and salmon.

As our interest in eating fish has grown, the distribution of fish and seafood has also improved so that a good quality, steady supply should be assured. Regrettably, environmentalists warn that some of our favorite fish and seafoods are becoming endangered by overfishing and irresponsible aquaculture. Although this environmental news means that food writers, chefs and consumers need to choose very carefully the fish they promote and cook with, it doesn't mean that we need to quit cooking and eating these foods entirely. The recommendations I make today as I write this book are made responsibly; however, when it comes time to choose fish for use in these recipes, I ask that you stay informed about the latest developments by consulting experts such as the Audobon Society, www.audobon.com.

Tips for Swimmingly Successful Fish Dinners

If your goal in cooking meals from scratch is to fish for compliments, you'll need to know how to select fish properly to be successful.

Long ago, when First Nations fishermen came home with the day's catch, their preferred cooking technique was to impale cleaned, freshly caught fish on strong green twigs, and plant the bending twigs into the ground so that the fish leaned over an open fire. Because the fishermen caught, cleaned and cooked their catch immediately, the resulting meals must have been delicious despite the lack of fancy marinades and interesting sauces.

Today's home cooks seldom catch their own ingredients, so we all need to know how to buy and store fish to ensure that the meals we serve will be as fresh and delicious as possible. There are a number of fish-counter options at most stores. In fact, frozen and fresh fish are sold whole, as sides, fillets, steaks, pieces and even chunks, in the case of large fish such as tuna.

I always recommend buying fish in a store that has a high turnover. Don't be too shy to ask which days of the week fish are delivered and buy accordingly.

Whether you purchase whole or semi-prepared fish, only buy fish that has firm, moist flesh that's not watery. If pressed lightly the flesh of the fish should bounce back without leaving an indentation.

When purchasing whole fish, make sure the eyes are clear, shiny and not sunken. Regardless of cut, size or origin, truly fresh fish smells clean and sweet, never "fishy" or similar to ammonia in any way.

Refrigerate and use fresh fish and seafood quickly, ideally within a day or two. If the weather is warm and fish is on your shopping list, take along a cooler to transport the fish home.

If nice quality fresh fish isn't available, frozen is a good alternative; however, inspect the packaging. If the fish is wrapped in a single layer of store-applied plastic wrap, it's likely that the fish was frozen because it was too old to sell as a fresh product.

If your store carries plant-packed frozen fish, opt for individually flash frozen fillets or steaks since they are usually more uniform and visually appealing than block-pressed fish. Likewise, flash frozen fish fillets and steaks thaw considerably more quickly than blocks, so you can be cooking (and eating!) sooner.

So fast and easy to prepare yet so classically elegant! I love to serve this simple fish entrée because it tastes like a fancy dinner yet the ingredients are quite reasonably priced and it takes only a few minutes to prepare enough to feed the whole family.

Trout, a member of the salmon family, thrive in freshwater rivers and streams. Although there are varieties of trout that grow as large as 50 pounds (22 kilograms), most grocery stores and fishmongers sell fillets from smaller fish. If only whole trout are on display at the fish store, ask the counter attendant to fillet it for you. Although it is easy to do at home, the bones and skin may attract every cat in the neighborhood to your garbage can!

Trout Almondine

PREP: 5 minutes | **COOK:** 10 minutes | **YIELD:** 8 servings

¼ cup (50 mL) butter
⅔ cup (150 mL) sliced almonds
¼ cup (50 mL) thinly sliced green onions
3 lb (1.5 kg) trout, salmon trout or arctic char fillets
3 tbsp (45 mL) lemon or lime juice
½ tsp (2 mL) each salt and pepper
Lemon wedges

Melt the butter in a large, nonstick skillet set over medium-high heat. Cook until the butter no longer sizzles and is lightly browned. Stir in the almonds and the green onions. Cook, stirring, for 1 minute or until the nuts are golden. Remove the nuts and onions from the butter using a slotted spoon. Reserve.

Sprinkle the trout evenly with salt and pepper. Working in batches, place fillets into the hot pan. Cook each piece of fish for 5 minutes or until the edges start to curl and the bottom is golden. Gently turn over and cook for 3 to 4 minutes longer or until the fish flakes easily when tested with a fork. Sprinkle the cooked fillets evenly with lemon juice. Arrange the fish on a serving platter. Return the almonds and green onions to the pan. Reheat, stirring, for 30 seconds. Pour the pan juices, almonds and green onions evenly over the fish. Serve with lemon wedges.

Since the era of ancient Rome, aficionados have held whisper thin, oval-shaped sole fillets in esteem for their delicate flavor and toothsome texture. True sole are a European breed of fish with the most famous variety being Dover sole. If sole isn't available, you can substitute another flat, white fish such as turbot or flounder.

Featuring vibrant colors and distinct, full flavors, this oven-steamed sole recipe can be made with frozen or fresh sole fillets. Steaming is an ideal way to cook great tasting meals like this one because it locks in flavor without adding a lot of additional fat. Serve this fish with fluffy brown rice for a flavorful, sophisticated yet healthful supper.

Coriander Pesto Sole

PREP: 15 minutes | **COOK:** 15 to 20 minutes | **YIELD:** 6 servings

2 tbsp (30 mL) lemon juice
1 cup (250 mL) lightly packed fresh coriander leaves
¼ cup (50 mL) ground almonds
2 cloves garlic, minced
¾ tsp (4 mL) each salt and pepper
¼ cup (50 mL) olive oil
1 cup (250 mL) each thinly sliced red and orange peppers
2 tbsp (30 mL) hoisin sauce
6 boneless sole fillets, about 1½ lb (750 g)

Preheat the oven to 375°F (190°C). Combine the lemon juice, coriander leaves, almonds, garlic, salt and pepper in a food processor and pulse the motor until smooth. With the machine running, drizzle in the olive oil until all the ingredients are combined into a paste. Reserve.

Toss the peppers with the hoisin sauce. Spread the peppers evenly in the bottom of a greased, 13- by 9-inch (3 L) casserole dish. Spread out the sole fillets, overlapping if necessary, on top. Spoon an equal amount of the coriander mixture onto each fillet and spread it evenly over the fish. Cover tightly with foil.

Bake for 15 to 20 minutes. Uncover and broil the fish for 2 to 4 minutes or until lightly browned.

Poppy seeds add crunchy texture and a vaguely nutty flavor to many of the traditional sweet and savory recipes commonly made in central Europe, the Middle East and India. This particular recipe includes commonly used Indian spices such as cumin, coriander seed and turmeric. Because these flavoring ingredients are used in such small quantities, the end result is a very mild, delicately flavored sauté that is unlike traditional Indian recipes.

Tiny gray-blue poppy seeds have a high, albeit healthy, essential oil content. This quality means that they can become rancid quickly, so purchase poppy seeds frequently and in small amounts and store all leftover seeds in the refrigerator or freezer.

Spread finely grated orange zest on a paper towel and microwave at High for 30 seconds to remove some of the moisture and make it easier to sprinkle over the fish.

Buttery Poppy Seed Sole

PREP: 5 minutes | **COOK:** 2 minutes | **YIELD:** 2 to 4 servings

½ tsp (2 mL) each salt and pepper
¼ tsp (1 mL) each ground cumin, coriander and turmeric
3 tbsp (45 mL) olive oil
1 clove garlic, minced
4 sole fillets, about ¾ lb (375 g)
¼ cup (50 mL) poppy seeds
1 tbsp (15 mL) butter
1 tsp (5 mL) very finely grated orange zest

Stir the salt with the pepper, cumin, coriander and turmeric in a small bowl. Blend in 2 tbsp (30 mL) of the olive oil and the garlic. Set aside. Pat the fish dry. Brush the oil mixture all over each piece of fish. Spread poppy seeds on a plate. Press one side of each portion of fish into the poppy seeds to coat.

Heat the butter and the remaining oil in a large skillet set over medium-high heat. Add the fish, poppy seed side down, and cook for 2 to 3 minutes, turning once, or until both sides are golden and the fish flakes easily with a fork. Transfer to a platter and sprinkle all over with orange zest.

Until several years ago, tilapia was relatively unheard of in North America. Tilapia is low in fat and has a fine texture and light-colored flesh. It is native to Africa, where it is an important food source. In some areas tilapia is called St. Peter's fish or Hawaiian sun fish. Today tilapia appears regularly on restaurant menus and is available at almost every retail fish counter. Tilapia gained in popularity in North America when stocks of other popular fish such as cod and halibut became depleted from overfishing. If you can't find tilapia for this recipe, farm-raised catfish makes a good substitution and goes well with the Creole flavors in this entrée.

Creole cooking is the refined hybrid cuisine that emerged in the eighteenth century when Spanish settlers established communities in New Orleans. The Creole pantry contains a full-flavored mélange of influences including French, Spanish and African ingredients. Unlike humbler Cajun dishes, Creole cooking uses many more tomatoes (found in the ketchup in this recipe) and generally is less spicy.

Cornmeal-capped Tilapia with Creole Sauce

PREP: 10 minutes | **COOK:** 10 minutes | **YIELD:** 4 servings

CREOLE SAUCE:
- ¼ cup (50 mL) tartar sauce
- 1 tbsp (15 mL) ketchup
- 1 tsp (5 mL) minced celery
- 1 tsp (5 mL) Dijon mustard
- ½ tsp (2 mL) hot pepper sauce

FISH:
- ½ cup (125 mL) each fine cornmeal and all-purpose flour
- 2 tsp (10 mL) chili powder
- ½ tsp (2 mL) each salt and pepper
- 4 tilapia fillets, about 1¼ lb (625 g)
- 1 egg, beaten
- 3 tbsp (45 mL) vegetable oil

CREOLE SAUCE: Blend the tartar sauce with the ketchup, celery, mustard and hot pepper sauce until well combined. Reserve.

FISH: Stir the cornmeal with the flour, chili powder, salt and pepper in a shallow dish. Dip each fillet in the egg and then into the cornmeal mixture until evenly coated on both sides. Discard any remaining cornmeal mixture.

Heat half of the oil in a large, nonstick skillet set over medium-high heat. Fry the fish fillets, in two batches, for 3 to 4 minutes per side or until golden. Use a large, flexible metal spatula to turn the fish. Between batches, wipe out the pan with paper towel and add more oil. Serve the fish with the Creole sauce on the side.

72

Sometimes the simplest dishes can be the most satisfying. Such is the case with this easy preparation for haddock fillets. Ready in mere minutes, this combination of readily available ingredients is always pleasing to the palate and virtually seasonless. Serve this appealing grilled fish with boiled new potatoes or as a partner to your favorite pasta dish; it's even good on a bun with tartar sauce, lettuce and tomato!

Haddock is very similar to cod in flavor and texture. Many stores sell frozen haddock, which makes it easy to pick up a box to keep on hand for evenings when you just don't know what you want to make for supper.

Lemon Dijon Buttered Haddock

PREP: 5 minutes | **COOK:** 8 minutes | **YIELD:** 4 servings

¼ cup (50 mL) Dijon mustard
3 tbsp (45 mL) lemon juice
3 tbsp (45 mL) melted butter
2 tbsp (30 mL) each chopped fresh tarragon and parsley
½ tsp (2 mL) coarsely cracked fresh pepper
¼ tsp (1 mL) salt
1½ lb (750 g) haddock fillets, fresh or thawed from frozen

Stir the mustard with the lemon juice, butter, tarragon, parsley, pepper and salt until well combined. Reserve. Preheat an indoor or outdoor grill to medium-high.

Brush the fish evenly with the butter mixture and set on the warmed grate. Grill, turning once, for 2 to 4 minutes per side, or until the fish flakes easily when tested with a fork.

73

Many stylish eateries have been serving fish topped with a crust for several years. The allure of encrusted fish rests in the wonderful contrast between the moist, flaky fish on the inside and the flavorful, crunchy texture on the outside. Recently a few frozen fish companies have launched products that duplicate this eating experience, but such recipes to prepare at home are still difficult to find in cookbooks.

In this easy to follow recipe (designed especially for home cooks), the encrusted fish trend is made family friendly by featuring popular flavors such as bacon and Cheddar cheese. This yummy, kid-pleasing topping combo paired with mild tasting, flaky haddock ensures this recipe will be a hit with the whole family.

Bacon and Cheddar-topped Haddock

PREP: 10 minutes | **COOK:** 10 minutes | **YIELD:** 4 servings

1 lb (500 g) haddock fillets, thawed if frozen
½ cup (125 mL) regular or light mayonnaise
1 tsp (5 mL) Dijon mustard
1 cup (250 mL) toasted fresh bread crumbs
½ cup (125 mL) each chopped, cooked bacon and coarsely shredded
   Cheddar cheese
¼ cup (50 mL) finely chopped fresh parsley
2 tbsp (30 mL) minced sun-dried tomatoes
1 tbsp (15 mL) melted butter

Lay the haddock fillets on a lightly greased baking sheet. Preheat the oven to 450°F (230°C).

Stir the mayonnaise with the mustard, bread crumbs, bacon, cheese, parsley, sun-dried tomatoes and butter until evenly combined. Spoon the crumb mixture evenly over the fish, patting lightly with the back of the spoon to ensure the coating clings to the fish.

Bake for 6 to 8 minutes (15 minutes if starting with frozen fish) or until the haddock flakes easily with a fork. Broil for 1 to 2 minutes to brown the topping.

Halibut is a flatfish found in the cold waters of both the Atlantic and Pacific oceans. Although it is a versatile, mild-tasting fish often used for fish and chips, that's not the only way to eat it. This recipe combines the delicate flavor of halibut with the popular appeal of garlic bread in a dish that's sure to be a hit with adults and kids, whether they're fish lovers or people who only eat fish occasionally (or who may just be trying it for the first time!).

According to experts at the Monterey Bay Aquarium in California, Pacific halibut stocks, found along the Pacific coasts of both the U.S. and Canada, are managed in an ecologically sound manner making them the preferred choice when purchasing halibut. So, when shopping for halibut, be sure to look for the Pacific halibut available at many grocery stores.

To make the bread crumbs, break a baguette or French bread into small pieces then chop roughly with a chef's knife. Toast in the preheated oven for 2 to 4 minutes or until just golden.

Cheesy Garlic Crumb-topped Halibut

PREP: 10 minutes | **COOK:** 10 minutes | **YIELD:** 4 servings

1½ cups (375 mL) lightly toasted, coarsely chopped French
    bread crumbs (see tip)
3 tbsp (45 mL) chopped fresh parsley
1 tbsp (15 mL) dried basil leaves
¼ tsp (1 mL) each salt and pepper
¼ cup (50 mL) melted, unsalted butter
2 tsp (10 mL) minced fresh garlic
½ cup (125 mL) each shredded Parmesan and mozzarella cheese
4 skinless, boneless halibut fillets, about 1½ lb (750 g)

Preheat the oven to 450°F (230°C). Toss the bread crumbs with the parsley, basil, salt and pepper. Stir the melted butter with the garlic. Drizzle the garlic butter over the crumb mixture, tossing to combine. Add the Parmesan and mozzarella cheeses and toss to combine.

Press an equal amount of the crumb mixture onto the top of each fillet. Transfer to a foil-lined baking sheet. Bake for 8 to 10 minutes; tent with foil during the last 3 minutes of baking if topping becomes too browned.

Much debate about farmed versus wild salmon and Atlantic versus Pacific salmon continues in the media and among fish lovers. Adding to the confusion, some farm-raised salmon is now being labeled as "naturally raised" and "organic." What consumers really need to know when making their purchase choice is that salmon connoisseurs, advocates for sustainable seafood and many health experts all recommend wild salmon over farmed fish. However, wild salmon is less consistently available and almost always considerably more expensive than farmed fish from either coast so you might not always be able to get what you want.

Regardless of what kind of fresh salmon you choose, the visual effect of this recipe is impressive. The elegant, long, slender ribbons of cucumber that are used as a bed for the coral-colored salmon make this recipe a wonderful choice for summertime entertaining. And the light, creamy dressing isn't too rich or too filling during hot weather either.

Creamy Salmon and Cucumber Salad

PREP: 10 minutes | **COOK:** 5 minutes | **YIELD:** 4 servings

2 cups (500 mL) fish broth, clam juice or chicken broth
1 lb (500 g) skinless, boneless salmon fillets, thawed if frozen, about 4 pieces
1 English cucumber
¼ cup (50 mL) each buttermilk and mayonnaise
1 tsp (5 mL) Dijon mustard
1 tbsp (15 mL) chopped fresh dill
1 green onion, finely chopped
¼ tsp (1 mL) each salt and pepper
Lemon wedges (optional)

Bring the fish broth to a boil in a large, deep skillet. Add the salmon and reduce the heat to low. Simmer the fish, uncovered, very gently for 5 minutes (10 minutes if starting with fish that is frozen). Turn the fish once during cooking. Cover the fish with a piece of waxed paper; cool to room temperature in the cooking liquid. (Once cooled to room temperature, the fish can be removed from the liquid and refrigerated for up to 1 day.)

Using a vegetable peeler or a mandolin, cut the cucumber lengthwise into long, thin ribbons. Place in a colander to drain for 5 to 10 minutes.

Meanwhile, whisk the buttermilk with the mayonnaise. Stir in the mustard, dill, green onion, salt and pepper. Divide the cucumber evenly among 4 plates. Top each bed of cucumber with a piece of fish. Drizzle the buttermilk dressing evenly over each plate. Garnish with lemon wedges if desired.

Another encrusted fish entrée, this particular recipe is more complex in flavor than the Bacon and Cheddar-topped Haddock (page 73) or Cheesy Garlic Crumb-topped Halibut (page 74).

This recipe is ideal for evenings when you crave a restaurant-style meal but prefer to eat at home. Combining popular ingredients such as sun-dried tomatoes and fresh Mediterranean herbs with goat cheese and crusty bread creates a topping that is full-flavored but that does not overpower the distinctive taste of the salmon.

Mediterranean Salmon

PREP: 10 minutes | **COOK:** 8 to 10 minutes | **YIELD:** 4 servings

¼ cup (50 mL) finely chopped, oil-packed sun-dried tomatoes
1½ tsp (7 mL) chopped fresh rosemary leaves
1 tsp (5 mL) each dried basil and oregano leaves
⅔ cup (150 mL) coarse fresh focaccia or Italian loaf bread crumbs (see tip on making bread crumbs, page 74)
¼ cup (50 mL) chèvre-style goat cheese
2 tbsp (30 mL) melted butter
2 tbsp (10 mL) balsamic vinegar
1 tsp (5 mL) finely grated lemon zest
4 skinless, boneless salmon fillets, about 1½ lb (750 g)

Blot the oil from the sun-dried tomatoes and toss them with the rosemary, basil, oregano and focaccia crumbs. Crumble the goat cheese into the crumb mixture and toss to combine.

Stir the butter with the balsamic vinegar and lemon zest. Toss this mixture with the crumb mixture until combined. Sprinkle a layer of the flavored crumbs evenly over each piece of fish. Press each fillet gently with the back of a spoon so that the topping mixture clings to the fish.

Preheat the oven to 450°F (230°C). Bake the fish, coated side up, on a lightly greased or nonstick, foil-lined baking sheet for 8 to 10 minutes. Tent the fish loosely with foil for the last 3 minutes of baking if the topping starts to become too brown.

This *Asian-inspired* preparation for salmon is a great choice for any time of year. Although I've also tested this recipe using bottled lime juice, the taste is far superior when it is made with freshly squeezed juice. Because this fish entrée tastes good both warm and at room temperature, it's a good option for entertaining or for families on the run where everyone will be eating dinner at a different time.

Lime Soy-glazed Salmon

PREP: 25 minutes | **COOK:** 8 minutes | **YIELD:** 6 servings

½ cup (125 mL) soy sauce
¼ cup (50 mL) lime or lemon juice
3 tbsp (45 mL) honey
2 tbsp (30 mL) vegetable oil
1 tbsp (15 mL) each minced fresh ginger and honey mustard
1 tsp (5 mL) hot pepper sauce
2 lb (1 kg) skinless, boneless salmon fillets
2 tbsp (30 mL) chopped fresh coriander leaves or parsley
½ tsp (2 mL) toasted sesame seeds

Combine the soy sauce with the lime juice, honey, vegetable oil, ginger, mustard and hot pepper sauce in a small saucepan. Bring mixture to a boil and cook until slightly thickened. Cool. Divide the glaze in half.

OVEN INSTRUCTIONS: Line a baking sheet with foil and grease lightly. Place the salmon fillets on the foil and brush with half of the glaze. Let stand for 15 minutes.
Preheat the broiler to high. Set the pan on the middle rack of the oven and broil the salmon, without turning, for 6 to 8 minutes, or until browned but still coral colored in the center. Brush the fillets with the reserved glaze. Sprinkle the coriander and sesame seeds evenly over the cooked fish.

GRILLING INSTRUCTIONS: Place the salmon on a well-oiled grate of an indoor or outdoor grill preheated to medium-high. Cook for 6 to 8 minutes, turning the fish halfway through using a large, flexible spatula. Fish should still be coral colored in the center. Finish as directed above.

Reinventing salmon salad for this century is easy if you focus on fresh Asian flavors for inspiration. Creating a complete meal with this simple salad as the main course is also easy. Serve with toasted garlic bread or a cup of noodle-rich soup and you have a light, flavorful meal that can be made in minutes.

Canned salmon offers a completely different taste and texture experience from fresh salmon. Although many people find the bones and skin in canned salmon unpleasant, mashing the bone into the fish creates a tremendously good, non-dairy source of calcium, a nutrient that many busy people (especially adult women) lack on a regular basis.

Teriyaki Salmon Salad

PREP: 5 minutes | **COOK:** none | **YIELD:** 2 servings

- 2 tbsp (30 mL) teriyaki sauce
- 1 tbsp (15 mL) lime juice
- 2 tsp (10 mL) brown sugar
- 2 tbsp (30 mL) toasted sesame oil
- 5 cups (1.25 L) mesclun salad greens
- ¼ cup (50 mL) fresh coriander leaves
- 1 tin (7½ oz/213 g) canned salmon
- 1 tsp (5 mL) toasted sesame seeds

Whisk the teriyaki sauce with the lime juice and brown sugar. Drizzle in the sesame oil, still whisking. Combine the greens with the whole coriander leaves.

Drain the salmon and flake it into chunks with a fork. Add the salmon to the greens. Drizzle the dressing over the greens mixture and toss gently to combine. Sprinkle the salad with sesame seeds.

This casserole features the fresh flavors of springtime but uses ingredients that are available in grocery stores year round. Not only is this one-dish meal easy to make, it's also so sophisticated tasting you'll be eager to serve it to company!

Firm, lean, mild-flavored cod is a popular fish that is relatively inexpensive compared to other fish and seafoods. Although wild cod is on several watch lists as an endangered fish, farmed varieties are becoming more readily available. So, be a responsible shopper and ask your fishmonger if the cod is farmed. If it isn't, substitute either farmed halibut, haddock or excellent Alaskan black cod instead.

Asparagus and Cod Bake

PREP: 20 minutes | **COOK:** 20 minutes | **YIELD:** 4 servings

2 tbsp (30 mL) minced, peeled onion
2 tbsp (30 mL) butter
½ tsp (2 mL) each salt, pepper, nutmeg and dried tarragon leaves
2 tbsp (30 mL) all-purpose flour
½ cup (125 mL) white wine or chicken broth
1 cup (250 mL) milk
1 tbsp (15 mL) each lemon juice and finely grated lemon zest
½ lb (250 g) blanched asparagus spears
1 lb (500 g) cod or haddock fillets
2 to 3 cups (500 to 750 mL) warm, cooked wild rice blend

Sauté the onion in the butter in a medium saucepan set over medium heat. Add the salt, pepper, nutmeg and tarragon; cook, stirring often, for 3 minutes. Whisk in the flour; cook for 1 minute. Gradually whisk in the wine and then the milk. Bring to a boil. Reduce the heat to low and simmer, stirring, for 5 minutes or until sauce is thickened and smooth. Stir in the lemon juice and zest. Remove from the heat.

Preheat the oven to 350°F (180°C). Pat the fish dry. Spoon two-thirds of the warm sauce into a lightly greased 13- by 9-inch (3 L) casserole dish. Arrange the asparagus in an even layer over the sauce. Place the fish fillets over the asparagus; spoon the remaining sauce evenly over the fish.

Cover the casserole and bake for 10 minutes. Uncover and bake for 10 minutes longer or until the fish flakes easily with a fork. Serve the fish, vegetables and sauce on a bed of wild rice blend.

Although it might sound strange, I didn't make (or taste!) my first tuna casserole until I started writing this book. I was so impressed with the results that I had to share this easy, classic comfort food with you. But first I ran it by a panel of experts—and all the tuna casserole devotees who taste-tested this entrée gave it two forks up!

I've made one small change to the traditional recipe: I added a tomato-crumb topping, which cuts the richness of the tuna mixture and makes the finished dish look so scrumptious you'll want to try a bite as soon as it comes out of the oven.

Tomato-topped Tuna Casserole

PREP: 15 minutes | **COOK:** 30 minutes | **YIELD:** 4 to 6 servings

CASSEROLE:
3 cups (750 mL) short pasta such as penne, rotini or gemelli
1 tbsp (15 mL) butter
3 green onions, chopped
2 celery ribs, thinly sliced
½ tsp (2 mL) each dried thyme leaves and salt
¼ tsp (1 mL) pepper
2 cans (6 oz/170 g each) chunk light tuna, drained
1 cup (250 mL) regular or light mayonnaise
¼ cup (50 mL) sour cream
2 tsp (10 mL) Dijon mustard

TOPPING:
1 large tomato, thinly sliced
½ cup (250 mL) whole wheat bread crumbs
1 clove garlic, minced
¾ cup (175 mL) shredded mozzarella or Cheddar cheese

CASSEROLE: Preheat the oven to 350°F (180°C). Boil the pasta in a large pot of boiling, salted water for 8 to 10 minutes or until al dente. Drain well and reserve.

Meanwhile, melt the butter in a small skillet set over medium heat. Add the green onions, celery, thyme, salt and pepper. Sauté for 5 minutes or until softened.

Using a fork, flake the tuna in a large bowl into bite-size pieces. Add the mayonnaise, sour cream and mustard; blend until combined. Mix in the onion mixture. Stir in the pasta and transfer to a buttered 8-cup (2 L) casserole dish.

TOPPING: Arrange the tomato slices in even rows over the top of the casserole. Toss the crumbs with the garlic until evenly combined. Add the cheese and toss to combine. Sprinkle evenly over the tomatoes. Bake the casserole for 30 minutes or until bubbly and very hot.

MAKE AHEAD: Cover casserole and refrigerate for up to 24 hours. Increase cooking time to 45 minutes if taking the casserole straight from the refrigerator.

This entrée, featuring fresh tuna steaks and chow mein noodles in a sesame-accented dressing, is so fast and easy to prepare that your family might think you picked up gourmet take-out! Fresh tuna has become a common item in upscale grocery stores. Odds are that what you'll find is actually "fresh, previously frozen." Since tuna are such large, deep-sea fish, almost all of the fresh tuna available has been frozen on the fishing boats and then thawed to be cut and displayed at the store.

Chow mein noodles are pale yellow, long strands that are usually sold in vacuum-sealed, block-shaped packages in the deli section of major grocery stores. Occasionally they are sold frozen and some stores—especially those in Asian neighborhoods—even offer dried ones for sale. If you can't find any of these varieties, substitute regular or whole wheat spaghetti for the chow mein noodles.

Grilled Sesame Tuna and Noodles

PREP: 10 minutes | **COOK:** 2 minutes | **YIELD:** 4 servings

1 tbsp (15 mL) each toasted sesame oil, soy sauce and honey
1 tbsp (15 mL) very finely chopped green onion or chives
1 tbsp (15 mL) lime juice
1 clove garlic, minced
2 tbsp (30 mL) vegetable oil
½ tsp (2 mL) toasted sesame seeds
4 fresh tuna steaks, each 1 inch (2.5 cm) thick
¼ tsp (1 mL) each salt and pepper
4 cups (1 L) hot chow mein noodles

Preheat the grill to medium-high. Combine the sesame oil, soy sauce, honey, green onion, lime juice and garlic in a small bowl. Whisk until well blended. Still whisking, drizzle in the vegetable oil. Stir in the sesame seeds. Brush the tuna steaks with half of the sesame mixture and sprinkle each portion evenly with salt and pepper. Grill the tuna for 1 to 2 minutes per side or until medium-rare. Remove the fish from the grill and set aside.

Toss the noodles with the remaining half of the sesame mixture. Divide the noodles evenly among 4 dinner plates. Top each portion with a tuna steak.

Salade Niçoise is a classic dish named for the town of Nice in southern France. Although this salad is one of the best known dishes from the area, the term "Niçoise" refers to a number of dishes from the region that include the following ingredients: tomatoes, black olives, garlic and anchovies. In addition to these ingredients, Salade Niçoise also always contains green beans, tuna and eggs.

My updated version of this classic uses fresh tuna, which is readily available thanks to the popularity of sushi. To save time (including eliminating the cooking time entirely), you can substitute canned tuna. I recommend using chunk light tuna packed in broth or water for the best flavor and texture.

Haricots verts is French for green beans. However, in North America (where what we call green beans are thicker and shorter than the French bean), haricots verts is usually used to describe young, thin green beans. French beans is another term green grocers use interchangeably with haricots verts.

If using canned tuna, simply open and drain, then flake the tuna into a bowl. Drizzle with dressing and toss to combine. Arrange an equal amount of tuna over each portion of salad before serving; garnish as directed.

Seared Tuna Salad Niçoise

PREP: 10 minutes | **COOK:** 4 minutes | **YIELD:** 4 servings

DRESSING:
1 tbsp (15 mL) each white wine vinegar and lemon juice
1 clove garlic, minced
1 tsp (5 mL) each minced capers and chopped dill
½ tsp (5 mL) finely grated lemon zest
½ tsp (5 mL) each honey and Dijon mustard
¼ tsp (1 mL) each salt and pepper
½ cup (125 mL) extra virgin olive oil

SALAD:
4 fresh tuna fillets
½ tsp (2 mL) each salt and pepper
1 lb (500 g) cooked haricot verts or green beans
2 cooked new potatoes, cut into wedges
¼ cup (50 mL) each thinly sliced yellow pepper and red onion
¼ cup (50 mL) halved, pitted, small black olives
1 tbsp (15 mL) non-pariel or other small capers
2 hard-cooked eggs, quartered
4 anchovy fillets (optional)

DRESSING: Whisk the white wine vinegar with the lemon juice. Stir in the garlic, capers, dill, lemon zest, honey, mustard, salt and pepper. Whisking, gradually add oil. (The dressing can be made up to 2 days ahead and covered tightly and refrigerated.) Divide the dressing in half.

SALAD: Preheat the grill to high. Brush the fish all over with half of the dressing and sprinkle evenly with salt and pepper. Place the fish on the preheated grate and cook, turning once, for 1 minute per side or until well seared on the outside but still very rare on the inside (add an extra 1 minute for medium-rare and an extra 2 minutes for medium doneness). Remove the fish from the grate using a flexible, very thin, metal spatula. Brush the fish all over with more dressing.

Meanwhile, combine the beans, potatoes, yellow pepper, red onion, olives and capers in a mixing bowl. Toss with the remaining dressing. Divide the dressed vegetables between 4 dinner plates. Slice each piece of tuna in half on the diagonal and arrange on top of each salad. Garnish with egg wedges and anchovies (if using). Mizuna and shiso are Japanese greens. Mizuna is often a component of mesclun mixed greens. It has spike tipped, feathery leaves that are sometimes sold in elastic-bound bunches.

Showcasing the choicest cut of tuna on a bed of Asian greens, this fish dish has dramatic visual impact. Although the look and taste scream "chef-prepared," the recipe itself takes less than 10 minutes of active cooking time, which means that you have lots of time to do other things when you choose this entrée for your evening meal.

Shiso—also called perilla and Japanese basil in some stores—is the green, serrated-leaf herb that Japanese chefs use to separate sushi and sashimi on platters. Many Japanese restaurants use a plastic substitute instead of this perishable fresh green herb, a cousin to mint and basil, since fresh shiso is only available in summer months from Asian markets. However, if you happen to find this delicate green at the market, pick some up to experience its fresh, mild flavor.

Ask the fish monger to cut the tuna into a rectangle that is about the same size and thickness as a piece of pork tenderloin.

SEE PHOTO INSERT

Rosemary-orange Seared Tuna and Greens

PREP: 5 minutes | **MARINATE:** 15 minutes
COOK: 60 to 90 seconds | **YIELD:** 4 servings

¼ cup (50 mL) each orange juice and olive oil
2 tbsp (30 mL) cider or white wine vinegar
1 tsp (5 mL) each Dijon mustard and liquid honey
1 tbsp (15 mL) finely chopped fresh rosemary
2 tsp (10 mL) finely shredded orange zest
1 clove garlic, minced
1 lb (500 g) centre-cut, sashimi-grade tuna (see tip)
½ tsp (2 mL) each coarsely ground black pepper and fleur de sel or
    coarse sea salt (approx)
6 cups (1.5 L) mizuna, shiso or mesclun greens
1 tbsp (15 mL) vegetable oil
Rosemary sprigs and long strips of orange zest

Whisk the orange juice with olive oil, vinegar, mustard and honey. Stir in rosemary, orange zest and garlic. Reserve one half. Add the tuna to the other half and let marinate at room temperature for about 15 minutes.

Arrange the greens to make a rectangular-shaped bed on four large serving plates.

Heat the vegetable oil in a cast iron or other heavy skillet over medium-high heat until very hot. Sprinkle tuna all over with half the pepper and salt. Sear on all sides and each end in the hot skillet for 15 to 20 seconds per side.

Drizzle reserved orange mixture over greens. Slice tuna thickly and fan out along the length of the greens. Sprinkle the remaining salt and pepper along the length of the tuna and garnish with additional rosemary and orange zest.

Although the ingredient list for the fresh-tasting marinade used in this recipe is longer than many of the other recipes in this book, the flavor of the finished dish is so incredibly nuanced, complex and satisfying that it is well worth the extra few moments of preparation time.

Butterflied shrimp look so very elegant on dinner plates that whatever else you make to go with this entrée doesn't need to be elaborate. For a quick and delicious meal you can save a little of the reserved portion of the marinade and drizzle it over the shrimp served very simply on a bed of baby salad greens. Or you can serve the cooked shrimp over hot couscous or risotto blended with wilted spinach, Swiss chard or rapini.

Grilled Honey Dijon Butterflied Shrimp

PREP: 15 minutes | **COOK:** 10 minutes | **YIELD:** 8 servings

MARINADE:
2 tbsp (30 mL) lightly packed fresh dill
1 tbsp (15 mL) chopped, peeled red onion
1 tbsp (15 mL) each white wine vinegar and lemon juice
2 tsp (10 mL) each honey and Dijon mustard
2 tsp (10 mL) finely grated lemon zest
1 tbsp (15 mL) finely chopped capers
½ tsp (2 mL) each salt and pepper
1 clove garlic, minced
¼ tsp (1 mL) hot pepper sauce
¼ cup (50 mL) extra virgin olive oil
½ tsp (2 mL) hot pepper flakes

SHRIMP:
2 lb (1 kg) jumbo shrimp, in shells
¼ tsp (1 mL) each salt and coarsely ground pepper
Lemon wedges

MARINADE: Combine the dill, red onion, white wine vinegar, lemon juice, honey, mustard, lemon zest, capers, salt, pepper, garlic and hot pepper sauce in a blender or food processor. Blend until well combined. With the motor running, drizzle in the oil. Stir in the hot pepper flakes. (The marinade can be made up to 3 days ahead and covered tightly and refrigerated.)

SHRIMP: Starting from the tail end, slice into the shrimp shells and almost all the way through the meat of each shrimp so that they can be opened up to lie flat. Toss the shrimp with half the marinade mixture. Reserve the other half.

Preheat the grill to medium-high. Remove the shrimp from the marinade and sprinkle evenly with salt and pepper. Lightly grease the grate and place the shrimp on the grill, cut side down. Grill the shrimp, basting often with the reserved marinade, for about 3 minutes per side or until cooked through. Serve with lemon wedges on the side.

Stir-frying is a wonderfully fast and healthy cooking technique that's not just for Asian cuisine. In this recipe, familiar flavors such as thyme, garlic and butter jazz up a quick, fresh and light tasting seafood entrée. This shrimp dish can be served over rice like an Asian stir-fry, or as a tasty topping for a baked potato. Or you can try something a little different and use it as a filling for wraps. The recipe is easily doubled for extra guests or leftovers.

SEE PHOTO INSERT

Easy Shrimp and Corn Stir-fry

PREP: 10 minutes | **COOK:** 8 minutes | **YIELD:** 4 servings

1 lb (500 g) frozen, peeled and deveined raw shrimp
2 tbsp (30 mL) butter
2 cups (500 mL) each corn kernels and trimmed green beans
1 tsp (5 mL) dried thyme leaves
2 cloves garlic, thinly sliced
1 lime
½ tsp (2 mL) each salt and pepper

Place the shrimp in a colander and rinse under cold water until no longer frozen together and the ice crystals are all melted. Drain well and pat dry on paper towel.

Melt the butter in a skillet or wok set over medium-high heat. Add the shrimp, corn, green beans, thyme and garlic. Stir-fry for 5 minutes or until the shrimp is bright pink. Halve the lime and juice one half. Stir the lime juice, salt and pepper into the shrimp. Taste and add more lime, salt or pepper as necessary. Cut the remaining lime half into wedges. Serve the shrimp with lime wedges on the side.

This isn't quite ravioli because the noodles aren't sealed around the edges, and it's not quite lasagna because it's not prepared in layers in a lasagna pan. But the finished dish looks sort of like ravioli, so ravioli is what I called it! Whatever name you want to give it, this dish is elegant and upscale looking, yet so easy to prepare that you shouldn't wait until you have company to make it. It's an ideal meal for busy people who want to enjoy flavorful foods served up with style anytime.

Unlike dried pasta, fresh lasagna noodles don't come in uniform sizes. When cutting the fresh noodles, the finished noodles should be about the size of the palm of your hand so that they are an appropriate size to sandwich most of the filling. If trimming is necessary to make the noodles the right size, reserve the scrap pieces of pasta in a tightly closed container and use them to make a pasta side dish or dinner for one later in the week.

SEE PHOTO INSERT

Shrimp "Ravioli" with Asparagus and Shiitake Mushrooms

PREP: 15 minutes | **COOK:** 20 minutes | **YIELD:** 4 servings

- **1 tbsp (15 mL) vegetable oil**
- **1 small onion, peeled and sliced**
- **2 cups (500 mL) sliced shiitake or cremini mushroom caps**
- **1 lb (500 g) fresh or thawed, frozen shrimp, thawed and cleaned**
- **1 tsp (5 mL) cornstarch**
- **½ cup (125 mL) orange juice**
- **2 tbsp (30 mL) soy sauce**
- **2 tsp (10 mL) minced ginger**
- **1 tsp (5 mL) finely grated orange zest**
- **3 cloves garlic, minced**
- **2 tsp (10 mL) butter**
- **2 to 4 fresh lasagna noodles**
- **1 bunch asparagus, about 1 lb (500 g)**
- **1 green onion, thinly sliced**

Heat the oil in a nonstick skillet or wok set over medium heat. Add the onion and cook, stirring often, for 5 minutes. Increase the heat to medium-high and add the mushroom caps. Sauté for 3 minutes or until lightly browned. Add the shrimp and toss to combine.

Whisk the cornstarch into the orange juice until smooth. Add the soy sauce, ginger, orange zest and garlic to the orange juice mixture. Pour this mixture into the pan with the shrimp and bring to a boil. Cook for 4 to 5 minutes or until the shrimp is pink and the sauce is thickened and glossy. Add the butter and stir until melted. Remove the shrimp mixture from the heat; reserve and keep warm.

Bring a large pot of salted water to a boil. Meanwhile, cut the lasagna noodles to make a total of 8 smaller noodles, each about the size of the palm of your hand. Reserve. Bend the asparagus until it snaps at its natural breaking point. Discard the ends.

Cook the trimmed asparagus spears in the boiling water for 1 minute. Add the noodles and cook for 2 to 3 minutes longer or until the noodles are tender.

Gently lift each noodle from the hot water using tongs or a slotted spoon. Shake off excess water and arrange one noodle on each of 4 dinner plates. Drain the asparagus spears. Top each noodle with a few spears of asparagus and an equal portion of the shrimp mixture and its sauce. Top with a second noodle and a bit more of the shrimp mixture and sauce. Sprinkle with green onion. Serve immediately.

In Europe, mussels are so immensely popular that they are routinely farmed to meet the demand. Since this bivalve is not part of the cooking repertoire of many North Americans, the vast stocks of wild mussels along our coastlines often thrive. You might even be able to see some clinging to the tidal rocks if you happen to be swimming at a beach north of Malibu as I did several years ago!

Mussles are inexpensive and available at almost any grocery store. They have a lightly sweet, surprisingly earthy flavor that is reminiscent of mushrooms. This speedy mussel recipe features popular South Pacific flavors such as kaffir lime leaves and fresh coriander. Although fresh kaffir lime leaves can be difficult to find in smaller communities, they freeze well—so if you are able to find them, stock up so that you have a ready supply. Or, feel free to use dried kaffir lime leaves if they are more readily available.

If fresh or dried kaffir lime leaves aren't available, substitute 1 tbsp (30 mL) lime juice and ½ tsp (2 mL) granulated sugar for the leaves.

SEE PHOTO INSERT

Chili Lager Steamed Mussels

PREP: 10 minutes | **COOK:** 5 minutes | **YIELD:** 4 to 6 servings

4 lb (2 kg) fresh mussels, preferably small
½ cup (125 mL) apple juice
3 fresh kaffir lime leaves
¼ cup (50 mL) butter
3 shallots, minced, or ½ cup (125 mL) minced onion
2 cloves garlic, minced
1 tbsp (15 mL) minced red chilies (approx)
¾ cup (175 mL) lager-style beer
2 tbsp (30 mL) finely chopped fresh coriander leaves

Pick over the mussels, discarding any whose shells stay open when you tap them. Scrub the remaining mussels with a kitchen brush. Pull out the fibrous, net-like beards that are attached to the inner edge of the shells; then use your fingers to snap the beards off along the edge of the shell and discard. Rinse the mussels well and drain. Reserve.

Heat the apple juice in a saucepan until steaming. Add the lime leaves and let stand for 5 minutes.

Melt half the butter in a deep skillet or wok set over medium heat. Add the shallots, garlic and chilies. Cook, stirring often, for 5 minutes. Add the apple juice, lime leaves and beer; bring to a boil. Simmer for 5 minutes.

Increase heat to medium-high. Stir in the reserved mussels and coriander leaves. Cover and steam for 3 to 5 minutes or until mussels are opened. Stir in the remaining butter until combined. Discard any unopened mussels and the lime leaves. Ladle an equal amount of the mussels and juices into serving bowls.

Pasta

Statistics reveal that pasta has been one of our top 10 favorite dinners for the last 20 years. Given our frequent dinnertime choice to eat sauce-coated noodles, it's hard to believe that North Americans haven't been eating pasta for centuries. In fact, pasta consumption here for many people was limited to spaghetti with meatballs and macaroni and cheese until the mid-1980s when restaurant chefs began to explore regional Italian flavors. Since then, the average consumer has gone from eating about 6 pounds of pasta per year (a per capita consumption rate that was relatively stable for over 15 years) to our current consumption rate of close to 14 pounds of pasta per person per year!

Research conducted by the National Pasta Association reveals that 40 percent of people claim spaghetti to be their favorite noodle-based supper, followed by lasagna (12 percent) in second place, and macaroni and cheese (6 percent) in third. Besides easy-to-follow ultimate versions of these three favorite recipes, there are also 17 more delicious ways to enjoy pasta for supper in this saucy chapter filled with twists and turns from start to finish!

Moms have been pleasing their families by making scratch mac and cheese for decades. And since the late 1930s, when Kraft first started making packaged macaroni and cheese, they have served make-do versions of this comfort food classic on busy nights when they lacked time to make the real thing. With generations of us having grown up eating these cheesy noodles, macaroni and cheese has long been the most popular comfort food.

Not only is my homemade version supremely cheesy and smooth, but it can be customized to suit your own definition of the classic. For those who grew up on the packaged stuff, this dish can be served creamy and saucy from the cooking pot. And, for those who have a hankering for Mom's old school version, this recipe can be topped with buttery crumbs and baked until a golden crust forms overtop. Either way, this mac and cheese is sublimely delectable and delightfully orange! The aged Cheddar cheese gives this casserole an especially cheesy flavor. If you'd like something a little less intense, mild or medium cheese will work well, too.

Cold pack cheddar cheese is a slightly crumbly but ultimately spreadable cheddar-flavored cheese product that has an intense cheesy flavor and a vibrant orange color.

Double Cheddar Mac and Cheese

PREP: 5 minutes | **COOK:** 15 minutes | **YIELD:** 6 to 8 servings

3 cups (750 mL) dry macaroni
2 tbsp (30 mL) butter
¼ cup (50 mL) very finely chopped or coarsely grated onion
1 clove garlic, minced
½ tsp (2 mL) each pepper and ground nutmeg
1 tbsp (15 mL) all-purpose flour
1½ cups (375 mL) milk
1 pkg (8 oz/250 g) cold pack Cheddar cheese
1 cup (250 mL) shredded aged Cheddar cheese

Bring a large pot of salted water to a boil. Add the macaroni and cook for about 6 to 8 minutes, or according to package directions. Drain well.

Meanwhile, melt the butter in a deep skillet set over medium-low heat. Add the onion and cook, stirring often, for 5 minutes. Stir in the garlic, pepper and nutmeg. Sprinkle the flour evenly over the onion mixture and blend well. Add a splash of the milk and blend until well combined.

Gradually add the remaining milk, stirring constantly. Bring to a boil. Reduce the heat to low and simmer, stirring frequently, for 5 minutes. Break up the cold pack cheese and add it a little at a time to the milk mixture. Stir until completely incorporated. Gradually add the grated cheese, stirring well between additions. When all the cheese has been incorporated into the sauce, remove the pan from the heat. Blend the macaroni into the sauce mixture, stirring until evenly coated.

Variation

For baked mac and cheese, transfer the hot macaroni mixture to a buttered 8-cup (2 L) casserole dish. Preheat the oven to 400°F (200°C). Toss 1 cup (250 mL) fresh bread crumbs with 2 tbsp (30 mL) each melted butter and chopped fresh parsley. Sprinkle the crumb mixture evenly over the casserole. Place in the oven and bake for 10 to 15 minutes or until bubbly and browned.

Cook once, eat twice: Double this recipe and freeze one half, unbaked, as a casserole for another time. Thaw in the refrigerator overnight before baking, covered in foil, for about 40 minutes or until heated through. Broil until browned on top.

My colleague Amy Snider introduced me to the idea of shell pasta stuffed with cheese and veggies. After just a few bites I (and everyone else who tried this dish in our test kitchen) was smitten. Since this recipe has such broad appeal and is made with commonly available ingredients, it was immediately earmarked to be included in this collection of favorites.

Because this meatless pasta meal is a great option for feeding a crowd of mixed ages or a group that may include vegetarians, you may find that you use this recipe often.

SEE PHOTO INSERT

Broccoli Cheddar Stuffed Shells

PREP: 25 minutes | **COOK:** 40 minutes | **YIELD:** 6 servings

1 tbsp (15 mL) vegetable oil
1 small onion, peeled and chopped
1 small red pepper, chopped
1 clove garlic, minced
1 tsp (5 mL) each dried thyme leaves and black pepper
1 bay leaf
3 cups (750 mL) pasta sauce
1 can (796 mL) diced tomatoes, with juice
1 tsp (5 mL) red wine vinegar
24 dry jumbo pasta shells, about one 8-oz (250 g) box
1 pkg (8 oz/250 g) brick-style cream cheese, softened
1½ cups (375 mL) shredded Cheddar cheese
2 cups (500 mL) chopped, cooked broccoli florets

Heat the oil in a deep skillet set over medium heat. Add the onion, red pepper, garlic, thyme, black pepper and bay leaf. Cook, stirring often, until softened. Stir in all but ½ cup (125 mL) of the pasta sauce into the pan along with the tomatoes. Bring to a boil. Reduce the heat to low and simmer, uncovered, for 10 minutes. Stir in the red wine vinegar and discard the bay leaf. Reserve vegetable sauce.

Preheat the oven to 350°F (180°C). Cook the shells according to the package directions. Drain and rinse the pasta under cold running water until cool enough to handle. Drain well. Blend the cream cheese and remaining pasta sauce until smooth. Stir in 1 cup (250 mL) of the Cheddar cheese and the broccoli.

Spoon half of the reserved vegetable sauce into a 13- by 9-inch (3 L) casserole dish. Using a spoon, stuff each shell with an equal amount of the cheese mixture. Set the shells, stuffed side up, in the pan. Spoon the remaining vegetable sauce over the shells. Cover and bake for 20 minutes. Uncover and sprinkle with remaining cheese. Bake for 10 minutes or until the cheese is melted and bubbly.

Cook once, eat twice: Double this recipe and freeze one half (before topping with cheese and baking) for another night. Do not thaw. Bake directly from the freezer at 400°F (200°C) for 45 minutes or until the sauce is bubbly and shells are hot in the center. Add the ½ cup of Cheddar cheese and proceed as directed.

Ziti, the Italian word for bridegroom, is also the name of a pasta that is very similar in shape to penne, but thinner. In a way, this recipe is my modern version of a TV dinner. Fans of the television show *The Sopranos* will no doubt associate baked ziti (as I do) with the doyenne of that crime family, Carmella Soprano, who during the early seasons was always dropping off a pan of this cheesy-topped tomato and pasta casserole to her good buddy Father Phil.

SEE PHOTO INSERT

Classic Baked Ziti with Sun-dried Tomato Sauce

PREP: 10 minutes | **COOK:** 60 minutes | **YIELD:** 6 servings

SAUCE:
- 2 tbsp (30 mL) olive oil
- 1 onion, peeled and chopped
- ¼ cup (50 mL) each chopped fresh basil and blotted, oil-packed sun-dried tomatoes
- ½ tsp (2 mL) each dried oregano and thyme leaves
- 2 cloves garlic, minced
- 3 cups (750 mL) puréed or ground tomatoes
- ½ tsp (2 mL) pepper
- ¼ tsp (1 mL) each salt and granulated sugar (approx)
- 2 tbsp (30 mL) shredded or grated Parmesan cheese

PASTA:
- 4 cups (1 L) dry ziti or penne
- 1 cup (250 mL) shredded mozzarella cheese

SAUCE: Heat the oil in a deep saucepan or Dutch oven set over medium heat. Add the onion, basil, sun-dried tomatoes, oregano and thyme and cook, stirring often, for 8 minutes or until the onion is very soft. Add the garlic, tomatoes, pepper, salt and sugar. Bring to a boil. Reduce the heat to low and simmer for 20 minutes. Stir in the Parmesan cheese. Taste the sauce and add additional salt and sugar if necessary.

PASTA: Meanwhile, cook the ziti in a large pot of boiling, salted water for 7 to 9 minutes or until almost al dente. Drain well. Toss the pasta with the sauce and transfer to a well-greased 13- by 9-inch (3 L) baking dish. Sprinkle the mozzarella cheese evenly all over the casserole and cover with lightly greased foil. (Recipe can be assembled to this point and then refrigerated for up to 1 day.)

Preheat the oven to 350°F (180°C). Bake the ziti on the center rack of the oven for 30 minutes or until the casserole is bubbly. Remove the foil and broil for 1 to 2 minutes or until golden.

92

Like a store-bought TV dinner, my version of this classic Italian recipe is designed to be made, frozen and then reheated in the microwave so you can enjoy its comforting flavor without missing a moment of your favorite show! Part of the success of this entrée is that it borrows from the packaged foods world. Instead of blending all the ingredients together and then freezing the casserole, each part of the dish is frozen separately to maintain optimum texture and taste.

Freezer Baked Ziti

Assemble all the ingredients for Classic Baked Ziti with Sun-dried Tomato Sauce. Instead of tossing the pasta and noodles together, spoon the pasta onto one side of a glass baking dish or 6 heatproof single-serve freezer containers. Add the sauce to the other side before covering tightly. (The sauce will seep around the pasta a bit, but that's okay.) Reserve the mozzarella cheese in a separate container. To serve, microwave at High for 7 to 8 minutes or until the sauce is completely thawed. Stir the noodles and sauce together and sprinkle cheese evenly. Microwave for 1 to 2 minutes longer at High or until hot.

For single-serving frozen portions, microwave at High for 3 minutes or until sauce is completely thawed; stir and sprinkle each portion with mozzarella cheese; cook on High for 1 minute longer.

Speed cooking tip: Substitute 1 jar (700 mL) sun-dried tomato-flavored pasta sauce for sauce ingredients listed above. Proceed from the point that the Parmesan is added to the sauce.

Like many children, my son Oliver adores meatballs with spaghetti and tomato sauce; unfortunately, like many working moms, I rarely find the time to hand-roll seasoned, ground meat so that he can have his favorite comfort food.

Anxious to be a good mom, I compromised. Instead of rolling each portion of meat into a little ball, to speed up the process, in this recipe the meat is formed into a long, flat meatloaf that is cut into 1-inch (2.5 cm) cubes before cooking. The result is a batch of only slightly misshapen meat"balls" that are still filled with home-made goodness and flavor. This modern twist on spaghetti and meatballs received Oliver's enthusiastic seal of approval—and I think your family will cheer for it, too!

Spaghetti with Easy Meat "balls"

PREP: 20 minutes | **COOK:** 25 minutes | **YIELD:** 4 servings

MEATBALLS:
- 3 tbsp (45 mL) ketchup
- 1 small onion, peeled and coarsely grated
- 1 clove garlic, minced
- ½ tsp (2 mL) each dried oregano and basil leaves
- ½ tsp (2 mL) salt
- ¼ tsp (1 mL) pepper
- 1 egg, beaten
- ¼ cup (50 mL) fresh bread crumbs
- 1 lb (500 g) lean ground beef or chicken

PASTA:
- 12 oz (375 g) dry spaghetti
- 2½ cups (625 mL) pasta sauce
- Parmesan cheese
- Chopped fresh parsley (optional)

MEATBALLS: Preheat the oven to 400°F (200°C). Line a rimmed baking sheet with nonstick foil or grease the pan well.

In a large bowl, combine the ketchup, onion, garlic, oregano, basil, salt and pepper. Add the egg and blend well with a fork. Blend in the bread crumbs. Crumble the meat into the bowl. Gently combine the ingredients using a rubber spatula or your hands.

Turn the meat mixture out onto the prepared baking sheet. Pat into a rectangle that is about ¾ inch (5 cm) thick. Use a knife to cut the meat mixture into squares without separating. Bake for 25 to 30 minutes or until the meat is no longer pink in the center. Using a metal spatula, break the meat into individual pieces; discard any liquids that accumulated in the pan during cooking. Reserve meatballs.

PASTA: Meanwhile, bring a large pot of salted water to a boil and cook the pasta for 8 to 10 minutes or until al dente. Drain well. Divide evenly between 4 pasta bowls.

Place the meatballs and the sauce in a saucepan or microwaveable dish. Stir very gently to combine. Heat on the stovetop or in the microwave until very hot. Spoon the sauce over the warm pasta. Sprinkle each bowl with grated Parmesan cheese and parsley (if using).

Lasagna is a favorite home-cooked meal for many people but it is time-consuming to prepare all those layers of cheese, sauce and noodles. Not surprisingly, sales of frozen lasagna entrées have increased steadily along with the growing number of households with two working parents. Unfortunately, no matter how expensive it is, frozen, packaged lasagna always seem to have a processed taste that is predominantly salty.

To make it easier to enjoy delicious home-style lasagna, I created this lazy version of the classic Italian casserole. By using broken or roughly chopped fresh lasagna noodles this recipe is much faster and far less messy to make than the traditional layered version and still has the texture of the original dish. In my opinion, this shortcut recipe is a weeknight winner!

Skillet Lasagna

PREP: 10 minutes | **COOK:** 25 minutes | **YIELD:** 6 servings

1 tbsp (15 mL) vegetable oil
1 onion, peeled and chopped
2 cloves garlic, minced
2 tsp (10 mL) dried basil leaves
1 tsp (5 mL) each dried oregano and thyme leaves
¼ tsp (1 mL) each salt and pepper
¾ lb (375 g) lean ground beef
3 cups (750 mL) tomato or pasta sauce
1 cup (250 mL) water
6 sheets fresh lasagna noodles
1 cup (250 mL) ricotta or cottage cheese
½ cup (125 mL) grated Parmesan cheese
1 cup (250 mL) shredded mozzarella cheese

Heat the oil in an ovenproof Dutch oven or wok set over medium heat. Add the onion, garlic, basil, oregano, thyme, salt and pepper to the pan. Cook for 5 minutes or until the onion is softened.

Increase the heat to medium-high; crumble in the beef and cook until browned, about 5 minutes. Stir in the tomato sauce and the water and bring to a boil. Tear the noodles into bite-size strips and add to the sauce mixture. Reduce the heat to medium-low, partially cover and simmer for 15 minutes, or until the noodles are tender.

Preheat the broiler to high. Stir the ricotta with the Parmesan cheese. Spoon the ricotta mixture into the center of the meat sauce and noodle mixture in the Dutch oven. Sprinkle the top evenly with mozzarella cheese. Transfer the pan to the oven and broil for 2 to 3 minutes or until the cheese is melted and bubbly.

Whole wheat spaghetti has come a long way since it became readily available about a decade ago. The first commercial versions were notoriously gummy once cooked. Today, however, there are many brands of good-quality, whole wheat pastas on the market. The benefits of eating whole wheat pasta are numerous and not just health related. Although whole wheat pasta contains fiber (which by now you know is good for your health), it also has a mild, almost nutty flavor that adds depth to meatless dishes and pairs very well with the ground pine nuts that are an ingredient in most pesto products.

This simple, straightforward pasta supper features an uncooked sauce that takes mere seconds to stir together. The flavors and texture of the sauce along with the distinctive flavor of the whole wheat noodles makes this a satisfying meatless entrée you'll want to prepare again and again.

To make Parmesan cheese curls, use a vegetable peeler to peel very thin strips from a wedge of Grana Padano or Parmigiano-Reggiano cheese.

Garden Fresh Pasta Toss

PREP: 5 minutes | **COOK:** 12 minutes | **YIELD:** 4 servings

1 pkg (12 oz/375 g) dry whole wheat spaghetti
½ cup (125 mL) deli-made fresh pesto or Nutless Basil Pesto (page 43)
1 tbsp (15 mL) balsamic vinegar
1 tsp (5 mL) grated lemon zest
½ cup (125 mL) chopped roasted red peppers
¼ cup (50 mL) finely diced sun-dried tomatoes
Salt and pepper
2 tbsp (30 mL) toasted pine nuts
Parmesan cheese curls

Cook the spaghetti in a large pot of boiling, salted water for 10 to 12 minutes until al dente, or according to package directions. Drain well.

Meanwhile, stir the pesto with the balsamic vinegar and lemon zest in a large bowl.

Add the hot spaghetti, red peppers and sun-dried tomatoes. Toss to combine.

Add salt and pepper to taste. Garnish with toasted pine nuts and Parmesan curls.

I often have a package of smoked salmon in my freezer so that on nights when I have no time to shop and no time to wait for take-out, I can still make this gourmet yet almost instant meal for dinner. If you are starting with frozen smoked salmon, place the unopened package in the sink and, as the water for the pasta comes to a boil, run a steady stream of cold water over the fish. It will thaw in just a few minutes.

This recipe can be served as a bowl-style meal with no accompaniment, or, if that doesn't feel complete enough for you, serve it with a simple lettuce, cucumber and tomato salad.

Lemon-lime Bowties with Smoked Salmon and Peas

PREP: 5 minutes | **COOK:** 12 minutes | **YIELD:** 4 servings

3 cups (750 mL) dry farfalle, about 12 oz (375 g)
1 cup (250 mL) frozen small peas
⅓ cup (75 mL) butter
¼ cup (50 mL) grated Parmesan cheese (approx)
1½ tsp (7 mL) each finely grated lime and lemon zests
½ tsp (2 mL) coarsely ground pepper
3 oz (90 g) smoked salmon, chopped into bite-size pieces
Salt

Cook the pasta in a large pot of boiling, salted water according to package directions or until al dente, about 12 minutes. Place the peas in the bottom of a large colander. When the pasta is cooked, drain it over the peas and let stand for 1 minute. Meanwhile, return the pasta pan to the stovetop. Decrease the heat to low. Melt the butter and stir in the cheese, lemon and lime zests, pepper and salmon. Add the drained pasta mixture and toss to combine. Taste and add salt if necessary.

Whether you use rotini or fusilli, short spiral-shaped pasta is so well liked because the ridges capture and hold sauce and flavorful bits wonderfully. This pasta and peppers dish is an interesting fusion of Mediterranean and Asian flavors. The main reason this combination works is because the peppers, although glazed to taste sweet and sour (Asian), are a natural partner for the tomatoes, oregano and Parmesan cheese (Mediterranean).

To help make this kind of flavor fusion pleasing and not confusing to the palate, in this recipe I call for tamari rather than soy sauce. Although both sauces are made from soy beans, tamari has a mellower flavor that doesn't overwhelm the other flavors in this colorful dish.

Rainbow Rotini with Chicken

PREP: 10 minutes | **COOK:** 15 minutes | **YIELD:** 4 servings

2 cups (500 mL) dry whole wheat rotini or other short pasta
2 tbsp (30 mL) olive oil
1 onion, peeled and thinly sliced
2 skinless, boneless chicken breasts, thinly sliced, about 1 lb (500 g)
2 cloves garlic, minced
2 tsp (10 mL) dried oregano leaves
½ tsp (2 mL) each salt and pepper
1 each red, yellow and green pepper, sliced
1 tbsp (15 mL) red wine vinegar
1 tsp (5 mL) each honey and tamari (or soy sauce)
1 can (19 oz/540 mL) stewed tomatoes, with juices
1 tbsp (15 mL) freshly grated ginger
1 tbsp (15 mL) chopped fresh parsley
¼ cup (50 mL) freshly grated Parmesan cheese

Cook the pasta in a large pot of boiling, salted water for 9 minutes or until al dente. Drain well and reserve.

Heat 1 tbsp (15 mL) of the olive oil in a deep, nonstick skillet or a wok set over medium-high heat. Add the onion and cook, stirring often, for 5 minutes. Add the remaining olive oil, chicken, garlic, oregano, salt and pepper. Increase the heat to high and stir-fry for 2 minutes. Add the peppers and cook for 2 minutes longer. Stir in the red wine vinegar, honey and tamari.

Push the vegetables to the sides of the pan. Pour in the tomatoes and their juices; bring to a boil and cook for 3 minutes or until the juices thicken. Stir in the ginger, cooked pasta and parsley. Cook, stirring, for 2 minutes or until the pasta is heated through. Stir in the Parmesan cheese.

Because springtime is the season for asparagus, wild mushrooms and tarragon, I look forward to making this pasta supper each winter as the meal roster of stews, soups and casseroles starts to become tedious.

I recommend using a textured pasta such as penne rigate or fusilli for this recipe. Such pasta shapes have lots of nooks and crannies to catch the yummy flavorful bits suspended in this light-bodied wine and butter sauce.

Penne with Mushrooms and Asparagus

PREP: 15 minutes | **COOK:** 15 minutes | **YIELD:** 4 servings

8 cups (2 L) hot, cooked penne rigate or other short pasta
¼ cup (50 mL) butter
½ cup (125 mL) thinly sliced, peeled red onion
3 cloves garlic, minced
½ tsp (2 mL) each hot red pepper flakes, salt and pepper
3 cups (750 mL) stemmed, chopped wild or button mushrooms
2 cups (500 mL) asparagus tips
½ cup (125 mL) white wine
1 tbsp (15 mL) grated lemon zest
2 tbsp (30 mL) lemon juice
2 tsp (10 mL) chopped fresh tarragon
½ cup (125 mL) raw or frozen peas
Coarsely shredded Parmesan cheese

Melt half of the butter in a skillet set over medium heat. Add the onion and cook, stirring often, for 5 minutes or until softened. Stir in the garlic, hot pepper flakes, salt and pepper. Increase the heat to medium-high. Add the mushrooms and asparagus tips and stir-fry for 5 minutes or until the asparagus is tender.

Stir in the wine, scraping to remove any cooked-on bits. Add the remaining butter, lemon zest, lemon juice and tarragon. Cook for 1 minute. Add the peas. Toss with the pasta; garnish each serving with cheese.

99

Alfredo sauce, one of the most soothing rich pasta sauces ever to cling to a noodle, is named for Roman restaurateur Alfredo di Lello, who created the sauce during the roaring, decadent twenties—before we had an awareness of cholesterol.

I often wonder why anyone buys prepared Alfredo sauce from a store when it's so fast and easy to make your own. In fact, it confounds me that anyone even thought to create a commercial version! The recipe below is a classic version of Alfredo sauce, but that doesn't mean you can't experiment with it. Stir in a heaping spoonful of pesto or a bit of tomato sauce to vary the flavor. Or add more protein by stirring in drained canned clams, slivers of smoked salmon or chopped grilled chicken.

15-minute Fettuccine Alfredo

PREP: 5 minutes | **COOK:** 10 minutes | **YIELD:** 4 servings

12 oz (375 g) dry fettuccine
¼ cup (50 mL) butter
¼ cup (50 mL) very finely chopped shallots or onions
¼ tsp (1 mL) white or finely ground black pepper
¼ cup (50 mL) white wine (optional)
1¼ cups (300 mL) 35% whipping cream
1¼ cups (300 mL) grated Parmesan cheese
Pinch ground nutmeg
Salt
Chopped fresh parsley (optional)

Cook the pasta in a very large pot of boiling, salted water for 9 to 10 minutes until al dente, or according to package directions. Drain well.

Meanwhile, melt the butter in a deep skillet or wide saucepan set over medium heat. Add the shallots and pepper. Cook the shallot mixture for 3 to 5 minutes or until translucent. Stir in the wine (if using) and boil for 1 minute.

Stir in the cream and heat until steaming (if you added the wine above, you will have to lower the heat under the pan back to medium; remove the pan from the stovetop for 30 to 60 seconds to let it cool a bit before adding the cream). Reduce the heat to low immediately and stir in the Parmesan cheese and nutmeg until the sauce is smooth. Keep warm until pasta is cooked. Toss the drained pasta with the sauce and add salt to taste. Garnish with parsley (if using).

Authentic Bolognese sauce is a zesty, full-bodied meat and tomato mixture that is the backbone of Northern Italian cooking. Once you try this authentic Bolognese sauce recipe, you won't want to toss your spaghetti with store-bought pasta sauce again! This recipe makes a big batch of sauce so that you can freeze family-size portions to have on hand to help ease weeknight cooking crunches. It's as easy to use as bottled but tastes so much better.

The secret ingredient to a true Bolognese sauce is milk, which is added in such a small amount that you don't even know it's there. It works its magic by mellowing and blending the stronger flavors of the white wine, garlic and tomatoes. Another key ingredient is bacon. Also added in small amounts, the bacon helps to deepen and extend the flavor of the veal or beef, and the fat from the bacon helps to emulsify the sauce.

Cool the sauce, uncovered, before chilling, covered. Freeze in batches of 2 cups (500 mL) each, which is just the right amount to cover 8 cups (2 L) (about 4 servings) of cooked pasta.

Make-ahead Rich and Meaty Bolognese Sauce

PREP: 30 minutes | **COOK:** 1 hour 30 minutes | **YIELD:** 8 cups (2 L)

2 each peeled onions, carrots and celery stalks, coarsely chopped
5 cloves garlic
¼ cup (50 mL) extra-virgin olive oil
1½ tsp (7 mL) salt
¾ tsp (4 mL) pepper
1 tsp (5 mL) each dried basil, oregano and thyme leaves
¼ cup (50 mL) chopped, uncooked bacon
1½ lb (750 g) ground veal or beef
1 cup (250 mL) dry white wine
¼ cup (50 mL) tomato paste
1 can (28 oz/796 mL) crushed or puréed tomatoes
½ cup (125 mL) milk

Place the onions, carrots, celery and garlic in a food processor. Pulse the motor until the vegetables are finely chopped. Place the vegetables and oil in a large, heavy pot set over medium heat. Stir in the salt, pepper, basil, oregano and thyme. Cook, stirring occasionally, until softened, about 5 minutes.

Add the bacon and the veal to the pot with the vegetables. Cook over medium-high heat, stirring and breaking up lumps of veal with a wooden spoon, until the meat is no longer pink, about 6 minutes. Stir in the wine, tomato paste, crushed tomatoes and the milk. Reduce the heat to low and simmer gently for 1 to 1½ hours.

Bucatini is the length of spaghetti and a bit thicker around. Because it is hollow down its center, bucatini is probably the most slurpable pasta ever invented (making it an instant hit with kids!). It is an excellent noodle for this pasta dish because it holds up well when tossing the ingredients together (finer pastas such as spaghetti break apart too easily).

This pasta toss features fine-quality cheese, white wine and pancetta (a salty, unsmoked Italian bacon) in an egg-thickened sauce. It's an elegant dish that is gourmet enough to make for guests or for those times when you want to treat your family.

Bucatini Carbonara with Pancetta and Swiss Chard

PREP: 5 minutes | **COOK:** 12 minutes | **YIELD:** 4 servings

1 tsp (5 mL) olive oil
½ cup (125 mL) chopped pancetta or bacon, about 2 oz (60 g)
1 onion, peeled and finely chopped
⅓ cup (75 mL) dry white wine
10 oz (300 g) dry bucatini or spaghetti
3 cups (750 mL) lightly packed, sliced Swiss chard or spinach leaves, well rinsed
3 eggs
¾ cup (175 mL) finely grated Parmigiano-Reggiano or Grana Padano cheese
1 tsp (5 mL) coarsely ground pepper
Salt

Heat the oil in a Dutch oven or wok set over medium-high heat. Add the pancetta and cook, stirring often, for 3 to 5 minutes or until browned. Reduce the heat to medium and add the onion. Cook, stirring often, for 5 minutes. Stir in the white wine. Cook for 1 minute, scraping the bottom of the pan with a wooden spoon to remove any cooked-on bits. Remove from the heat and set aside.

Meanwhile, cook the pasta in a large pot of boiling, salted water for about 12 minutes until al dente, or according to package directions. Place the rinsed greens into the colander. Add the pasta and drain well.

Whisk the eggs with half the cheese and the pepper. Place the pasta and Swiss chard mixture into the pan containing the onions. Slowly add the egg mixture and toss the ingredients over medium heat until well combined and very warm, about 2 minutes. Taste and add more salt if necessary. Divide the pasta mixture between 4 serving bowls and sprinkle each serving with additional cheese. Serve immediately.

Pasta Puttanesca is a classic, throw-together Italian dish. It features olives, capers and hot pepper flakes in a tomato-based sauce. A similar recipe, Spaghetti with Capers and Olives, appears on page 102, but that one is tossed with an oil-based sauce, which makes it higher in calories from fat. If you find the combination of olives, capers and hot pepper flakes appealing but want to keep the calories from fat down, this Puttanesca recipe is a good choice since just a small amount of oil is used for sautéeing (if you serve it with meat as suggested, the calories from fat will increase).

Linguine is a favorite noodle of mine. Long and thready like spaghetti but flat and slightly more substantial, one of the nice things about linguine noodles is that when you twirl them around your fork, more of the scrumptious sauce sticks to the pasta with each bite. If you don't like your food too spicy, use a smaller amount of the hot pepper flakes.

Spicy Linguine Puttanesca

PREP: 25 minutes | **COOK:** 20 minutes | **YIELD:** 4 servings

3 tbsp (45 mL) olive oil
4 cloves garlic, minced
½ cup (125 mL) each chopped pitted green and black olives, such as gaeta or kalamata olives
¼ cup (50 mL) drained capers
½ tsp (2 mL) each dried oregano leaves and hot pepper flakes
¼ tsp (1 mL) salt
1 can (19 oz/540 mL) diced tomatoes, with juices
½ cup (125 mL) shredded fresh basil or chopped parsley
12 oz (375 mL) dry linguine
Grated Parmesan cheese

Heat the olive oil in a deep skillet set over medium heat. Add the garlic to the oil and sauté for 1 minute. Then add the olives, capers, oregano, hot pepper flakes and salt. Sauté for 1 minute.

Add the tomatoes, with their juices, and bring to a boil. Reduce the heat to medium-low. Simmer, stirring often, for 10 minutes or until slightly thickened. Remove the sauce from the heat and stir in the basil.

Meanwhile, cook the pasta in a very large pot of boiling, salted water for 9 to 10 minutes until al dente, or according to package directions. Drain well. Toss with the pasta sauce and add cheese to taste. If you'd like to serve this pasta dish with meat, add a lightly breaded veal cutlet or a grilled chicken breast to each serving.

Aglio e olio means "garlic and oil," so naturally pasta dishes that feature aglio e olio sauces always include generous amounts of garlic and fruity, flavorful olive oil as main ingredients. Standing up to these two strong flavors isn't easy so most variations of this Roman-style pasta dish contain other assertive ingredients. In this speedy recipe, I've used a gutsy combination of capers, olives, hot pepper flakes and lemon zest to make a full-flavored taste experience.

This pasta entrée is very wine friendly and so flavorful that meat won't be missed; however, if you'd like to make it more substantial, you can add ingredients such as a handful of grilled shrimp or calamari rings to each serving.

Spaghetti with Capers and Olives

PREP: 15 minutes | **COOK:** 20 minutes | **YIELD:** 4 to 6 servings

12 oz (375 g) dry spaghetti
½ cup (125 mL) extra virgin olive oil
6 cloves garlic, minced
1 tsp (5 mL) salt
½ tsp (2 mL) hot pepper flakes
¼ cup (50 mL) chopped pitted black olives
2 tbsp (30 mL) drained capers
1 tsp (5 mL) finely grated lemon zest
¼ cup (50 mL) finely chopped fresh parsley
3 tbsp (45 mL) grated Parmesan cheese

Cook the pasta in a very large pot of boiling, salted water for 9 to 10 minutes until al dente, or according to package directions. Drain well.

Meanwhile, heat the olive oil in a skillet set over low heat. Cook the garlic, stirring often, with the salt and hot pepper flakes for about 10 minutes or until the garlic is just slightly golden. Stir in the black olives, capers and lemon zest. Add the parsley and cheese and toss the sauce with the hot cooked noodles.

If you've been to Italy you'll know that prosciutto is an incredibly popular ingredient in Italian cuisine. I remember stepping into Italian delis and being awed by the sight of rows of whole prosciutto haunches—some with the hoof and a tuft of ankle fur still attached—dangling from every available area of ceiling space. In North America prosciutto has grown in popularity since the 1980s when Cal-Ital cuisine began to influence chefs all over the continent. Soon after, this ingredient became widely available to home cooks, too.

Although prosciutto means ham in Italian, it is more specifically a seasoned, salt-cured but unsmoked pork product. It can be cooked (*cotto*) or raw (*crudo*). Both the *crudo* and *cotto* versions of prosciutto can be eaten right out of the package (although the *crudo* version hasn't been cooked, it has been cured). Either kind can be used in this tasty recipe.

Spaghetti with Roasted Tomato, Prosciutto and Olive Sauce

PREP: 10 minutes | **COOK:** 20 minutes | **YIELD:** 4 servings

3 cups (750 mL) grape or cherry tomatoes
½ cup (125 mL) extra virgin olive oil
2 tbsp (30 mL) balsamic vinegar
½ tsp (2 mL) each salt, pepper and hot pepper flakes
¾ cup (175 mL) very thinly sliced proscuitto
½ cup (125 mL) halved, pitted salt-cured olives
6 cups (1.5 L) hot, cooked spaghetti
1 cup (250 mL) lightly packed shredded fresh basil or chopped fresh parsley
¼ cup (50 mL) very finely grated Parmesan cheese

Preheat the oven to 375°F (190°C). Halve each tomato and toss with the olive oil, balsamic vinegar, salt, pepper and hot pepper flakes until well coated. Stir in the prosciutto and olives. Transfer this mixture to a large, rimmed baking sheet and shake to spread out the ingredients evenly.

Bake the tomato mixture for 15 to 20 minutes, stirring occasionally, or until the tomatoes are wrinkled and slightly dried and the prosciutto is crisping at the edges.

Scrape the contents of the pan, including any oil and cooked-on bits that you can scrape off easily, over the hot pasta. Add the basil and cheese. Toss to combine.

The word vodka comes from a Russian term that translates as "water of life." Interestingly, pasta is revered as a life force in Italy, too. For instance, food writer Ursula Ferrigno endorses pasta as the "soul of Italian life" in her pasta tribute book *Truly, Madly Pasta*.

Serve this peppered vodka pasta entrée when you want to shake up your dinner routine but don't want to spend all day in the kitchen. Vodka is prized by spirit enthusiasts for its purity and neutral flavor; however, in recipes like this one it adds an assertive, distinct but welcome touch. To temper some of the bolder flavors in this recipe, I add a splash of whipping cream to the sauce. This mellow addition blends the flavors and the result is a supper that is intriguing and exciting.

Penne with Peppered Vodka Sauce

PREP: 25 minutes | **COOK:** 15 minutes | **YIELD:** 4 servings

1 tsp (5 mL) hot pepper flakes
¼ cup (50 mL) vodka
12 oz (375 g) dry penne rigate
1 tbsp (15 mL) vegetable oil
¼ cup (50 mL) finely chopped onion
½ tsp (2 mL) each dried basil and oregano leaves
3 cups (750 mL) tomato sauce
½ cup (125 mL) 35% whipping cream
¼ cup (50 mL) finely chopped, pitted green olives
1 tbsp (15 mL) chopped fresh parsley
Grated Parmesan or Romano cheese

Place the hot pepper flakes in a microwaveable bowl or measuring cup. Add the vodka and microwave at High for 20 seconds. Let stand, covered, for 15 minutes.

Cook the pasta in a large pot of boiling, salted water for about 10 minutes until al dente, or according to package directions. Drain well.

Meanwhile, heat the oil in a saucepan set over medium heat. Cook the onion, stirring often, for 5 minutes or until softened. Stir in the basil and oregano. Strain the vodka into the saucepan; discard the pepper flakes. Stir in the tomato sauce and bring the sauce mixture to a boil. Reduce the heat to low and simmer the sauce for 5 minutes. Remove the pan from the heat. Stir in the whipping cream.

Toss the penne with the sauce, olives and parsley and serve with Parmesan or Romano cheese on the side.

Cook once, eat twice: Make a double or triple batch of the sauce and freeze in batches. To use, gently melt in a heavy-bottomed saucepan set over low heat. Stir often to avoid scorching. Do not boil.

Bruschetta is a ubiquitous dinner starter that appears on countless restaurant menus. Although the word *bruschetta* comes from an Italian word (*bruscare*) that means to "roast over the coals," the version that has become so wildly popular and is served in many restaurants today is usually garlic toast crowned with a raw tomato, onion and olive oil topping.

In this recipe, I've omitted the bread but used the same flavors and ingredients to make a very fast pasta toss. You get to savor the terrific taste of bruschetta as part of the main dish and not just as an appetizer. For best results, be sure to use the ripest, reddest tomatoes you can find.

Pasta with Bruschetta Sauce

PREP: 10 minutes | **COOK:** 10 minutes | **YIELD:** 4 servings

3 cups (750 mL) dry pasta such as penne
1 cup (250 mL) finely diced, peeled, sweet white onion
2 cups (500 mL) chopped, seeded plum or vine-ripened tomatoes
¼ cup (50 mL) each chopped fresh parsley and basil
2 cloves garlic, minced
1 tbsp (15 mL) red wine vinegar
½ tsp (2 mL) each salt and pepper
⅓ cup (75 mL) extra virgin olive oil
½ cup (125 mL) grated Parmesan cheese

Cook the pasta in a large pot of boiling, salted water for about 10 minutes until al dente, or according to package directions.

In a large pasta bowl, combine the onion, tomatoes, parsley, basil, garlic, red wine vinegar, salt and pepper. Toss to combine.

Drizzle the olive oil over the tomato mixture and toss gently. Add the pasta and toss to combine. Sprinkle the cheese over top of the noodles.

Preparing an elegant, fresh meal when you've just come home from a long day at work is well worth the effort when you use good-quality ingredients such as sweet butter, sage and fresh ravioli filled with squash or spinach. In this recipe, silky little pasta pillows are enrobed in a nutty butter sauce that tastes chef-prepared. Whether you serve this entrée to company or to your family, you'll be sure to receive accolades.

Because this pasta dish is quite rich, I find it to be a very satisfying meal when served with a simply dressed salad. If you have a robust appetite, however, you may want to serve this ravioli with grilled chicken, veal chops or a piece of baked fish.

If the skillet is not large enough to hold all the ingredients, add the nuts and skillet ingredients to the reserved hot pasta instead and toss them gently until coated.

Squash Ravioli with Browned Butter, Walnuts, Sage and Garlic

PREP: 10 minutes | **COOK:** 10 to 12 minutes | **YIELD:** 4 to 6 servings

1 pkg (24 oz/700 g) fresh, ready-to-cook squash or spinach ravioli
½ cup (125 mL) California walnut halves
⅓ cup (75 mL) butter
3 cloves garlic, thinly sliced
½ cup (125 mL) lightly packed fresh sage leaves
¼ cup (50 mL) very finely grated Parmesan cheese

Bring a large pot of water to a boil and cook the ravioli until it floats to the top of the pot, from 2 to 4 minutes. Drain well and keep warm.

Heat a large, dry skillet over medium heat. Add the walnuts and toast, stirring often, until golden, about 4 minutes. Remove the nuts from the pan.

Add the butter and garlic to the skillet. Cook, stirring often, until the butter stops sizzling and is beginning to turn amber, about 5 minutes. If the garlic starts to scorch, remove it from the pan using a slotted spoon and reserve with the nuts.

Stir in the sage leaves and cook, stirring, until wilted and slightly browned, from 1 to 2 minutes. Stir in the reserved nuts and pasta. Toss the ingredients gently to coat. Serve sprinkled with cheese.

Add an exotic touch to your dinner-time repertoire quickly and easily with this spicy, warm salad. Indonesian noodle cups (or salad rolls) are popular at the fast food-style Asian restaurants located in big North American cities. This concept of eating spiced noodles and other mixtures wrapped in a lettuce leaf has become so popular that recently one of Canada's leading grocery chains launched a bagged, pre-washed lettuce leaf product that is crisp yet flexible enough to use like a wrap or taco shell and which is the perfect size for cradling savory mixtures.

This recipe calls for rice stick noodles, which are the ¼-inch (0.5 cm) wide rice noodles that are used to make Pad Thai. Once cooked, these noodles grow to about double in width. If rice noodles aren't available or aren't to your taste, you can substitute cooked basmati rice or fettuccine instead.

Indonesian Beef Noodle Cups

PREP: 20 minutes | **COOK:** 15 minutes | **YIELD:** 8 servings

PEANUT DRESSING:
  ½ cup (125 mL) hoisin sauce
  ¼ cup (50 mL) smooth peanut butter
  ¼ cup (50 mL) orange juice
  1 tbsp (15 mL) rice wine vinegar
  1 tsp (5 mL) chili paste or hot pepper sauce
  ¼ tsp (1 mL) minced garlic
SALAD:
  4 oz (125 g) rice stick noodles
  1 tbsp (15 mL) vegetable oil
  ¼ cup (50 mL) each finely chopped, peeled onion, carrot and celery
  2 cloves garlic, minced
  ½ tsp (2 mL) ground cinnamon
  ¼ tsp (1 mL) each ground cardamom, nutmeg, salt and pepper
  1 lb (500 g) lean ground beef
  1 cup (250 mL) mung bean sprouts, well rinsed
  8 whole iceberg or Boston lettuce leaves
  Sliced yellow pepper

DRESSING: Whisk the hoisin sauce with the peanut butter, orange juice, rice wine vinegar, chili paste and garlic until smooth. Reserve.

SALAD: Place the rice noodles in a bowl and cover with boiling water. Let stand for 5 minutes; drain well. Fluff the noodles with a fork. Reserve.

Meanwhile, heat the oil in a large skillet set over medium heat. Cook the onion, carrot and celery, stirring often for 5 minutes, or until lightly browned. Stir in the garlic, cinnamon, cardamom, nutmeg, salt and pepper. Increase the heat to medium-high. Crumble in the ground beef and cook, stirring often, for 6 to 8 minutes or until the meat is well browned. Toss the beef mixture with the bean sprouts and rice noodles. Spoon the noodle mixture into lettuce "cups." Drizzle evenly with peanut dressing and garnish with yellow pepper.

Peanut-enhanced sauces are a hall-mark of many Southeast Asian cuisines. This particular recipe is inspired by the take-out noodles my friends and I used to pick up years ago to eat on movie nights. This sauce, which is sweet, spicy and tart all at once, goes very well with a cold, frosty beer. Yum!

I think rice noodles really are best for this recipe. However, if you prefer a wheat noodle, you can make this dish with Japanese, wheat-based udon noodles or, in a pinch, even linguine.

Pea-nutty Cold Noodles with Shrimp

PREP: 5 minutes | **COOK:** 5 minutes | **YIELD:** 4 servings

¼ cup (50 mL) smooth peanut butter
¾ cup (175 mL) hoisin sauce
¼ cup (50 mL) lime juice
2 tsp (10 mL) brown sugar
1 tsp (5 mL) hot pepper sauce
¼ tsp (1 mL) each salt and pepper
2 cloves garlic, minced
8 oz (250 g) thick rice stick noodles
1 cup (250 mL) diced firm tofu
¾ cup (175 mL) each thinly sliced snow peas and red pepper
3 green onions, sliced
2 cups (500 mL) cold cooked shrimp
3 tbsp (45 mL) chopped fresh coriander

Whisk the peanut butter with the hoisin sauce, lime juice, brown sugar, hot pepper sauce, salt, pepper and garlic in a small saucepan set over medium heat. Bring to a boil, stirring often; remove from the heat. Cool.

Place the rice noodles in a bowl and cover with boiling water. Let stand for 5 minutes or according to package instructions until the noodles are al dente. Drain and rinse the noodles under cold running water. Drain well. Fluff with a fork. Toss the noodles with the peanut sauce, tofu, snow peas, red pepper, green onions and shrimp. Garnish with coriander.

Pizza

I was surprised to learn that in a society where take-out pizza options abound, so many of us cite pizza as one of the top 10 things we make for dinner. This finding truly underlines the fact that pizza is one of our very favorite foods.

The roots of pizza may reach back as far as Ancient Egypt where flatbread was (and still is) popular. Today, this single-layer cousin of the hot sandwich has become one of the world's most popular foods. Pizza was available in Italian immigrant neighborhoods almost as soon as these populations became established in North American cities; but pizza didn't become immediately popular with non-Italians. It took pizza-addicted soldiers returning home from World War II battles in Italy to popularize this pie in North America.

The topping combinations for pizza are truly infinite. In this chapter, I present several crust options, a basic sauce recipe and then recipes for interesting pizzas and pizza-inspired foods that you likely won't find on take-out menus. The crust and the sauce recipes can be used to make all of the pizzas found in this chapter; or to save time, you can buy deli-made dough and use a bottled sauce. Whichever method you choose, you'll be surprised at how quickly and inexpensively you can make a fabulous homemade pizza for dinner! Please read my colleagues' inspired pizza combinations on pages 120-121.

My husband Martin Kouprie is an amazingly accomplished chef and co-owner of the acclaimed Pangaea restaurant in Toronto. Years ago, when we were first married, he shared his excellent pizza dough recipe with me when I was writing an article. To make this recipe faster and less messy, I've modified Martin's recipe by using quick-rising yeast and the food processor. Honey is the crucial ingredient that makes this recipe better than others. Not only does the honey give the yeast a quick boost, but it helps the crust to brown and crisp quickly.

When making any yeast-leavened dough, the temperature of the water used to moisten the dry ingredients and activate the yeast is crucial. The water should be 105°F to 115°F (43°C to 47°C)—hot but not so hot that you burn yourself when you immerse and hold your finger in it for a few seconds. If the water is too hot, it will kill the yeast.

If you don't have time to make your own dough, you can substitute 12 oz (375 g) of deli-made pizza dough wherever this recipe is called for.

Thin and Crispy Basic Pizza Crust

PREP: 15 minutes | **REST:** 30 minutes | **YIELD:** 1 pizza crust (4 servings)

1½ cups (375 mL) all-purpose flour
1 tsp (5 mL) quick-rising yeast
¾ tsp (4 mL) salt
1 tbsp (15 mL) honey
1½ tsp (7 mL) olive oil, plus extra for oiling the bowl
½ cup (125 mL) warm water, 105°F to 115°F (43°C to 47°C)

Blend the flour, yeast and salt in a food processor fitted with a metal blade; add the honey and oil. With the motor running, drizzle in the water; mix for 1 minute or just until a ball forms.

Knead the dough on a lightly floured surface into a smooth ball; transfer the dough to a lightly oiled bowl, turning to coat it all over with oil. Cover and let the dough rise for 30 minutes. Stretch the dough into about a 12-inch (30 cm) circle and transfer to a lightly floured pizza pan or baking sheet; fold under the edge to make a rim. If time permits, let the dough rest for another 30 minutes before topping.

Cook once, eat twice: Double this recipe and use half the dough tonight. Stretch the rest over a pizza pan, wrap tightly and freeze for up to two weeks.

As health professionals are increasingly recognizing and telling us, the nutritional benefits of including fiber, antioxidants and other essential nutrients that come from unrefined grains in our diets is very important. In fact, in 2005, 66 percent of consumers reported that they wanted to include more whole and unrefined grains in their diets. As a result, many pizza restaurants, both gourmet and take-out, have added whole wheat crust as an option to their menus. This whole wheat pizza crust recipe is easy to make. The gourmet pizzeria-style thin and crisp crust that it produces has a very appealing flavor that kids will eat willingly—so you won't even have to convince them that it's good for them!

Whole Wheat Pizza Crust

PREP: 15 minutes | **REST:** 30 minutes | **YIELD:** 1 pizza crust (4 servings)

¾ cup (175 mL) each whole wheat and all-purpose flour
1 tsp (5 mL) quick-rising yeast
¾ tsp (4 mL) salt
1 tbsp (15 mL) honey
1½ tsp (7 mL) olive oil
½ cup (125 mL) warm water, 105°F to 115°F (43°C to 47°C)

Blend the flours, yeast and salt in a food processor fitted with a metal blade; add the honey and oil. With the motor running, drizzle in the water; mix for 1 minute or just until a ball forms.

Knead the dough into a smooth ball on a lightly floured surface; transfer the dough to a lightly oiled bowl, turning to coat it all over with oil. Cover and let the dough rise for 30 minutes. Stretch the dough into about a 12-inch (30 cm) circle and transfer to a lightly floured pizza pan or baking sheet; fold under the edge to make a rim. If time permits, let the dough rest for another 30 minutes before topping.

I love to cook but cleaning the kitchen is really not my idea of fun. To limit the time I spend cleaning, I make this pizza dough after dinner *before* I wash up. That way I have just one mess to clean up but two meals as a result. Knowing that I have this dough waiting for me in the refrigerator gives me great peace of mind and makes hectic days that much less stressful.

This dough recipe yields quite a large pizza, which means that there are often leftovers that can be put in lunchboxes the following day.

If you don't have a baking sheet, you can use a regular round pizza pan. The pizza will have a thicker crust with fewer servings. If you prefer a thinner crust, use only half the dough and freeze the rest to use another time.

Overnight Party-size Pizza Crust

PREP: 20 minutes | **REST:** overnight
COOK: 20 minutes | **YIELD:** 1 large pizza crust (6 servings)

2 ¼ tsp (11 mL) active dry yeast, 1 pouch
2 cups (500 mL) all-purpose flour
¾ cup (175 mL) warm water, 105°F to 115°F (43°C to 47°C)
1 tsp (5 mL) salt
1 tbsp (15 mL) olive oil

Combine the yeast and 1 tbsp (15 mL) of the flour with the water. Whisk until well combined and set aside for 5 minutes or until the mixture looks frothy and creamy.

Place the remaining flour and salt in a large bowl. Add the yeast mixture and the oil. Stir, using a large spoon, until the dough starts to come away from the edge of the bowl.

Turn the dough out onto a floured work surface and knead for 6 to 7 minutes or until the dough becomes soft and elastic. (Alternatively, knead it in a stand mixer fitted with a dough hook for 3 minutes at medium speed.)

Transfer the dough to a clean bowl that has been lightly coated with oil or cooking spray. Cover tightly with plastic wrap and let the dough rise in the refrigerator overnight.

To use, remove the dough from refrigerator and punch down the dough to remove all the air. Roll the dough to fit a 15- by 10-inch (37 x 25 cm) greased, rimmed baking sheet. Let stand for 30 minutes. Preheat the oven to 450°F (230°C). Add pizza sauce and toppings to taste. Bake the pizza for 15 to 20 minutes or until the bottom is crispy and golden.

This distinctive base for pizza is in-fused with herbal and other classic Italian flavors. The oil from the pesto enriches this dough and makes it more bread-like than the other thin-and-crispy-style pizza crust recipes in this book. This dough is a good choice for people who like a thicker crust pizza.

For the fresh prepared pesto called for in this recipe, you can either use fresh deli-made pesto or make your own (see the recipe for Nutless Basil Pesto on page 43).

Pesto-flavored Focaccia Pizza Crust

PREP: 10 minutes | **REST:** 30 minutes
COOK: 20 minutes | **YIELD:** 1 large, thick-crust pizza (6 servings)

3 cups (750 mL) all-purpose flour
5 tsp (25 mL) quick-rising dry yeast
1 tbsp (15 mL) granulated sugar
¼ tsp (1 mL) salt
1½ cups (375 mL) warm water, 105°F to 115°F (43°C to 47°C)
3 tbsp (45 mL) fresh prepared pesto
Cornmeal (optional)

Combine the flour, yeast, sugar and salt in a food processor bowl fitted with a metal blade. Pulse the motor until the ingredients are well blended. With the motor run-ning, add the water and process just until the dough starts to form a ball.

Add the pesto and pulse the motor until the ingredients are well combined. Turn the dough out onto a lightly floured board or other clean work surface and knead 6 to 10 times or until the pesto is evenly distributed in the dough.

Cover the dough with a clean kitchen towel or a large inverted bowl and let it stand for 15 minutes. Dust a greased 16- by 12-inch (40 x 30 cm) baking sheet with a little cornmeal (if using). Roll or press and stretch the dough by hand into a large oval; transfer the dough to the prepared baking sheet. Top as desired and let stand for 15 minutes. Preheat oven to 425°F (230°C). Bake the pizza for 20 minutes or until the bottom is crispy and golden.

If you don't have the time or patience to make a yeast-based pizza crust but making homemade pizza from scratch is something you'd like to try, then this thick and bready (but not doughy) quick-bread crust alternative is for you! You don't need any special equipment and all the ingredients, including the baking soda and baking powder, which are the leavening agents, are common pantry items.

Biscuit-style Pizza

PREP: 10 minutes | **COOK:** 20 to 25 minutes | **YIELD:** 1 pizza crust (4 servings)

1 cup (250 mL) milk
½ tsp (2 mL) white vinegar
2¼ cups (550 mL) all-purpose flour
1 tbsp (15 mL) finely chopped fresh rosemary leaves (optional)
2 tsp (10 mL) each baking powder and granulated sugar
½ tsp (2 mL) each baking soda and salt
¼ cup (50 mL) vegetable shortening or butter
½ cup (125 mL) pizza or pasta sauce
Toppings
Shredded cheese

Stir the milk with the vinegar and set aside for 5 minutes. Meanwhile, use a fork to stir the flour with the rosemary, baking powder, granulated sugar, baking soda and salt. Cut in the shortening (using a pastry blender or two knives) until crumbly. Preheat the oven to 400°F (200°C).

Make a well in the flour mixture and pour in the soured milk. Stir until most of the flour has been incorporated and a ragged dough forms. Turn the dough out onto a clean, lightly floured surface and knead just until the dough comes together into a smooth ball. Pat the dough evenly onto a lightly greased 12-inch (30 cm) pizza pan.

Spread the sauce evenly over the dough and sprinkle with desired toppings and just enough cheese to cover the toppings. Bake for 20 minutes or until golden on the bottom. Cool on a rack for 10 minutes before slicing and serving.

Cheese lovers will adore this pizza crust that incorporates string cheese right into the dough! Dress each section with a different combination of pizza toppings or use just one combination on the whole pie, the choice is yours. My preference is to dress the pizza with one set of toppings and then cut it into quarters so that each portion has a cheese filled ridge filled with melted cheese down its center.

Criss-cross Cheese-filled Pizza Crust

PREP: 20 minutes | **REST:** 2 hours
COOK: 20 minutes | **YIELD:** 1 pizza crust (4 servings)

2¼ tsp (11 mL) active dry yeast, 1 pouch
2 cups (500 mL) all-purpose flour
¾ cup (175 mL) warm water, 105°F to 115°F (43°C to 47°C)
1 tsp (5 mL) salt
2 tbsp (30 mL) olive oil, plus more for oiling the bowl
4 mozzarella cheese strings

Combine the yeast and 1 tbsp (15 mL) of the flour with the water. Whisk until well combined. Set aside for 5 minutes or until the mixture looks frothy and creamy.

Place the remaining flour and the salt in a large bowl. Add the yeast mixture and the oil. Stir, using a large spoon, until the dough starts to come away from the edge of the bowl.

Turn the dough out onto a floured work surface and knead for 6 to 7 minutes or until the dough becomes soft and elastic. (Alternatively, knead it in a stand mixer fitted with a dough hook for 3 minutes at medium speed.)

Transfer the dough to a clean bowl that has been lightly coated with oil or cooking spray. Cover tightly with plastic wrap and let rise in a warm place for 1½ hours or until doubled in bulk. Punch down the dough to remove all the air.

Cut off one-quarter of the dough and set aside. Roll the remaining dough into a 13-inch (33 cm) circle. Arrange the dough over a lightly greased 12-inch (30 cm) pizza pan. Turn under the edge to make a thick rim around the pan. Roll the remaining dough out into 2 long strips, one 10 inches long by 3 inches wide (25 cm x 7.5 cm) and one 11 inches long by 3 inches wide (27.5 cm x 7.5 cm). Place 2 cheese strings down the length of each piece of dough. Wrap the dough around the string cheese to enclose. Place the longer piece across the pizza pan, crimping the edges of the cheese-filled dough into the rim. Cut the other length of cheese-filled dough roll in half. Arrange the two pieces of dough like spokes, at 90 degree angles from the first set of cheese wrapped pieces so that the pizza is divided into four.

Dress the pizza with either four separate topping combinations or just one. Let stand for 30 minutes before baking. Preheat the oven to 425°F (230°C). Bake the pizza on the bottom rack for 20 to 25 minutes or until the pizza is golden around the edges and on the bottom.

Ideally, sauces for pizza should be thicker and less chunky than most pasta sauces. A rich, concentrated flavor is key so that you only need to spread a minimum amount of sauce over the crust to achieve maximum flavor. Looser, more liquid and less intensely flavored sauces aren't recommended for pizza since the more sauce you add, the more difficult it is to achieve a crispy crust.

Although there are many commercial pizza and tomato sauces on the market that can be used to make homemade pizza quickly, I like to know exactly what's in the food I eat. This recipe doubles or triples easily, so, when you have time, make up batches of this wholesome pizza sauce and then stash 1 cup (250 mL) portions in the freezer for pizza nights.

To peel tomatoes, score an "X" in the pointed end of each tomato using a sharp knife. Immerse the tomatoes in boiling water for about 5 seconds. Drain and plunge immediately into ice water. The skins should slip off easily. To seed the tomatoes, slice them in half crosswise and use your fingers or a spoon to remove the seeds.

Basic Pizza Sauce

PREP: 20 minutes | **COOK:** 35 minutes | **YIELD:** 2 cups (500 mL)

- 2 tbsp (30 mL) extra virgin olive oil
- 1 onion, peeled and finely chopped
- 1 carrot, peeled and finely chopped
- 1 stalk celery, finely chopped
- ¼ cup (50 mL) chopped fresh parsley
- 2 cloves garlic, minced
- ½ cup (125 mL) chopped fresh basil
- 1 tbsp (15 mL) each chopped fresh thyme and oregano
- 2½ lb (1 kg) peeled, seeded, chopped Roma (or plum) tomatoes
- ½ tsp (2 mL) each salt and pepper
- 1 tsp (5 mL) each granulated sugar and red wine vinegar (approx)

Heat the oil in Dutch oven set over medium heat. Add the onion, carrot, celery and parsley. Cook, stirring occasionally, for 5 minutes. Stir in garlic, basil, thyme and oregano. Cook, stirring often, for 5 minutes.

Add the tomatoes and stir until well combined. Bring to a boil. Reduce the heat to low and simmer for 20 to 30 minutes or until tomatoes are cooked down. Stir in the salt and pepper. Taste and add sugar and red wine vinegar as required to balance the flavor. Cool to room temperature. Purée the sauce, in batches if necessary, in a food processor or blender.

Prepare a container of this spread to keep in the refrigerator when you know you've got a busy week ahead of you. Then, when dinner needs to be made in a hurry, just slather the spread on pitas, bagels, baguettes or tortillas to create personal cheese pizzas in no time flat! Let older kids know that this pizza spread is in the fridge so that they can make their own healthy snacks or light suppers when parents are running late. Customize this pizza sauce as you would a take-out pizza. Just before using, stir a little chopped sweet pepper, mushrooms, pepperoni or olives into the spread.

SEE PHOTO INSERT

Super Pizza Spread

PREP: 5 minutes | **COOK:** none | **YIELD:** 1⅔ cups (400 mL) spread (enough for one 14-inch/35 cm pizza or 6 small tortilla or pita pizzas)

1 cup (250 mL) tomato sauce
½ tsp (2 mL) each dried oregano and basil leaves
1 small clove garlic, minced
1 green onion, chopped
3 tbsp (45 mL) grated Parmesan cheese
½ cup (125 mL) shredded mozzarella cheese

Blend the tomato sauce, oregano, basil, garlic, green onion, Parmesan and mozzarella cheeses until well combined. Store in a clean, dry container, tightly covered. Refrigerate for up to 1 week.

119

The Italian word "capra," meaning goat, lends its name to this robustly flavored, gourmet, thin-crust pizza. Although many pizzerias make Caprese pizza with mild bocconcini cheese, my version attempts to be more authentic by using goat cheese.

Chèvre-style goat cheese is a snow white, creamy textured, slightly crumbly cheese with a tart finish; like olives, this cheese is sometimes an acquired taste. Bocconcini on the other hand, is a fresh mozzarella cheese that is much milder tasting and considerably firmer in texture than chèvre. If you and your dining companions generally prefer milder flavored cheeses, choose the bocconcini. However, if you like zesty, pungent cheeses, go for the chèvre; it will be sure to please! Both chèvre and bocconcini are sold in the deli section at the supermarket.

Caprese Pizza

PREP: 15 minutes | **COOK:** 15 minutes | **YIELD:** 4 to 8 servings

1 portion pizza dough (pages 110-115)
1 cup (250 mL) Basic Pizza Sauce (page 116)
¼ cup (50 mL) grated Parmesan cheese
1 log (4 oz/125 g) chèvre-style goat cheese
¼ cup (50 mL) shredded basil leaves

Preheat the oven to 450°F (230°C). Stretch the pizza dough to fit a lightly greased 12-inch (30 cm) pizza pan. Let the dough rest for 5 minutes. Spread the pizza sauce evenly over the crust. Sprinkle with the Parmesan cheese. Slice the goat cheese into disks and arrange evenly over the sauce. Sprinkle the pizza evenly with basil. Bake for 12 to 15 minutes or until the bottom of the crust is crisp and brown.

Speed cooking tip: Substitute store-bought pizza sauce and pizza dough rather than the recipes suggested here.

By 1953 there were at least 15,000 pizzerias in the United States. While most of these restaurants sold pizzas that were baked on flat, disk-shaped pizza pans, a different kind of pizza tradition had already been established in Chicago. Born at Pizzeria Uno, which opened in 1943, Chicago-style pizza was (and still is) made in a high-sided pan so that toppings can be layered one or more inches deep! Deep dish pizza, which is sort of a pizza-flavored casserole, makes a great change from the more familiar, ubiquitous take-out pizzas most of us often eat.

The art of making this style of pizza is to get the crust crispy and brown from edge to center. That's why it must be baked on the lowest rack of the oven where the heat is the highest.

Chicago-style Deep Dish Pizza Pie

PREP: 15 minutes | **COOK:** 30 minutes | **YIELD:** 4 servings

**1 portion Thin and Crispy Basic Pizza Crust (page 110) or Whole Wheat
    Pizza Crust (page 111)**
2 tsp (10 mL) cornmeal (optional)
1 tbsp (15 mL) vegetable oil
1¾ cup (425 mL) thinly sliced onions
2 cloves garlic, minced
1 tsp (5 mL) each dried basil and oregano leaves
½ tsp (2 mL) hot pepper flakes (approx)
8 oz (250 g) mushrooms, thinly sliced
1½ cups (375 mL) Basic Pizza Sauce (page 116)
1 cup (250 mL) thinly sliced pepperoni
2 cups (500 mL) Italian-style shredded cheese or mozzarella

Preheat the oven to 475°F (240°C). Roll the dough out to make an 11-inch (26 cm) circle. Lightly grease a 9-inch (23 cm) round cake pan. Dust the pan evenly with cornmeal (if using) by shaking the pan to distribute the grains evenly over the bottom and up the sides of the pan. Press the rolled dough into the bottom and up the sides of the prepared pan. Reserve.

Heat the oil in a skillet set over medium heat. Add the onion and sauté for 5 minutes. Stir in the garlic, basil, oregano and hot pepper flakes. Add the mushrooms and cook for 2 to 3 minutes or until lightly browned. Stir in the pizza sauce. Stir in half the pepperoni.

Spoon the sauce mixture into the prepared pan. Sprinkle evenly with cheese and top with the remaining pepperoni slices. Bake the pizza on the lowest rack in the oven for 20 minutes or until the pizza crust is golden and the topping is bubbly.

121

Inspired Pizza Combinations

Although I wish I could say that I'm a rare talent who can write a great recipe book effortlessly all on my own, the truth is this book exists thanks to the hard work of a talented group of people. Each recipe in this collection was developed and then tested and retested by trained recipe testers who made suggestions, which in many cases improved my original ideas immensely. In fact, I am indebted to the efforts and insights of the food experts who work with me on a daily basis to track trends, test recipes and create new food products for corporate clients.

Each of the key members of our team brings their own informed perspective to their work. To showcase this exceptional pool of talent and to thank them publicly for being involved in the creative process that produced this book, here are some inspired pizza combinations from the home kitchens of our team members. Combine these topping suggestions with the sauce and crust recipes in this chapter to enjoy these pizza combinations at your house!

CHARMAINE BROUGHTON, SENIOR RECIPE TESTER AND PRODUCT DEVELOPER
"Food is a big part of my life on a physical, vocational and even a psychological level. As a result, my favorite pizza toppings are closely tied to my day-to-day life.

One day I had an overwhelming, unexplained craving for something salty. This was not a potato chip situation—this craving was deeper and more urgent. I let my culinary imagination kick into high gear and the result was a whole wheat crust pizza brushed with olive oil and generously topped with chopped green olives, herbs, anchovy fillets, grated Asiago cheese and a little diced pineapple. I ate this pizza frequently over the next nine months as my belly grew and the source of my craving became apparent to the entire world!

As a marathon runner, I find the typical runner's carb-loading meal of pasta leaves me feeling sluggish so I eat this pre-race pizza instead: Brush a whole wheat pita lightly with barbecue sauce, top with ¼ lb (250 g) cooked, ground sirloin, chopped fresh basil, thinly sliced sun-dried tomatoes and sprinkle with your favorite shredded cheese. It's a winning combination!"

SABRINA FALONE, PANTRY MANAGER AND RECIPE TESTER
"Pizza was a regularly consumed food for my Italian family. Although the classic toppings are always pleasing, two of my favorite pizzas are very non-traditional.

Because it was my brother's favorite, my grandmother often made an olive-oil–dressed pasta mixture that contained cauliflower, anchovies, caramelized onions, roasted garlic and Romano cheese. I never liked this pungent mixture until I started spooning the sauce over toast. Eventually I tried using this mixture as a topping for pizza and the result was a hit! Unfortunately this zesty pizza combo has such an assertive aroma that it has been dubbed the *Anti-intimacy Pizza* so only make it if you are craving personal space as well as pizza.

My boyfriend Reg and I are opposites in our attitudes toward food. I'll try anything, while his dining preferences are limited to a few basic foods. I was thrilled to discover a stir-fry pizza combination that pleases us both. Instead of tomato sauce, I use a little hoisin or honey garlic sauce and then add toppings such as pineapple, red pepper, grilled pork or chicken and mozzarella cheese."

TRACEY SYVRET, SENIOR RECIPE TESTER AND FOOD STYLIST

"My most memorable and mouth-watering pizza-topping combos are culinary souvenirs I brought back from my travels to Europe. Both of these pizzas begin with simple, regional ingredients and end in combinations of flavors that approach the mystical."

In Orange, a thriving marketplace in Provence, close to the vineyards of the Côtes du Rhône, I visited a gourmet food shop whose name translates to "The Three Little Pigs." There I ate a cheese-free pizza that combined creamy and sweet caramelized onions with the salty brine of black olives. Perfection!

At an outdoor market in Bastia, Corsica, I found another unbelievable pizza. The crust was brushed with oil infused with fresh mint and was then topped with slices of fresh tomato and rounds of creamy goat cheese. Sublime!"

AMY SNIDER, VP, SENSORY EXCELLENCE PROGRAM

"As a professional food writer I sometimes feel obligated to try new foods and to be an adventurous eater; although that can be enjoyable, I still find myself craving the fun foods that friends like to share. Likewise, I find the best pizzas in my repertoire are the ones that combine great snack foods with the pizza concept.

Lingering over a glass of wine while nibbling on cheese and crackers is one of the ways I enjoy relaxing with friends; this enjoyable experience inspired one of my favorite pizza combinations: starting with mini, prepared pizza crust bases, I spread an even layer of mango salsa, chutney or fig spread over the top and then sprinkle with crumbled goat cheese before baking until crisp.

My Buffalo Chicken Wing Pizza is fun to serve to friends. I start with a combination of buffalo wing sauce and pizza sauce and then proceed with layers of Cheddar and mozzarella shredded cheese blend, sliced green onions and cooked chicken fingers tossed in more buffalo sauce. Once baked, I slice the pizza into thin wedges and serve it with a thick, creamy blue cheese salad dressing for dipping."

Umami is the Japanese word used to describe the complex, often salted and always rich, full-flavor of foods such as homemade chicken broth, sautéed mushrooms and miso. Smoked mussels are a high umami food that elevates this pizza from basic to a superb taste experience.

Smoked mussels are inexpensive and pair well with cheese, cream and other dairy products. Available in the canned fish section of any grocery store, smoked mussels are a great item to stock in your pantry since they instantly add flavor and protein to dishes like this one.

Smoked Mussel and Gruyère Pizza

PREP: 15 minutes | **COOK:** 15 minutes | **YIELD:** 4 to 8 servings

1 portion Whole Wheat Pizza Crust (page 111)
½ cup (125 mL) Basic Pizza Sauce (page 116)
2 cans (3 oz/85 g each) smoked mussels, well drained
1½ cups (375 mL) shredded Gruyère or mozzarella cheese
2 tbsp (30 mL) chopped fresh parsley

Preheat the oven to 450°F (230°C). Stretch the dough into about a 12-inch (30 cm) circle and transfer to a lightly floured pizza pan or baking sheet; fold under the edge to make a small rim. Spread the sauce evenly over the crust. Scatter the mussels evenly over the sauce. Sprinkle the pizza evenly with the cheese and parsley. Bake, on the bottom rack, for 12 to 15 minutes or until the bottom of the crust is crisp and brown.

Variation

Substitute escargots for the mussels. Prepare crust as directed; spread with sauce. Drain a 7-oz (200 g) can of escargots and place in a skillet with 1 tbsp (15 mL) butter and 1 minced clove garlic. Sauté for 3 minutes. Scatter escargots evenly over the sauce and proceed as directed.

This rustic-looking pizza is wonderfully full-flavored and impossible to find on a take-out menu. Since tomatoes are a main ingredient, pesto is used as the sauce for this gourmet-style pizza. You can use either fresh pesto from the deli or make your own Nutless Basil Pesto (page 43) if you have time. Roasting the tomatoes removes much of their moisture and concentrates the flavor of these pizza-perfect fruits so that the finished pizza has a rich, intense tomato flavor.

SEE PHOTO INSERT

Oven-dried Tomato, Asiago and Pesto Pizza

PREP: 15 minutes | **COOK:** 30 minutes | **YIELD:** 4 to 8 servings

4 small Roma (or plum) tomatoes, halved and seeded
½ cup (125 mL) fresh basil pesto or Nutless Basil Pesto (page 43)
1 tbsp (15 mL) balsamic vinegar
1 portion of pizza dough (pages 110-115)
1½ cups (375 mL) shredded Asiago cheese

Preheat the oven to 375°F (190°C). Set the tomatoes on a foil-lined baking sheet. Bake in the oven for 15 minutes. Blend 2 tbsp (30 mL) of the pesto with the balsamic vinegar in a separate bowl. Drizzle the pesto-balsamic mixture over the tomatoes. Reduce the oven temperature to 275°F (140°C). Bake the tomatoes for an additional 30 minutes or until reduced to about half their original size. Cool to room temperature. Increase the oven temperature to 450°F (230°C).

Stretch the pizza dough to fit a lightly greased 12–inch (30 cm) pizza pan. Let the stretched dough rest for 5 minutes. Brush evenly with the remaining pesto and sprinkle with all but ½ cup (125 mL) of the cheese. Arrange the cooled tomatoes on top. Sprinkle the pizza with the remaining cheese. Bake for 12 to 15 minutes or until the bottom of crust is crisp and brown.

Cook once, eat twice: Make a double batch of tomatoes and reserve the extra to toss with hot pasta and a few handfuls of baby spinach another night.

MAKE AHEAD: Prepare the pesto (if using homemade) and tomatoes up to 2 days before making the pizza. Reserve tightly covered in separate containers in the refrigerator.

Gorgonzola is an Italian town near Milan and the cheese produced there is considered one of the grand culinary accomplishments of the region. When aged, Gorgonzola is one of the more pungent blue-veined cheeses; however, the texture is creamy and melts nicely, making it a great topper for pizza.

When I make this particular pizza for dinner, it is almost always for adults since most kids aren't big fans of heady blue cheeses like gorgonzola, and the caramelized onions and fresh figs don't always suit their tastes either. When served as a main course, all this pizza needs on the side is a very mildly dressed, leafy green salad. It works well as an appetizer too, accompanied by a glass of red wine.

Make mini versions of this pizza as party appetizers!

SEE PHOTO INSERT

Caramelized Onion, Fig and Gorgonzola Pizza

PREP: 45 minutes | **COOK:** 15 minutes | **YIELD:** 4 to 8 servings

2 tbsp (30 mL) butter
1 Spanish or 3 medium cooking onions, peeled and sliced
1 clove garlic, minced
1 tsp (5 mL) dried thyme leaves
½ tsp (2 mL) each salt and pepper
2 tbsp (30 mL) granulated sugar
¼ cup (50 mL) dry sherry
1 tsp (5 mL) Worcestershire sauce
1 portion pizza dough (pages 110-115)
3 fresh green or purple figs, cut into 6 wedges each
4 oz (125 g) Gorgonzola, Cambazola or another creamy blue-veined cheese

Melt the butter in a large skillet set over medium-low heat. Add the onions, garlic, thyme, salt and pepper. Cook, stirring often, for 10 minutes or until the onions are softened. Decrease heat to low and cook, stirring occasionally, for 30 minutes or until the onions are just beginning to brown.

Sprinkle in the sugar and increase the heat to medium. Cook, stirring often, until the onions are very brown but not scorched. Add the sherry and Worcestershire sauce. Stir to scrape up any brown bits. Cool to room temperature.

Stretch the pizza dough to fit a greased 12-inch (30 cm) pizza pan. Let the stretched dough rest for 5 minutes. Spread the cooled onions evenly over the crust. Scatter the figs evenly over the onion layer and crumble the cheese over the top.

Bake the pizza on the lowest rack of the oven for 12 to 15 minutes or until the bottom of the crust is crisp and golden.

Variations

Add sliced prosciutto for a meaty pizza.

No time to spare? Spread this topping mixture over the surface of a halved loaf of Italian-style bread or naan (Indian-style flatbread). Broil and serve pieces with a green salad for a complete meal.

When I first became a "foodie," I thought that oil-topped pizzas were extremely chic and refined. In fact, feeling quite urbane, I made regular trips to an Italian bakery just to indulge in a potato and olive oil pizza that was sold by the slice.

As it turns out, in Italy it is not uncommon or at all special for pizza to be topped with olive oil! In fact, although most people on this side of the Atlantic are most familiar with pizzas that have a tomato sauce layer, in Italy pesto, cream sauce and olive oil are all often used instead. In the case of my starch-on-starch topping combination, fruity extra virgin olive oil is the ideal choice since it allows the flavor of the potato to shine through where a tomato sauce would likely mask the taste of that mild-flavored vegetable completely.

If you can't find one of the smoked cheeses for this pizza, unsmoked (regular) mozzarella will work. You can still add smoky flavor by adding 1 tsp (5 mL) chipotle-flavored hot pepper sauce to the olive oil and rosemary mixture that the potatoes and onions are tossed in.

Smoky Potato and Red Onion Pizza

PREP: 15 minutes | **COOK:** 15 minutes | **YIELD:** 4 to 8 servings

1 small, unpeeled new potato, preferably red-skinned
½ cup (125 mL) very thinly sliced red onion rings
¼ cup (50 mL) extra virgin olive oil
1 tbsp (15 mL) chopped fresh rosemary leaves
3 cloves garlic, minced
½ tsp (2 mL) coarsely ground pepper
1 portion pizza dough (pages 110-115)
1 cup (250 mL) shredded, smoked Italian cheese such as mozzarella, provolone, scamorza or caciacovalli
¼ cup (50 mL) grated Parmesan cheese

Preheat the oven to 450°F (230°C). Using a chef's knife, food processor or mandolin, very thinly slice the potato into disks that are about ⅛ inch (3 mm) thick. Place the potato and onion slices in a large bowl. Add 2 tbsp (30 mL) of the oil, the rosemary, garlic and pepper. Toss until evenly combined.

Stretch the dought to fit a lightly greased 12-inch (30 cm) pizza pan. Let the stretched dough rest for 5 minutes. Brush the dough evenly with the remaining oil. Arrange the potato slices over the dough in overlapping circles. Scrape the onions and any oil mixture remaining in the bowl over the potatoes and spread evenly. Sprinkle the cheeses evenly over the vegetables. Bake for 14 to 15 minutes or until the bottom of the crust is crisp and brown.

This kid-pleasing pizza is easy to make since there's no crust to be blended or kneaded. To make this recipe even easier and faster to prepare, you can subsitute leftover grilled chicken if you have any on hand, or you can use leftover steak.

I recommend Greek-style, pocketless pitas; they are moister and have a texture more similar to pizza dough than the drier, thinner pocket-style pitas; however, any kind of flatbread from naan to thin focaccia can be used as a base for this pizza.

If using an indoor grill, cover using a disposable foil pan.

Cowboy Grilled Chicken Mini Pizzas

PREP: 10 minutes | **COOK:** 20 to 22 minutes | **YIELD:** 4 pizzas

2 skinless, boneless chicken breasts, about 1 lb (500 g)
½ cup (125 mL) barbecue sauce
¼ cup (50 mL) Basic Pizza Sauce (page 116)
4 Greek-style pitas
2 cups (500 mL) shredded Cheddar cheese
½ cup (125 mL) thinly sliced red pepper
¼ cup (50 mL) frozen corn kernels, thawed, or canned black beans, drained and rinsed
2 green onions, sliced

Preheat an outdoor or indoor grill to medium-high. Grease the grate well. Brush the chicken with ¼ cup (50 mL) of the barbecue sauce. Grill the chicken, covered and turning once, for 12 to 15 minutes or until cooked through. Let the cooked chicken rest for 5 minutes. Slice. Reduce the grill heat to medium.

Stir the remaining barbecue sauce with the pizza sauce. Spread the sauce mixture evenly over one side of each pita. Divide chicken, cheese, red pepper, corn and green onions evenly over the sauce-covered pitas.

Set the pizzas on the grill. Cover and cook for about 6 minutes or until the cheese is melted and the pitas are toasted.

Stromboli is a Philadelphia pizza specialty that is somewhat similar to an open-ended, large calzone. This folded pizza is named for a particularly active volcano located near Sicily, because, as the stromboli bakes, the cheese and sauce often flow out of the ends like a scrumptious, savory lava.

Keep the fillings for stromboli simple so that the finished dish isn't too messy to handle. Ideally the finished stromboli will be easy to pick up and eat out of hand after a brief cooling period.

SEE PHOTO INSERT

Family-size Stromboli

PREP: 15 minutes | **COOK:** 20 minutes | **YIELD:** 4 servings

1 portion pizza dough (pages 110-115)
2 cups (500 mL) shredded mozzarella cheese
½ cup (125 mL) shredded or grated Parmesan cheese
⅔ cup (150 mL) Basic Pizza Sauce (page 116)
½ cup (125 mL) thinly sliced pepperoni
1 egg, beaten
½ tsp (2 mL) poppy seeds

Preheat the oven to 450°F (230°C). Roll or stretch the pizza dough out into a large rectangle, about 11 by 15 inches (27.5 x 37 cm). Place the dough on a greased baking sheet.

Blend the cheeses and reserve. Spread the sauce down the center of the dough, leaving a wide, uncovered border of dough along each side. Sprinkle a little cheese and a layer of pepperoni over the sauce. Repeat the layers until all of the cheese and pepperoni has been used.

Fold one side of the dough over the filling and brush the edge with egg. Fold over the other side to overlap the dough. The folded stromboli should look like a letter that has been folded to be put into an envelope. Pinch the top fold to form a seam that will seal the dough together, leaving the ends open. Brush the top of the stromboli evenly with beaten egg and sprinkle with poppy seeds.

Using a sharp knife, cut slashes every two or three inches down the length of the dough. Bake for about 20 minutes or until the stromboli is golden brown and the cheese is bubbling at the ends. Cool for about 10 minutes before slicing into thick portions.

These *hand-held pizza-like* sandwiches fall into the same casual, family supper realm as tacos or fajitas. Besides being a good hot dinner choice, calzones can also be enjoyed at room temperature—which means that they can be made ahead and packed in school lunches or set aside for teens to reheat for afterschool snacks.

Although authentic calzones are usually filled with pizza toppings, these half-moon shaped, stuffed breads can hold all manner of fillings from chili to ham and cheese. My fun, fast food-inspired version is guaranteed to be a hit with kids of all ages since it mimics the flavor of one of our most loved quick meals, the cheeseburger.

Cheeseburger Calzones

PREP: 15 minutes | **COOK:** 15 minutes | **YIELD:** 4 servings

½ tsp (2 L) vegetable oil
¼ lb (125 g) extra lean ground beef
½ cup (125 mL) ketchup
2 tbsp (30 mL) each green relish and mustard
1 tsp (5 mL) Worcestershire sauce
1 portion pizza dough (pages 110-115)
2 cups (500 mL) shredded Cheddar cheese
½ cup (125 mL) small red onion, thinly sliced (optional)

Preheat the oven to 425°F (220°C). Heat a nonstick skillet over medium-high heat. Add the oil. Crumble in the ground beef and cook, stirring often, until browned. Stir in the ketchup, relish, mustard and Worcestershire sauce. Cook for 3 minutes or until mixture is thickened and bubbly. Cool slightly.

Divide the dough into 4 equal portions. Roll each portion out into a thin circle on a lightly floured surface. Spoon an equal amount of meat mixture onto half of each dough circle, leaving a ½-inch (1 cm) uncovered edge. Sprinkle the meat evenly with cheese and top with sliced onion (if using). Fold the dough over and pinch the edges until each calzone is tightly sealed. Transfer the raw calzones to a greased baking sheet.

Bake on the lower rack of the oven for 15 minutes or until the crust is golden. Cool for 5 to 10 minutes before serving.

This recipe is great for those times when you just can't deal with preparing a pizza dough. These savory pancakes are a fast, novel and fun dinner that combines the appeal and ease of pancakes with the savory flavors of pizza. Not only is this recipe simple to make, but it also gets a high rating for kid appeal—and it's good for you. The cornmeal in these fluffy pancakes adds fiber, an essential part of a healthy diet.

If you don't have buttermilk, make sour milk by stirring 1 tsp (5 mL) lemon juice or white vinegar into regular milk and letting it stand for 5 minutes.

Pizza Pancakes

PREP: 10 minutes | **COOK:** 20 minutes | **YIELD:** 4 to 6 servings

1½ cups (375 mL) fine cornmeal
½ cup (125 mL) all-purpose flour
1½ tsp (7 mL) chili powder
1 tsp (5 mL) dried oregano leaves
1 tsp (5 mL) baking powder
½ tsp (2 mL) baking soda
½ tsp (2 mL) salt
2 cups (500 mL) buttermilk or sour milk (see note)
1 tbsp (15 mL) granulated sugar
2 tbsp (30 mL) vegetable oil
1 egg, beaten
½ cup (125 mL) finely chopped pepperoni or ham
1 green pepper, diced
1 cup (250 mL) pizza sauce
1 cup (250 mL) shredded mozzarella cheese

Mix the cornmeal with the flour, chili powder, oregano, baking powder, baking soda and salt in a medium bowl. Stir until well combined. In a separate bowl, stir the buttermilk with the sugar, vegetable oil and egg. Whisk until well blended. Add the cornmeal mixture and stir until the ingredients are just blended. Stir in the pepperoni and green pepper.

Heat a nonstick griddle or a large heavy skillet over medium-high heat. When the pan is hot, spray with nonstick cooking spray. Pour about ¼ cup (50 mL) of the batter onto the pan to make each pancake.

Cook each pancake for 2 to 3 minutes or until the bottoms are golden and bubbles start to form. Turn and cook the pancakes for 2 minutes longer. While the pancakes are still in the pan, top each one with about 1 tbsp (15 mL) of pizza sauce and mozzarella. Remove the pancakes from the griddle and keep warm in the oven until all the pancakes are ready to serve.

Although pizza is a family favorite, sometimes it isn't the perfect choice for dinner. The entire family will like this pizza-inspired main course because it delivers the flavors they love and is more comforting and substantial than an ordinary slice of 'za. It's got all the flavor of pizza and all the comfort of mashed potatoes! To complete the meal, serve with a crisp Caesar salad.

If using oil-packed sun-dried tomatoes, blot them dry on paper towel to remove excess oil.

Deep Dish Potato "Pizza"

PREP: 10 minutes | **COOK:** 35 minutes | **YIELD:** 4 servings

2 cups (500 mL) mashed, cooked potatoes
¼ cup (50 mL) milk
1 tbsp (15 mL) butter
1 tbsp (15 mL) all-purpose flour
½ cup (125 mL) grated Parmesan cheese
¼ cup (50 mL) each finely chopped sun-dried tomatoes and fresh basil
1 cup (250 mL) shredded mozzarella cheese
⅓ cup (75 mL) very thinly sliced pepperoni

Preheat the oven to 425°F (220°C). Whip the mashed potatoes with the milk and butter using an electric mixer on medium speed. Blend in the flour and Parmesan cheese and transfer to a well-greased, 10-inch (25 cm) shallow round baking dish. Bake for 30 minutes.

Toss the sun-dried tomatoes with the basil and sprinkle evenly over the potato base. Sprinkle evenly with mozzarella cheese. Scatter pepperoni over top. Bake for 5 minutes, or until cheese is melted and crust is set. Run a knife around the edge of the dish. Let stand for 5 minutes before slicing into wedges and lifting out onto serving plates.

Pork

Pork has a long tradition as a well loved, satisfying and comforting dinnertime choice. In fact, the Dutch settlers who colonized New York City were so fond of fresh pork that their pigs became a nuisance as they roamed what is now the lower part of Manhattan. Eventually a long wall had to be built both to keep the swine from rampaging through spaces that were designed for people and to protect the livestock from poachers. A commercial road was built along this wall; aptly—and now famously—that thoroughfare was named Wall Street.

Although pigs no longer roam around the Big Apple, apples and pork are still a good combination in a cooking pot. Inspired recipes like Brie and Cranapple Stuffed Pork Tenderloin and Cheese-wrapped Sausages with Onions and Apples in this chapter are delicious proof.

On health, heritage and hedonism...

When I was growing up, pork chops were a staple in my mother's repertoire of meals. I remember my mom's broiled or grilled chops being thick, juicy and full of their own wonderful flavor. At that time pork wasn't just another white meat. It was a distinctive, tasty meat deserving of its own category.

Home cooks like my mother were trained to cook pork until it was white and firm all the way through. Trichinosis, a parasitic disease caused by a species of round-worm was for many years a risk to pork consumers because pigs were not always raised on quality feed. By cooking the meat until well done, health officials felt the risk of trichinosis was eliminated. Today, feeding processes have been improved so that commercially sold pork is trichinosis free and food scientists now know that trichina is killed at 137°F (60°C), a temperature far below the currently recommended finished cooking temperature of 160°F (71°C).

While ensuring the pork producers were feeding pigs healthfully, pork marketing agencies in Canada and the US also worked to breed pork to be leaner and milder tasting so that it could better compete with chicken. As a result most of the pork sold today in supermarkets tastes less assertive and is so much leaner than it was in the seventies that it can't be cooked until well done without becoming dry and flavorless. Although better sales are the result of these marketing driven changes, for those of us who remember the juicy taste of the pork of yesteryear, this popularity has come at a price.

Due to the recent rise of the slow food movement that has reminded chefs and gourmets of the benefits and pleasures of eating regionally produced, heritage food products, great tasting pork is becoming more available once again. If you're inter-ested in enjoying the flavor and goodness of traditional pork, visit a butcher who sells heritage brands of pork. Some, such as Berkshire and Duroc are even being produced in organic versions.

134

Just like the gourmet pork chops you expect to find at a traditional chop house restaurant, these gorgeous chops feature a long, elegant bone (a preparation technique that butcher's call "Frenched") and glistening sauce. In fact, even before anyone takes a bite you're likely to hear a few "oohs" and "ahs"!

Although this recipe is so simple to make that it is an ideal weeknight choice, it's such a showstopper that you'll never regret choosing it as an entrée for entertaining. The key to making this dish a success is to cook the chops only until they are just barely pink in the center and not any longer so that the inside is as succulent and flavorful as the saucy exterior. Serve these impressive chops with baked sweet potatoes and sautéed snap peas for a supper that is colorful as well as delicious and nutritious!

If using an indoor grill, cook the chops at medium-high heat to get the best browning. Cover the grill with a disposable foil pan to maintain the optimum temperature.

Chop House BBQ Pork Chops

PREP: 5 minutes | **COOK:** 16 minutes | **YIELD:** 6 servings

½ cup (125 mL) steak sauce
3 tbsp (45 mL) honey or brown sugar
2 tbsp (30 mL) lemon juice
2 tbsp (30 mL) minced onion
1 tbsp (15 mL) chopped fresh thyme or 1½ tsp (7 mL) dried thyme leaves
1 tsp (5 mL) Dijon mustard
1 clove garlic, minced
¾ tsp (4 mL) each salt and pepper
6 thick, French cut, bone-in pork chops

Stir the steak sauce with the honey, lemon juice, onion, thyme, mustard and garlic. Reserve half of this marinade for basting; pour the rest over the pork chops. Marinate for at least 30 minutes at room temperature or up to 24 hours in the refrigerator.

Preheat the grill to high. Remove the pork chops from the marinade and sprinkle evenly with salt and pepper. Grease the grate well. Place the chops on the grate and reduce the heat to medium.

Grill the chops for 6 to 8 minutes per side, basting often with reserved marinade, or until an instant-read thermometer inserted into the chop from the side reads 160°F (71°C). Brush the chops all over with any remaining marinade before serving.

Pork and beans has been a successful food marriage since cowboys and covered wagons traveled the dusty trails that used to criss-cross North America. While the trail rider's version of pork and beans was popular because it was hearty but inexpensive to make, this version is all that and more. In fact, this comfort-food meal is decidedly gourmet.

Showcasing golden, thick, meaty chops served on a mélange of ordinary canned beans accented with Louisiana-style ingredients, this simple supper has bistro-style panache. Serve with warm crusty rolls and a green salad for a perfect meal for family or guests!

Seared Pork Chops and Creole Beans

PREP: 5 minutes | **COOK:** 40 minutes | **YIELD:** 4 servings

2 tbsp (30 mL) each fancy molasses, mustard and tomato paste
1 tbsp (15 mL) cider vinegar
4 thick pork chops, about 1½ lb (750 g)
1 tsp (5 mL) pepper
1 tbsp (15 mL) vegetable oil
1 can (14 oz/398 mL) baked beans in tomato sauce
¾ cup (175 mL) diced green pepper
¼ cup (50 mL) chili sauce
½ tsp (2 mL) ground allspice

In a small saucepan, bring the molasses, mustard, tomato paste and cider vinegar to a boil. Cool slightly.

Preheat the oven to 375°F (190°C). Sprinkle the pork chops all over with pepper. Heat the oil in a skillet set over medium-high heat. Add the chops to the skillet and brown on each side for 1 to 2 minutes or until golden. Transfer to a warm plate. Brush the molasses mixture all over the browned pork chops.

Stir the beans, green pepper, chili sauce and allspice together in a greased 13- by 9-inch (3 L) baking dish. Nestle the pork chops into the beans. Cook, loosely covered, for 20 minutes; uncover and cook for 10 to 15 minutes more until the chops are cooked through.

This fast and easy supper is wonderfully comforting. The cinnamon adds a family-friendly spiciness that makes this the perfect dinner choice for a mixed-ages group. Serve these saucy chops with mashed potatoes and steamed broccoli for a healthy, hearty dinner that everyone will love!

To keep preparation time as short as possible, choose thin, butterflied loin chops that will remain juicy and tender when cooked quickly. For the apples, I like to use Granny Smiths because they are tangy and crunchy; however, any firm apple that is suitable for pie making (such as Northern Spy, Spartan or Idared) will work well, too.

Diner-style Breaded Pork Chops with Apples

PREP: 15 minutes | **COOK:** 20 to 25 minutes | **YIELD:** 4 servings

CHOPS:
  2 tbsp (30 mL) vegetable oil, divided
  1 onion, peeled and thinly sliced
  ½ tsp (2 mL) dried thyme leaves
  1 Granny Smith apple, peeled and sliced
  1 small clove garlic, minced
  ¼ cup (50 mL) apple juice
  ⅓ cup (75 mL) all-purpose flour
  ½ tsp (2 mL) each salt, pepper and ground cinnamon
  4 thin pork loin chops, about 1½ lb (750 g)
  1 egg, beaten

PAN GRAVY:
  1 tbsp (15 mL) each butter and all-purpose flour
  1 cup (250 mL) chicken broth
  1 tsp (5 mL) cider vinegar

CHOPS: Heat half of the vegetable oil in a large nonstick skillet set over medium heat. Add the onion and thyme; cook, stirring often, for 5 minutes. Add the apples and increase the heat to medium-high. Sauté until browned. Stir in the garlic and cook for 1 minute. Remove the skillet from the heat. Stir in the apple juice, scraping the brown bits from the bottom of the pan. Transfer the apple mixture to a clean bowl and reserve.

Meanwhile, place the flour, salt, pepper and cinnamon in a plastic bag. Shake to combine. Dip each pork chop into the egg and then shake it in the flour mixture until coated all over. Return the skillet to the stovetop and set over medium-high heat; add the remaining vegetable oil. Add the chops to the pan and cook for 2 to 4 minutes on each side or until browned all over and cooked through. Remove the chops from the pan and keep warm in a 200°F (100°C) oven.

PAN GRAVY: Melt the butter in the same skillet; stir in the flour. Gradually add the broth and cider vinegar, stirring constantly to prevent lumps from forming. Bring the broth mixture to a boil and reduce heat to medium-low. Simmer the gravy gently, stirring occasionally, for 3 to 5 minutes, or until thickened. Stir in the reserved apple mixture. Transfer the chops to a platter and top with the apple and gravy mixture.

Although these pork chops feature many of the same ingredients as the Cinnamon Maple Pork Tenderloin recipe that appears on page 147, the taste is quite different. Here sage is one of the main stars and hot pepper sauce adds a spicy note that spreads its warmth evenly and appealingly into the aftertaste.

These chops are delicious when marinated for a short time, but the smoky flavor will deepen and better penetrate the meat if you have time to cover the prepared chops tightly and let them marinate in the refrigerator for several hours (or even overnight). Bring the meat to room temperature for 30 minutes before grilling.

 Try this sauce on chicken legs, too.

Sweetly Spiced Pork Chops

PREP: 15 minutes | **COOK:** 14 minutes | **YIELD:** 6 servings

2 cups (500 mL) smoky barbecue sauce
½ cup (125 mL) maple syrup
1 tbsp (15 mL) ground cinnamon
1 tsp (5 mL) crumbled dried sage leaves
1 tsp (5 mL) hot pepper sauce
2 cloves garlic, minced
3 green onions, finely chopped
6 thick pork chops, about 2½ lb (1.25 kg)
½ tsp (2 mL) each salt and pepper

Combine the barbecue sauce in a saucepan with the maple syrup, cinnamon, sage, hot pepper sauce and garlic; bring to a boil over medium-high heat. Reduce the heat to low and simmer for 10 minutes or until the sauce is very thick. Cool completely; stir in the green onions.

Meanwhile, preheat an indoor or outdoor grill to medium-high and grease the grate lightly. Sprinkle the pork chops evenly with salt and pepper; coat the seasoned meat all over with half the sauce. Grill the chops, basting often with the remaining sauce, for about 7 minutes per side or until only slightly pink in the center.

In this recipe, braised pork chops—an age-old favorite—get a modern update with the addition of seemingly diverse ingredients such as chili sauce, ginger, oregano, vinegar and teriyaki sauce. As wacky as this combination may sound, in the end these ingredients come together to make a zesty, saucy dish that is sure to make it onto your greatest hits list!

Although any kind of pork chop will work in this dish, I favor the bone-in variety for this slower-cooked recipe. Not only are they tastier in general, but the marrow from the bones flavors the sauce wonderfully and gives it more body. Also, whole chops will hold their shape better during the long cooking time than butterflied loin chops.

Braised Pork Chops with Peppers

PREP: 15 minutes | **COOK:** 40 minutes | **YIELD:** 4 servings

3 tbsp (45 mL) vegetable oil, divided
1½ cups (375 mL) thinly sliced onion
2 cloves garlic, minced
2 tsp (10 mL) dried oregano leaves
1 each red, yellow and green pepper, thickly sliced
½ cup (125 mL) chili sauce
2 tbsp (30 mL) red wine or balsamic vinegar
2 tbsp (30 mL) honey
1 tbsp (15 mL) teriyaki or tamari sauce
1 tsp (5 mL) minced ginger
¼ cup (50 mL) all-purpose flour
¼ tsp (1 mL) each salt and pepper
2 lb (1 kg) pork chops, about 4

Heat 1 tbsp (15 mL) of the oil in a deep skillet set over medium heat. Add the onion, garlic and oregano; cook, stirring occasionally, for 5 minutes or until softened.

Add the peppers. Stir-fry for 5 minutes or until the vegetables are browned at the edges but still crunchy. Stir in the chili sauce, vinegar, honey, teriyaki sauce and ginger. Cook, stirring, for about 1 minute or until the vegetables are well glazed. Remove the pan from the heat. Transfer the vegetables to a bowl, using a slotted spoon; leave the juices from the vegetables in the pan.

Mix the flour with the salt and pepper in a plastic bag or large bowl. Add the pork chops and shake or toss to coat. Return the skillet to the stove and set it over medium-high heat. Add the remaining oil to the juices still in the pan; add the pork and cook, turning as necessary, until it is browned on both sides, about 5 minutes. Spread the vegetables over the chops. Reduce the heat to low. Simmer, covered, for 20 minutes or until the chops are tender.

In this chop recipe, maple syrup, a flavor characteristic of parts of Eastern Canada and the Northeastern United States known for their chilly winter weather meets warm southwestern flavors such as toasty cumin and smoky chipotle. Together these rich ingredients provide a strong foundation of flavor that is capped off with the tangy and refreshing tastes of lime and coriander leaves. The result is a complex-flavored grilling sauce that is mild enough to please most palates.

Chipotle Maple Pork Chops

PREP: 10 minutes | **COOK:** 15 minutes | **YIELD:** 6 servings

½ cup (125 mL) pure maple syrup
2 chipotle peppers in adobo sauce or 1 tsp (5 mL) chipotle chili powder
2 tbsp (30 mL) vegetable oil
1 tbsp (15 mL) tomato paste
1 tbsp (15 mL) lime or lemon juice
½ cup (125 mL) loosely packed fresh coriander leaves
1 tsp (5 mL) ground cumin
2 cloves garlic
½ tsp (2 mL) each salt and pepper
6 large, bone-in pork chops, about 2½ lb (1.25 kg)

Preheat the grill to medium-high. Combine the maple syrup, chipotle peppers, oil, tomato paste, lime juice, coriander, cumin, garlic, salt and pepper in a blender or mini chopper. Purée until smooth. Divide in half.

Place half of the sauce mixture in a microwaveable bowl or measuring cup. Microwave at High until boiling. Reserve. Brush the other half of the sauce evenly over the chops. Sprinkle with salt and pepper.

Lightly grease the grate. Grill the chops for 5 to 7 minutes per side or until pale pink in the center, brushing often with cooked sauce. Let the chops rest for 3 to 5 minutes before serving.

This is one of my son Oliver's favorite suppers. You'll find that the combination of Asian flavors in this dish are a huge hit not only with kids but with people of all ages. Even if you don't usually eat much Asian cuisine, I encourage you to try this recipe; you'll be pleasantly surprised.

Bok choy is a type of Chinese cabbage that has a mild, pleasant flavor that makes it a great alternative to other green veggies such as green beans and broccoli. The white stalks on bok choy are crunchy while the leaves are tender and wilt easily, like spinach. These days, large, baby and even thumb-size bok choy are regularly available in most large supermarkets. Bok choy can be stored in the refrigerator for only about three days, so try to buy it the day you plan to make this dish.

Save the mildly flavored, nutrient-fortified bok choy cooking liquid for making soup or a sauce for a stir-fry later in the week.

SEE PHOTO INSERT

Honey Garlic Braised Pork Chops and Bok Choy

PREP: 10 minutes | **COOK:** 40 minutes | **YIELD:** 4 servings

¼ cup (50 mL) all-purpose flour
¼ tsp (1 mL) pepper
4 pork chops, about 1¼ lb (625 g)
1 tbsp (15 mL) vegetable oil
½ cup (125 mL) teriyaki sauce
3 tbsp (45 mL) honey
2 tbsp (30 mL) fresh lime juice
1 tbsp (15 mL) minced fresh ginger
1 tsp (5 mL) finely grated lime zest
1 tsp (5 mL) sesame oil
3 cloves garlic, minced
8 baby bok choy
1½ cup (375 mL) each low-sodium chicken broth and water
Thinly sliced green onions
Sesame seeds (optional)

Combine the flour with the pepper in a plastic bag or large bowl. Add the pork chops and shake or toss to coat all over. Heat the oil in a skillet set over medium-high heat. Add the chops and brown for 2 minutes on each side or until golden.

Meanwhile, combine the teriyaki sauce with the honey, lime juice, ginger, lime zest, sesame oil and garlic. Pour this mixture into pan and turn the chops to coat them all over in the teryaki mixture. Reduce the heat to low and cover the pan. Simmer, turning chops occasionally, for 35 minutes or until tender.

Meanwhile, wash the baby bok choy under cold, running water to remove any grit. Trim. Bring the chicken broth and water to a boil in a deep skillet or large saucepan. Add the bok choy and cook, partially covered, for 8 minutes or until the bases are fork tender. Reserve the bok choy in their hot liquid until the chops are cooked.

To serve, lift the bok choy from the pan and shake off the excess moisture. Arrange 2 pieces of bok choy on each of 4 dinner plates. Top with a chop, spooning over some pan juices. Sprinkle each serving with green onions and sesame seeds (if using).

Thick, juicy pork chops stuffed with cheese and roasted red peppers seem like a special occasion supper; however, this recipe is so fast and easy to make that you can serve it anytime. All you need to complete the meal is a side dish of pasta, polenta or risotto, all of which pair superbly well with the Mediterranean flavors in this entrée. Mashed potatoes would be a good choice, too, since they can sop up the pan juices.

If you don't have homemade roasted red peppers, buy the ones sold in Italian-style delis. If you must use the peppers sold in jars, just be sure that they are packed in water or oil and not a pickle-style brine.

Mozzarella-stuffed Pork Chops

PREP: 20 minutes | **COOK:** 30 minutes | **YIELD:** 4 servings

4 boneless pork loin chops, at least 1½ inch (4 cm) thick
½ tsp (2 mL) each salt and pepper
2 roasted red peppers
2 cups (500 mL) shredded mozzarella cheese
2 tbsp (30 mL) vegetable oil
2 tbsp (30 mL) maple syrup
1 tbsp (15 mL) each balsamic vinegar and rum or brandy
1 tbsp (15 mL) chopped fresh rosemary

Use a sharp knife to make a slit down the length of one side of each chop to create a deep pocket. Sprinkle the chops all over with the salt and pepper. Cut the roasted red peppers into large pieces and stuff an equal amount into each chop; smooth the peppers so that they lie flat. Divide 1 cup (250 mL) of the cheese equally between each chop, filling the pockets snugly. Secure the pockets closed with toothpicks. (The chops can be stuffed and reserved in the refrigerator for up to 4 hours.) Preheat the oven to 350°F (180°C).

Heat the oil in a large, ovenproof skillet set over high heat. Place the pork chops in the pan and reduce the heat to medium-high. Cook the pork chops for 4 minutes per side or until well browned. Meanwhile, whisk the maple syrup with the balsamic vinegar, rum and chopped rosemary.

Brush the chops all over with the glaze. Drizzle any extra glaze into the skillet and transfer to the preheated oven. Bake for 20 minutes or until cooked through, basting often with pan juices. Remove the chops to a serving platter and sprinkle with remaining cheese. Set the skillet over medium-high heat and boil the pan juices until reduced and thickened. Drizzle the pan juices over the cooked pork chops before serving.

For me, this easy recipe showcases the appeal of the gastropub trend that is so popular in the United Kingdom and seems to be burgeoning on this side of the Atlantic. Retro but still modern, satisfying yet still fresh tasting thanks to the fruit and herbs, dishes like this one form a bridge between the humble cooking of the past and today's more sophisticated tastes.

Serve this tangle of apples, onions and cheese-covered sausage over steamed spinach. Or mound it into toasted whole grain buns for a messy but fun hand-held supper option.

SEE PHOTO INSERT

Cheese-wrapped Sausages with Onions and Apples

PREP: 10 minutes | **COOK:** 35 to 40 minutes | **YIELD:** 6 servings

2 tbsp (30 mL) melted butter
1 Vidalia or Spanish onion, very thinly sliced
1 tbsp (15 mL) brown sugar or maple syrup
½ tsp (2 mL) dried thyme leaves and pepper
¼ tsp (1 mL) salt
1 clove garlic, minced
2 apples, peeled and sliced
2 tbsp (30 mL) chopped fresh parsley
6 bratwurst or other sweet pork sausages, about 1½ lb (750 g) total
¾ cup (175 mL) apple juice or chicken broth
3 slices Swiss cheese, halved on the angle

Heat the butter in a skillet set over medium heat. Add the sliced onion. Cook, stirring often, for 8 minutes or until softened. Stir in the brown sugar, thyme, pepper, salt and garlic. Increase the heat to medium-high. Add the apples and sauté for 8 to 10 minutes or until the apples and onion are golden. Scrape the apple mixture into a bowl. Stir in the parsley and reserve, covered.

Slash each sausage a couple of times on each side. Return the skillet to medium-high heat. Place the sausages, one cut side down, into the skillet. Cook, turning as needed, for 4 to 5 minutes or until browned all over.

Add the apple juice to the pan and reduce the heat to medium. Cook the sausages, partially covered, for 12 to 15 minutes longer or until they are cooked all the way through. Drape a slice of cheese over each sausage. Cover the pan and cook for 1 minute or until the cheese is melted. Serve the sausages with the apple mixture over top.

Sometimes dinner can be a real conundrum. Often when I feel like there isn't anything in the house that I can make for dinner, I find myself preparing this recipe. This entrée features ingredients that are true pantry basics such as saltine (soda) crackers, mustard and chutney (if chutney isn't one of your pantry basics, it will be after you've tried this recipe!). Together with precooked sausages that need only to be heated through, these simple ingredients are easily transformed into a hot, homemade supper. Because this recipe is so short and easy to make, it's ultra-convenient for busy nights.

Branston pickle and mango chutney are sweet and savory condiments. While Branston pickle is chunky and only slightly thickened, mango chutney is usually more jam-like in consistency. Both condiments have a spicy taste and tang that makes them wonderful flavor boosters in recipes like this one.

Serve these dressed-up sausages with a salad or steamed mixed veggies for a light supper. Or go with boiled potatoes and your favorite steamed green vegetable for a more conventional-looking dinner plate.

144

Chutney Sausage Crumble

PREP: 10 minutes | **COOK:** 20 minutes | **YIELD:** 4 servings

4 precooked, smoked sausages
15 unsalted saltine crackers
2 tbsp (30 mL) chopped fresh parsley
2 tbsp (30 mL) each softened butter, Pommery-style Dijon mustard and Branston pickle or mango chutney
1 tbsp (15 mL) brown sugar
2 tsp (10 mL) lemon juice

Preheat the oven to 400°F (200°C). Slit each sausage lengthwise almost all the way through, so that it falls open slightly.

Crumble the crackers in the food processor or with a rolling pin until they resemble coarse oatmeal. Blend the parsley with the butter, mustard, pickle, brown sugar and lemon juice. Add the crumbs and gently combine.

Divide the crumb mixture evenly between the sausages, using your fingertips to stuff the mixture into the slits in the sausages. Arrange the sausages, crumble side up, in a shallow casserole dish. Scatter any remaining crumb mixture over top. Cover and cook for 15 to 20 minutes. Uncover and broil for 2 to 3 minutes or until golden.

Juicy, rich sausages, sweet mustard and tangy sauerkraut make good culinary companions, but then add a buttery, crunchy topping and this meal becomes something extraordinary in an instant. This recipe may feature humble ingredients but it is far from boring. Serve this sausage and pickled cabbage combination with mashed potatoes for a comforting, farmhouse-style dinner.

The dried bread crumbs that are sold in cartons at the grocer's will give this topping a dusty texture so be sure to use fresh crumbs. To make fresh crumbs quickly, crumble a piece of sandwich bread between your fingers or chop it quickly in a mini chopper until finely chopped. If you have stale bread, use it to prepare a big batch of crumbs and then simply store them in the freezer in a tightly closed container.

Crunchy-topped Sausages on Sauerkraut

PREP: 5 minutes | **COOK:** 20 minutes | **YIELD:** 4 servings

    4 bratwurst or other sweet sausages
    3 tbsp (45 mL) honey mustard
    ¼ cup (50 mL) fresh bread crumbs
    4 tsp (20 mL) melted butter
    1 onion, thinly sliced
    2 cups (500 mL) sauerkraut, well drained
    2 green onions, chopped

Preheat the broiler to high. Slice the sausages in half down their length without cutting them all the way through. Gently flatten each sausage and place, cut side down, on a rimmed baking sheet. Place the sheet on the upper rack of the oven under the broiler; cook for about 6 minutes or until browned.

Turn the sausages and spread the cut surface evenly with the mustard. Sprinkle the bread crumbs evenly over the sausages. Drizzle with half the butter. Place the baking sheet on a rack that is at least 6 inches (15 cm) lower than the broiling element and broil the sausages for an additional 3 to 5 minutes or until topping is golden and sausages are cooked through.

Meanwhile, heat the remaining butter in a skillet set over medium heat. Add the onion and cook, stirring often, for 5 minutes or until softened. Increase the heat to medium-high and add the sauerkraut and green onion; cook, stirring often, for 3 to 5 minutes or until browned. Divide the sauerkraut mixture evenly among 4 dinner plates; top each plate with a sausage and serve.

Sticky, saucy spareribs are a popular restaurant item because although many people love to eat ribs, most people find that they take too much time and too much work to prepare at home. Many sparerib recipes require both partial cooking and then an additional cooking step to glaze the meat in its sauce.

My preferred method for making spareribs eliminates not only the messiest step but makes, in my opinion, superior ribs. By using a heavy-duty foil grill bag, no partial cooking is required. Instead, the ribs steam-cook and are glazed all in one step in either a closed barbecue or in the oven. The results are so tender, tasty and easy to accomplish that restaurant ribs may become a thing of the past in your home.

If foil grill bags are unavailable make your own with a large double layer of heavy-duty foil, folded in half and crimped tightly to seal. Proceed as directed.

Honey Dijon Spareribs

PREP: 10 minutes | **COOK:** 1 hour, 15 minutes | **YIELD:** 4 to 6 servings

¾ cup (175 mL) Dijon mustard
½ cup (125 mL) honey
⅓ cup (75 mL) steak sauce (such as A1 or HP)
¼ cup (50 mL) lemon juice
1 tbsp (15 mL) all-purpose flour
1 tbsp (15 mL) hot pepper sauce
3 cloves garlic, minced
1 tsp (5 mL) dried thyme leaves
½ tsp (2 mL) each salt and pepper
3 lb (1.5 kg) pork spareribs, cut into 3-rib portions
2 tbsp (30 mL) chopped fresh parsley (optional)

OVEN INSTRUCTIONS: Preheat the oven to 400°F (200°C). Stir the mustard with the honey, steak sauce, lemon juice, flour, hot pepper sauce, garlic, thyme, salt and pepper in a large bowl. Add the rib segments and toss to coat in the sauce mixture.

Transfer the ribs to a large foil grill bag set on a baking sheet. Spread the ribs out evenly. Fold the open end over twice and crimp to seal tightly. Transfer the baking sheet to the oven. Cook, carefully turning the bag over every 15 minutes, for 60 to 75 minutes or until the ribs are very tender and browned.

Wearing oven mitts to protect your hands from the steam, carefully cut open the bag. Sprinkle with chopped fresh parsley (if using).

GRILLING INSTRUCTIONS: Preheat the grill to medium. Place the sealed grill bag on a baking sheet; transfer the baking sheet to the grill, and slide the bag onto the grate. Close the lid and cook, flipping the bag every 15 minutes, for about 60 minutes, or until ribs are very tender and browned.

Once again, here is a rib recipe that eliminates the partial cooking step by using a foil grill bag to steam-cook the meat and glaze it simultaneously.

The flavor of these ribs is sweet and only slightly spicy since Thai sweet chili sauce is not nearly as hot as the unsweetened Asian chili sauces. Thai chili sauce is glossy, amber tinted and flecked with bits of suspended red pepper flakes. Conversely, Asian chili sauces such as *sambal olek* are chunkier and opaque. Nor is Thai chili sauce similar to the chunky cousin of ketchup known as chili sauce that is still a Canadian favorite. Although that version of chili sauce is sweet and tangy, it can't glaze meat in the same way as the Thai variety used in this recipe.

Perfect as an entrée served with rice or Asian-style noodles and stir-fried vegetables, these ribs can also be served as a casual party appetizer. Whichever way you serve them, make sure you have plenty of napkins handy—or better yet finger bowls—because these ribs are notoriously sticky!

Use this mixture on pork tenderloin or pork chops, too.

Thai Sweet Chili Ribs

PREP: 5 minutes | **COOK:** 1 hour, 15 minutes | **YIELD:** 4 to 6 servings

2 lb (1 kg) pork ribs, sliced into single-rib portions
1 tbsp (15 mL) all-purpose flour
1½ cups (375 mL) Thai sweet chili sauce
¼ cup (50 mL) hoisin sauce
1 tbsp (15 mL) sesame oil
Chives or green onions

GRILL INSTRUCTIONS: Preheat the grill to medium. Sprinkle the ribs evenly with flour. Stir the chili sauce with the hoisin sauce and sesame oil in a large bowl. Add the ribs and toss to coat them with the sauce mixture. Spread the ribs and sauce out in an even layer in a large foil grill bag set on a baking sheet. Fold over the open edge of the bag to seal tightly and fit around the food snugly. Crimp the seams tightly.

Slide the bag from the baking sheet onto the preheated grate. Close the lid. Cook, carefully turning the bag over every 15 minutes, for 60 to 75 minutes or until the ribs are very tender and browned. Wearing oven mitts to protect your hands from the steam, carefully cut open the bag. Arrange the ribs on a platter and sprinkle with chives before serving.

OVEN INSTRUCTIONS: Preheat the oven to 400°F (200°C). Place the sealed grill bag with the ribs spread out on a baking sheet. Cook, turning the bag over every 15 minutes, for 60 to 75 minutes or until the ribs are very tender and browned. Serve as above.

Spit-roasted suckling pig is often the crowning glory of an Indonesian Rice Harvest Festival. These festivals thank the rice god *Dewi Sri* for a blessed season. The meal that accompanies the celebration is an elaborate affair. In this yummy rib recipe I've gathered together the flavors and spirit of these festive meals in a single dish that can be prepared easily by home cooks. The gooey sauce, which is flavored with hoisin as well as fish sauce, is slathered over partially cooked ribs. As the racks brown on the grill, the sauce caramelizes, intensifying the flavor. The result: exotically flavored ribs that are well complemented by simple steamed rice on the side.

Although I personally prefer the meatiness of back ribs for this particular recipe, side ribs or spareribs (cut from the belly side of the pig) can be used to make this recipe, too.

Indonesian Glazed Pork Ribs

PREP: 10 minutes | **COOK:** 1 hour 30 minutes | **YIELD:** 6 servings

6 lb (3 kg) pork back ribs, about 4 racks
2 bay leaves
1 tsp (5 mL) peppercorns
1 onion, chopped
1½ cups (375 mL) ketchup
¼ cup (50 mL) hoisin sauce
3 tbsp (45 mL) lemon juice
2 tbsp (30 mL) each Worcestershire and soy sauce
1 tbsp (15 mL) Dijon mustard
2 tsp (10 mL) Asian fish sauce
4 cloves garlic, minced
2 tsp (10 mL) chili powder
1 tsp (5 mL) cayenne

Combine the ribs, bay leaves, peppercorns and onion in a large roasting pan. Add enough cold water to cover. Cover tightly with foil and place in a preheated 350°F (180°C) oven. Cook for 1 hour or until the ribs are tender enough to pierce easily with a fork. Cool the ribs in the cooking liquid. Drain off the liquid and transfer the ribs to a platter. (The ribs can be made to this point, brushed with the sauce, covered and refrigerated for up to 2 days.)

Stir the ketchup with the hoisin sauce, lemon juice, Worcestershire, soy sauce, mustard, fish sauce, garlic, chili powder and cayenne in a bowl. Preheat the grill to medium-high. Lightly grease the grate. Brush the sauce evenly over the ribs. Place the ribs on the grate and cook, basting often and turning as needed, for about 10 minutes or until well glazed and heated through. Alternatively, bake the ribs in a preheated 325°F (160°C) oven on a rimmed baking sheet for 25 to 30 minutes, basting often.

Pork tenderloin is one of my favorite weeknight meat choices since it is dependably tender and juicy. I also love that pork tenderloin cooks quickly and that there is no waste—every morsel is edible.

Families will love this recipe since it combines the familiar enduring, soothing flavors of maple and cinnamon. The heat of the grill intensifies the depth and character of the maple syrup and the cinnamon, making this entrée interesting and adventurous but still broadly appealing, too.

Cinnamon Maple Pork Tenderloin

PREP: 10 minutes | **MARINATE:** 30 minutes
COOK: 15 to 18 minutes | **YIELD:** 4 servings

2 pork tenderloins, about 1½ lb (750 g) total
3 tbsp (45 mL) maple syrup
2 tbsp (30 mL) olive oil
1 tbsp (15 mL) each balsamic vinegar and tomato paste
1 tsp (5 mL) ground cinnamon
½ tsp (2 mL) dried thyme leaves
½ tsp (2 mL) Dijon mustard
1 clove garlic, minced
½ tsp (2 mL) each salt and pepper

Slice the tenderloins lengthwise about halfway through the thickness of the meat so that each piece of meat can be butterflied to make a flat piece of meat of uniform thickness.

Whisk the maple syrup with the olive oil, balsamic vinegar, tomato paste, cinnamon, thyme, mustard and garlic until combined. Divide the mixture in half. Reserve one half and brush the other half evenly over the raw meat; cover and marinate the meat for at least 30 minutes at room temperature or for up to 24 hours in the refrigerator.

Preheat an indoor grill to medium-high or an outdoor grill to medium. Sprinkle the meat all over with salt and pepper and grease the grate. Place the meat on the hot grate. Grill for 5 minutes. Turn and brush evenly with the reserved maple mixture. Cook, brushing and turning as necessary, for 10 to 13 minutes or until an instant-read thermometer inserted into the side of the pork registers 160°F (71°C). Rest the cooked meat, loosely tented with foil, for 5 minutes before slicing.

Part of my job is tasting and evaluating all the promising new products that come on the market; as a result, my refrigerator is almost always crowded with bottles of partially used condiments. Likewise, because new products are coming through the door on almost a daily basis, it isn't unusual for me to feel a desperate need to make space. When that situation occurs, I usually try to use up the odds and ends by incorporating them into my own weeknight cooking.

Interestingly, many of the recipes that are born at times when the refrigerator shelves become crowded get made again because we really like them. Such was the case with this recipe that combines cranberry jelly (left over from writing an autumn-themed "Dana Recommends" column for my *Topline Trends* newsletter) with other ingredients in my pantry.

Sage Berry Pork Tenderloin

PREP: 5 minutes | **MARINATE:** 30 minutes
COOK: 25 minutes | **YIELD:** 4 servings

½ cup (125 mL) cranberry jelly, melted
2 tsp (10 mL) crumbled dried sage leaves or chopped fresh rosemary
1 tbsp (15 mL) each soy sauce and Dijon mustard
2 cloves garlic, minced
2 pork tenderloins, 1 lb (500 g) each
¾ tsp (4 mL) each salt and pepper

Stir the melted cranberry sauce with the sage, soy sauce, mustard and garlic. Place the tenderloins In a bowl and add half the cranberry mixture. (Reserve the other half for basting.) Turn the meat to coat it all over in the cranberry mixture. Let the pork stand for 30 minutes (or cover and refrigerate for up to 2 days). Preheat the oven to 400°F (200°C).

Sprinkle the tenderloins evenly with salt and pepper and place on lightly greased, foil-lined, rimmed baking sheet. Fold the small end of each tenderloin up under the thicker part of the loin so that the meat is an even thickness.

Place the tenderloins in a preheated oven and cook, basting often with reserved cranberry mixture, for about 25 minutes or until an instant-read thermometer inserted into the meat registers 160°F (71°C). Rest the cooked pork for 5 minutes before slicing into medallions.

The tried and true combination of cranberries and apples proves successful once again in this oven-cooked pork tenderloin entrée. To mimic, albeit on a smaller scale, the appeal of a roast loin of pork, two tenderloins are butterflied and then stacked, sandwich style, on either side of a savory cheese and fruit stuffing. The visual effect is rustic elegance and the flavor says "more, please"!

I like to serve this entrée with squash and a salad made from peppery greens such as chicory in the autumn and winter, and with steamed asparagus or green beans and boiled new potatoes in the spring and summer months.

Do not substitute 100% cranberry juice or cranberry juice blend for the cranberry cocktail. The added sugar in the cranberry cocktail helps the sauce to thicken and get glossy.

SEE PHOTO INSERT

Brie and Cranapple Stuffed Pork Tenderloin

PREP: 20 minutes | **COOK:** 40 minutes | **YIELD:** 4 servings

2 tbsp (30 mL) vegetable oil
½ onion, peeled and chopped
1 tsp (5 mL) dried thyme leaves
½ cup (125 mL) dried cranberries
½ cup (125 mL) chopped dried apples or pears
¼ cup (50 mL) cranberry cocktail or apple juice
½ cup (125 mL) cubed Brie or Camembert cheese
2 pork tenderloins, about ¾ lb (375 g) each
½ tsp (2 mL) salt and pepper
½ cup (125 mL) cranberry sauce
2 tbsp (30 mL) whole grain Dijon mustard
1 tbsp (30 mL) each maple syrup and cider vinegar

Heat half of the vegetable oil in a skillet set over medium-high heat. Add the onion. Cook, stirring often, until golden, about 6 minutes. Stir in the thyme, dried cranberries and apples. Cook, stirring often, for 4 minutes. Add the cranberry cocktail and reduce the heat to low. Cover and cook until the liquid is absorbed. Cool the mixture completely and stir in the cheese.

Preheat the oven to 400°F (200°C). Slice each pork tenderloin lengthwise about halfway through the thickness of the meat so that each piece of meat can be butterflied to make a flat piece of meat of a uniform thickness. Sprinkle the meat all over with salt and pepper.

Place one tenderloin, cut side up, on a rack set in a shallow roasting pan or on a rimmed baking sheet. Spread the cooled stuffing evenly over the top of the meat. Place the second pork tenderloin, cut side down, on the stuffing and press lightly to compress. Use your fingers to stuff back any filling that falls out from between the pieces of meat.

Stir the cranberry sauce with the remaining oil, mustard, maple syrup and cider vinegar. Brush ¼ cup (50 mL) of this mixture over the pork. Roast, basting occasionally with remaining sauce mixture, for 30 to 40 minutes or until an instant-read thermometer inserted into the thickest part of the meat registers 160°F (71°C). Rest the tenderloin for 5 minutes before slicing.

Peameal bacon is also sold as Canadian bacon or back bacon depending on where you live and where you shop. Unlike side bacon, which is best sliced thin and cooked until crisp, peameal bacon is lean and rather like a mildly flavored fresh ham that is lightly coated in cornmeal. Cut from the tender eye of the loin, it is an incredibly versatile cut of meat. Some cooks pan-fry thin peameal bacon slices until golden to add to sandwiches or to serve with eggs, while some recipes call for peameal bacon to be cooked slowly on a barbecue or grilled like a small roast.

Regardless of how it is prepared, peameal bacon is great value and makes a wonderful change from the ordinary. In this recipe, pantry staples such as mustard, marmalade, hot pepper sauce and green onions are combined to make a flavorful coating for a family-size peameal bacon roast.

Substitute pure maple syrup for the marmalade for an equally yummy version.

Mustard Marmalade Roasted Peameal Bacon

PREP: 10 minutes | **COOK:** 60 minutes | **YIELD:** 6 servings

½ **cup (125 mL) whole grain Dijon mustard**
½ **cup (125 mL) melted orange marmalade**
¼ **cup (50 mL) very finely chopped green onions**
½ **tsp (2 mL) hot pepper sauce**
2 **cloves garlic, minced**
2 **lb (1 kg) whole peameal bacon**

Preheat the oven to 375°F (190°C). Blend the mustard with the marmalade, green onions, hot pepper sauce and garlic. Slather thickly all over the top of the peameal bacon.

Place the meat on a rack in a baking pan and roast for 60 to 65 minutes or until an instant-read thermometer inserted into the center of the meat registers 160°F (71°C). Rest the peameal bacon for 5 minutes. Slice thickly before serving.

My mother always had ham steaks on her shopping list. She would cook one whenever someone in our family needed a fast dinner because they were in a rush to go somewhere before the family meal was ready. Likewise, a pan-browned ham steak and eggs was often the supper she prepared for anyone who arrived home after supper had been served.

Today, when so many of us treat coming home from work and school as a mere pit stop on our way to evening activities, ham steaks are still an ideal supper solution. Since ham steaks are already cooked, all you have to do is to heat them up in a skillet. While quite good tasting simply pan-fried in a bit of butter or oil, adding a glaze quickly transforms a ham steak from a make-do meal into an enjoyable dinner. The Asian-inspired glaze in this recipe is one of my favorites to use on ham steak since it coats the meat well but doesn't overpower the flavor of the ham.

Orange Teriyaki Ham Steak

PREP: 5 minutes | **COOK:** 5 minutes | **YIELD:** 1 serving

2 tbsp (30 mL) each soy sauce and honey
1 tsp (5 mL) each vegetable oil and rice wine vinegar or lemon juice
½ tsp (2 mL) each minced fresh ginger and finely grated orange zest
1 small clove garlic, minced
1 ham steak, about 6 oz (175 g)
Sesame seeds (optional)

Blend the soy sauce with the honey, oil, rice wine vinegar, ginger, orange zest and garlic in a medium-size skillet set over high heat. Bring to a boil.

Add the ham steak and turn to coat it in the glaze mixture. Cook, turning often, for 3 to 5 minutes or until the meat is well browned and glazed. Sprinkle with sesame seeds (if using) before serving.

Pork

Over the past decade, Latino flavors have become a permanent part of our culinary landscape. Nuevo Latino restaurants have set the pace by showcasing exotic ingredients with exciting presentations. Meanwhile, stylish bar menus routinely feature a proliferation of cool and refreshing cocktails such as mojitos and caiprinhas. These trends have begun to filter into the home cooking environment where time-starved but food-savvy cooks are eager to add sizzle to their meals. Learning about the unique methods of combining flavors in countries such as Cuba, Puerto Rico and the Dominican Republic is proving to be a popular hobby.

In this recipe, stew gets a spicy make-over and becomes faster to make than most traditional recipes. (If you're not a fan of spicy foods, you can still make this recipe; just use less hot pepper sauce.) Simmering less tender cuts of meat for long periods of time is the technique usually used to make stews; however, as a shortcut, this recipe uses a tender cut of meat, making a Latin-inspired, comfort food supper just minutes away!

30-minute Cuban Pork Stew

PREP: 15 minutes | **COOK:** 30 minutes | **YIELD:** 4 servings

2 tbsp (30 mL) butter
1 onion, peeled and chopped
1 stalk celery, chopped
1 pork tenderloin, cut in large chunks, about ¾ lb (375 g)
2 tbsp (30 mL) all-purpose flour
1 tbsp (15 mL) tomato paste or ketchup
1 clove garlic, minced
½ tsp (2 mL) ground allspice
¼ tsp (1 mL) each salt and pepper
2 cups (500 mL) chicken broth
2 sweet potatoes, peeled and coarsely chopped
1 green pepper, coarsely chopped
1 tsp (5 mL) jalapeño or other hot pepper sauce (approx)

Melt the butter in a deep saucepan set over medium heat. Add the onion and celery and cook, stirring often, for 5 minutes. Increase the heat to medium-high. Toss the pork with the flour until well coated. Add the meat and any loose flour to the pan. Cook, turning as necessary, until the meat is brown on all sides. Leave the meat in the pan.

Add the tomato paste, garlic, allspice, salt and pepper. Add 1 cup (250 mL) of the broth and stir to combine. Add the remaining broth and bring the pan juices to a boil; stir to scrape up any cooked-on bits. Add the sweet potatoes.

Partially cover and simmer the stew for 20 minutes or until the meat and vegetables are almost tender. Add the green pepper and cook for 10 minutes. Stir in the hot pepper sauce. Taste and adjust seasonings if necessary.

Sandwiches

If I were ever going to purchase a royal seat, I think I'd like to become the Countess of Sandwich. Not only is Sandwich a fitting name for someone in my profession, but I also love that I would be linked to the Earl of Sandwich (1718–1792), the British aristocrat whom history credits with having invented the sandwich, one of my favorite kinds of food. Everyone would love me if my name was Countess Sandwich! It's true. Proof of the popularity of sandwiches is all around. Consider the latest foodservice trends: As health concerns about fast food have emerged over the last decade, what have donut shops and burger joints added to their menus? Sandwiches. In fact, sandwich consumption has increased by more than 5 percent both at home and in restaurants over the last few years.

Besides being perceived as something healthy, other factors are contributing to the increased popularity of sandwiches as a dinnertime choice. For home cooks, sandwiches are a winning choice since they are fast and easy to make, portable and generally don't require utensils to be consumed. Sandwiches can also easily be customized to suit individual preferences. With this list of advantages going for them, it isn't surprising that sandwiches make sense as a suppertime solution in our busy, health-conscious culture.

Try some of the hearty sandwiches in this chapter such as the Family-size BLTs with Roasted Garlic Mayonnaise, the Knife and Fork Cheese and Beef Sandwiches and the Toasty Shrimp Naanwiches to experience first-hand how sandwiches can make dinner a royally satisfying meal!

I have a confession to make and I don't want anyone to tell my husband Martin (honey, if you're reading this, turn the page!). Here's my secret: I sometimes have overwhelming cravings for peanut butter. But there's one catch in my household—my beloved hubby is severely allergic to peanuts. As a result I feel very guilty about my love of peanut butter. I feel like I'm betraying my husband if I so much as think about having a peanut butter sandwich!

Whenever Martin is out of town I succumb to the occasional peanut butter binge—followed by thorough kitchen cleaning (even the slight whiff of peanuts can be life-threatening for someone allergic to peanuts). This sandwich recipe was born of one of these peanut butter indulgences. Part old-school peanut butter and jelly (or "PB&J" for aficionados) and part French toast, I can make a meal out of a couple of these sandwiches and a glass of milk, as I'm sure many of you can, too.

Substitute sliced, peeled banana for the jelly and proceed as directed.

Peanut Butter and Jelly Panini

PREP: 5 minutes | **COOK:** 5 minutes | **YIELD:** 2 servings

4 slices Italian-style bread, each ½ inch (1 cm) thick
¼ cup (50 mL) smooth or crunchy peanut butter
¼ cup (50 mL) grape jelly
2 eggs, beaten
2 tbsp (30 mL) milk
½ tsp (2 mL) pure vanilla extract

Preheat a panini maker or hinged grill to medium. Lay the bread out on a clean work surface and spread the peanut butter and then the jelly evenly over two of the slices. Top with the remaining bread.

Whisk the eggs, milk and vanilla together. Dip the sandwiches into the egg mixture until coated all over on both sides. Place the sandwiches on the panini maker and close the lid. (Do not put pressure on the lid; it doesn't need to be fully closed.) Cook for 1 to 2 minutes or until golden brown.

SKILLET METHOD: Heat a heavy skillet over medium heat. Melt 1 tsp (5 mL) of butter in the skillet and add the sandwiches. Cook for 2 minutes on each side or until golden.

Although there is much debate about whether this popular deli sandwich was named for Arthur Reuben (the owner of a famous deli in New York City called Reuben's) or for Reuben Kay (a gambling Omaha grocer said to have invented this sandwich when he became peckish during a long poker game), there is no doubt this is one of my favorite sandwiches. There's something so perfect about the combination of the rich corned beef and the tangy sauerkraut. And, although the snooty chef in me hates to admit it, a Rueben is fundamentally incomplete without the Thousand Island dressing. Sometimes you just have to let go of your pretensions.

Classic Reuben Sandwiches

PREP: 5 minutes | **COOK:** 6 minutes | **YIELD:** 2 servings

> 4 slices sourdough rye or marble rye bread
> 6 oz (180 g) shaved corned beef
> ½ cup (125 mL) sauerkraut, well drained
> 3 tbsp (45 mL) Thousand Island dressing
> 2 slices Swiss cheese
> 1 tbsp (15 mL) butter
> Kosher-style dill pickles

Arrange two slices of bread on a clean work surface. Top each slice with an equal amount of corned beef and sauerkraut. Drizzle the salad dressing evenly over this layer. Top with Swiss cheese slices.

Cap each sandwich with one of the remaining pieces of bread. Butter the outside of each slice of bread. Heat a skillet over medium heat. Add the sandwiches and cook, turning once or twice, for 2 to 3 minutes per side or until the bread is golden brown and the cheese is melted. Serve with pickles on the side.

BLT—the acronym for a bacon, lettuce and tomato sandwich—is one of the most enduring recipes in the sandwich world. Wikipedia, the online encyclopedia, cites that the first published recipe for this sandwich appeared in a 1929 cookbook called *Seven Hundred Sandwiches*. Although I haven't seen a copy of this book myself, I would bet that this early version contained pretty much the same ingredients as my family-size version. The only changes I've made to this classic are to add roasted garlic to the mayonnaise and to use leaf instead of iceberg lettuce.

Making one, loaf-size sandwich for the entire family is the same amount of work as making four smaller ones, but the look of the big one is a novelty that makes this dinner not just a sandwich, but a conversation piece to be eaten!

Family-size BLTs with Roasted Garlic Mayonnaise

PREP: 15 minutes | **COOK:** 15 minutes | **YIELD:** 4 servings

1 tsp (5 mL) butter
4 cloves garlic
¼ cup (50 mL) chicken broth or water
8 slices bacon
1 baguette
½ cup (125 mL) mayonnaise
Leaf lettuce
2 tomatoes, thinly sliced
Salt and pepper

Heat the butter in a small skillet set over medium heat. Add the garlic cloves and cook, stirring often, for 5 minutes or until well browned all over. Add the broth and bring to a boil. Cover the pan tightly and simmer for 5 to 10 minutes or until the garlic is very soft and all the liquid is evaporated. Cool to room temperature.

Meanwhile, in another skillet set over medium-high heat, cook the bacon, turning often, until it is crisp but not crumbly, about 6 to 8 minutes. Drain on paper towels.

Cut the baguette lengthwise through the center to make two layers. Mash the cooked garlic with a fork and blend with the mayonnaise until smooth. Spread this mixture evenly over both pieces of bread. Top bottom piece with a layer of bacon and then lettuce. Spread the tomato slices out over the lettuce and sprinkle with salt and pepper. Cap with the remaining piece of bread and cut into 4 equal-sized pieces.

Mediterranean flavors and good food experiences naturally go hand in hand. In this recipe, spicy salami adds zip and transforms the familiar, simple grilled cheese sandwich into a more substantial meal. Other tasty additions to this sandwich would be roasted sweet peppers or chopped pitted olives. Although butter may seem like an odd ingredient to slather over the outside of a Southern Italian-style grilled sandwich, truth be told, it just tastes so good on the bread that I always use it when I make this recipe.

As I've mentioned in several other places in this book, I recommend using either the Nutless Basil Pesto, which appears on page 43, or a deli-made fresh version of this ubiquitous Genovese sauce instead of the bottled pesto sold by the grocer. Not only is the flavor of fresh versions almost always much brighter and more pleasant tasting than a bottled pesto, but the color is much nicer and more appealing, too.

Genoa Grilled Cheese Sandwiches

PREP: 5 minutes | **COOK:** 10 minutes | **YIELD:** 4 servings

¼ **cup (50 mL) butter**
1 **tbsp (15 mL) fresh pesto**
8 **thick slices whole wheat or Italian-style bread**
8 **slices processed mozzarella cheese**
8 **slices spicy salami**
3 **tbsp (45 mL) each finely chopped oil-packed sun-dried tomatoes and fresh basil**

Preheat the grill to medium-high. Blend the butter with the pesto. Arrange the 8 slices of bread on a clean work surface. Spread the pesto and butter mixture evenly over one side of each of the bread slices. Flip 4 of the buttered slices of bread over and top each of these flipped slices with one piece of cheese and 2 salami slices. Toss the sun-dried tomatoes with the basil and sprinkle over the meat. Top with the remaining cheese and bread slices, buttered side facing out.

Grill the sandwiches for 3 to 5 minutes per side, occasionally pressing down gently with a metal spatula, until the cheese is melted.

Fun to look at and delicious to eat, these oven-baked sandwiches are definitely a change from the ordinary. They are easy to eat with one hand so are a good choice for a working supper or for when you find yourself eating dinner on the run. (It's not the ideal way to eat but, let's face it, it does happen occasionally in our busy lives.)

The combination of ingredients I've suggested has proven to be popular time and time again, but don't think these are the only ingredients you can use. My idea is only a template. Experiment and let your imagination and your pantry be your inspiration for fillings, cheeses and kinds of bread to make these warm, toasty sandwiches.

These sandwiches are also great served as an appetizer (4 to 6 servings).

SEE PHOTO INSERT

Baked Triangle Toast Sandwiches

PREP: 5 minutes | **COOK:** 8 minutes | **YIELD:** 3 servings

6 slices whole grain sandwich bread
2 tbsp (30 mL) mayonnaise (regular or light)
1 tbsp (15 mL) Dijon mustard
1 cup (250 mL) shredded Gruyère or Swiss cheese
6 slices Black Forest ham
18 blanched asparagus spears

Preheat the oven to 350°F (180°C). Line a baking sheet with foil or parchment paper. Lay the bread on a clean work surface. Blend the mayonnaise with the mustard and spread evenly over the bread slices. Sprinkle half of the cheese evenly over the 6 slices of bread. Top with ham slices (folding the meat as necessary) and sprinkle the remaining cheese over each slice. Place three asparagus spears diagonally over each slice of bread.

Bring the corners of the bread that are not being touched by asparagus together and fasten closed with a toothpick. Arrange the sandwiches points up on the prepared baking sheet and place on the bottom rack of the preheated oven. Bake for 5 to 8 minutes or until the bread is lightly golden and the cheese is melted.

This sandwich is an ideal choice for evenings when you feel like something different but don't want to spend a lot of time in the kitchen. The recipe can be doubled or quadrupled easily. Although it appears here as a dinner option, my son often requests this sandwich for breakfast, too.

You can mix and match the cheeses as you like. Good choices include Brie, a creamy blue or a nutty, flavored Gruyère. Mango chutney makes a great condiment.

Apple Cheddar Sandwich

PREP: 2 minutes | **COOK:** 6 minutes | **YIELD:** 1 serving

2 tsp (10 mL) softened butter
2 slices raisin or cinnamon raisin bread
¼ cup (50 mL) grated extra old Cheddar cheese
¼ Granny Smith apple, thinly sliced

Lay the bread out on a clean work surface. Butter one side of each slice. Flip the slices of bread over; sprinkle half the cheese over one slice. Layer the apple slices over the cheese. Sprinkle the remaining cheese evenly over the apple. Cap with the second piece of bread, butter side out.

Heat a small skillet set over medium heat. Transfer the sandwich to the pan. Cook for 2 to 3 minutes per side or until the bread is golden and the cheese is melted.

With the rise in popularity of hinged indoor grills over the last decade, panini sandwiches have became a hit with home cooks. We love toasty, hot sandwiches so much that submarine chains now offer grilled sandwiches, and recently grocers have hopped onto the sandwich band-wagon by launching frozen sandwiches that can be heated in the microwave. The instructions below are for cooking this panini sandwich on an outdoor grill, which gives the sandwich a truly fantastic flavor. It will have a different flavor when cooked on a hinged indoor grill (see the optional cooking instructions), but either method produces a delectable, mouth-watering suppertime option.

Skinless, boneless chicken thighs work best in this sandwich because they are fla-vorful, moist and economical, too. Do use fresh pesto if you can (page 43).

Grill-pressed Rosemary and Garlic Chicken Panini

PREP: 10 minutes | **COOK:** 30 minutes | **YIELD:** 4 servings

⅓ cup (75 mL) extra virgin olive oil
3 tbsp (15 mL) finely chopped rosemary
1 tbsp (15 mL) balsamic vinegar
½ tsp (2 mL) coarsely ground pepper
3 cloves garlic, minced
2 red peppers, quartered
8 skinless, boneless chicken thighs, about 1¼ lb (625 g)
¼ tsp (1 mL) salt
4 ciabatta- or focaccia-style buns
⅓ cup (75 mL) mayonnaise
2 tsp (10 mL) fresh pesto
4 thin slices provolone cheese, about 2 oz (60 g)

Preheat the grill to medium. Stir the olive oil with the rosemary, balsamic vinegar, pep-per and garlic. Measure out 2 tbsp (30 mL) of this mixture and rub it all over the quartered peppers. Place peppers on the grate. Cover and grill, turning often, for about 15 minutes or until peppers are softened and the skin is blistered. Transfer the peppers to a small bowl and cover tightly. Let the peppers cool slightly, then peel off and discard the skins.

Meanwhile, place the chicken and the remaining oil mixture in a large bowl; turn to coat the chicken all over with the seasoned oil. Marinate at room temperature until peppers are cooked or for as long as 2 hours in the refrigerator. Increase the grill heat to medium-high. Preheat a grill press or two bricks wrapped in foil on the grill for 5 minutes (see tips at right).

Sprinkle the chicken all over with salt before placing it on the grate. Set the grill press or bricks on top of the meat. Grill for 4 to 5 minutes. Remove the grill press and turn the chicken; replace the grill press. Cook for 5 minutes. Remove the chicken and keep warm. Place the buns, cut side down, on the grate until lightly toasted.

Stir the mayonnaise with the pesto. Slather all over both sides of the buns. Layer equal amounts of chicken and peppers on one side of each bun and then top each with a slice of cheese; cover with the top half of the buns. Stake with tooth-picks to hold sandwiches together. Return sandwiches to the grill. Cover and heat for 45 to 60 seconds or until the cheese is melted. Remove from the grate and serve warm.

HINGED INDOOR GRILL INSTRUCTIONS: Cook the peppers in a preheated 350ºF (180ºC) oven on a foil-lined, rimmed baking sheet for 20 to 30 minutes or until softened and wrinkly. Cook the chicken and then the sandwiches, on a hinged indoor grill according to the manufacturer's instructions.

Grill Pressing Tips:

INDOOR: The popularity of countertop, electric, hinged indoor grills has risen significantly in the last five years. While smaller ones with little or no temperature control are sometimes labeled "panini makers" or "sandwich presses," the larger format hinged grills with more temperature control, sold as appliances for cooking steaks, chops and full meals, are also suitable for making sandwiches like this one.

OUTDOOR: You can duplicate this cooking technique by using a grill press sold at a gourmet store. Such tools usually look a bit like an old-fashioned iron. If you don't have a grill press, simply wrap a clean brick in a double layer of heavy-duty foil. Be sure to heat the grill press or brick on the grill until very hot before using.

Although Philadelphia is famous for its cheese steak sandwich that combines thinly sliced steak and American processed cheese with sautéed onions, I think my warm cheese and beef sandwich might be a close contender to share the spotlight.

Instead of steak, my open-faced version of this sandwich uses very thinly sliced ribbons of rare roast beef. Each portion is finished with melted, aged Cheddar cheese and contains a juicy layer of sautéed onions. The end result is a sandwich that is a simple but very satisfying hot meal!

Knife and Fork Cheese and Beef Sandwiches

PREP: 20 minutes | **COOK:** 3 minutes | **YIELD:** 4 servings

2 tsp (10 mL) each butter and vegetable oil
3 onions, peeled and sliced
1 clove garlic, minced
½ tsp (2 mL) each salt and pepper
4 thick slices French bread
2 tbsp (30 mL) mayonnaise
2 tsp (10 mL) horseradish
12 oz (375 g) very thinly sliced rare roast beef
1 cup (250 mL) shredded, extra old Cheddar cheese

Melt the butter with the oil in a large skillet set over medium heat. Add the onions, garlic, salt and pepper. Cover and cook, stirring often, for 10 minutes or until the onions are softened. Remove the lid and increase the heat to medium-high. Cook the onions, stirring, for 8 to 10 minutes longer or until browned. Reserve.

Meanwhile, preheat the broiler to high. Place the bread on a baking sheet and lightly toast both sides under the broiler. Blend the mayonnaise with the horseradish and spread evenly over one side of each slice of bread. Arrange an equal amount of the beef over each slice. Top with a mound of onions and sprinkle evenly with cheese.

Broil the prepared sandwiches on the middle rack of the oven for 2 to 3 minutes or until the cheese is bubbly.

A *terrific compromise* between burgers and a sit-down-style steak dinner, these hearty sandwiches can be garnished with lettuce and tomato or eaten just as they are.

Flank steak is an inexpensive and excellent choice for this sandwich because it has a lot of flavor and is extremely lean; however, if cooked beyond medium doneness flank steak can become quite tough. Likewise, flank steak must be cut across its grain so that the strong muscles that run the length of this steak are easier to chew. If flank steak isn't available, choose skirt steak. It should be cooked and sliced the same way as flank.

Open-faced Seared Steak Sandwiches

PREP: 15 minutes | **MARINATE:** 30 minutes
COOK: 12 minutes | **YIELD:** 4 servings

1 cup (250 mL) barbecue sauce
1 clove garlic, minced
1 tbsp (15 mL) chopped fresh rosemary
1 tbsp (15 mL) olive oil
¼ cup (50 mL) mayonnaise
1 flank steak, about 1 lb (500 g)
2 large portobello mushrooms, about ½ lb (250 g)
2 halved, toasted ciabatta or other crusty rolls

Stir all but 2 tbsp (30 mL) of the barbecue sauce with garlic, rosemary and olive oil. Stir the remaining barbecue sauce with the mayonnaise and reserve. Coat the steak evenly with half the herb- and garlic-flavored marinade mixture and let stand at room temperature for 30 minutes or for up to 2 days in the refrigerator.

Preheat the grill to high. Scoop out and discard the soft dark gills on the mushroom caps. Toss the mushrooms with the remaining half of the marinade mixture. Grease the grate lightly. Place the steak and the mushrooms on the grate.

Cook the steak, turning once, for 10 to 12 minutes for medium-rare. Rest the cooked meat for 5 minutes; slice thinly across the grain. Continue to grill the mushrooms for 5 to 10 minutes longer or until tender. Slice thickly.

Divide the sliced steak and mushrooms evenly among each of the 4 halves of the rolls. Drizzle with the reserved mayonnaise mixture.

Sometimes controversy breaks out in our test kitchen. Food preferences can be very personal and even professional recipe writers and testers have biases about what is considered "right" or "wrong" for some classic recipes. Interestingly, such differences of opinion often arise when we're talking about the most common foods, the kind of fare Mom made when we were kids.

During the testing of this Sloppy Joe recipe, pantry manager Sabrina Falone and test kitchen director Amy Snider both had their own take on what makes a Sloppy Joe authentic. At Amy's house Sloppy Joes were served open-faced and eaten with a knife and fork like a hot beef sandwich. Meanwhile, at the Falone household, Sabrina's mom's Sloppy Joe mixture was spooned onto the bottom of a bun, capped off with the top piece of bread and then gingerly eaten out of hand.

After being a part of their discussion, I set to researching the nature of an authentic Sloppy Joe and discovered that there was simply no consensus on the matter. So, although you may choose to serve these saucy sandwiches Sabrina's way, I had to decide on writing instructions for one method or the other—I settled on serving these sandwiches open-faced. (What can I say, I'm a neat freak!)

Retro Sloppy Joes

PREP: 10 minutes | **COOK:** 20 minutes | **YIELD:** 4 servings

1 tbsp (15 mL) vegetable oil
1 small onion, peeled and finely chopped
1 cup (250 mL) sliced mushrooms
1 clove garlic, minced
½ tsp (2 mL) pepper
¼ tsp (1 mL) salt
1 lb (500 g) regular ground beef
1 green pepper, chopped
2 cups (500 mL) arrabiata- or marinara-style tomato sauce
4 hamburger buns
¼ cup (50 mL) shredded Cheddar cheese

Heat the oil in a skillet set over medium heat. Add the onion and cook, stirring, for about 3 minutes. Stir in the mushrooms. Increase the heat to medium-high and sauté for 3 to 4 minutes or until browned. Add the garlic, pepper and salt.

Crumble the meat into the vegetable mixture; cook, stirring often, for 5 to 7 minutes or until browned. Add the green pepper and the tomato sauce. Bring to a boil. Reduce the heat to low and simmer for 10 minutes.

Cut the buns in half; toast if you like. Spoon the meat mixture evenly over each bun half. Sprinkle an equal amount of cheese over each mound of meat. Serve 2 meat-and-cheese topped bun halves to each person.

Tartine is a French term that is used to describe a piece of bread that is spread with butter and then topped with various toppings. At the café in Toronto's boutique department store Holt Renfrew, stylish shoppers can choose from a dozen or so different tartine sandwiches accompanied by a salad of delicate mixed greens.

In this easy homemade tartine, I've replaced the traditional butter with a flavored, silky and rich cream cheese mixture. For the best taste and texture, make sure you use fresh, deli-style cream cheese.

Cucumber and Cream Cheese Tartines

PREP: 10 minutes | **COOK:** 4 minutes | **YIELD:** 4 servings

½ cup (125 mL) deli-style cream cheese
1 tbsp (15 mL) chopped, drained red and yellow banana pepper rings
2 tsp (10 mL) chopped, drained capers
¼ tsp (1 mL) finely grated lemon zest
2 oil-packed sun-dried tomatoes
½ English cucumber
4 large slices light sourdough rye bread
Alfalfa spouts, well rinsed (optional)

Preheat the broiler. Stir the cream cheese until creamy. Add the chopped banana peppers, capers and lemon zest. Blot the sun-dried tomatoes and chop finely; add to the cheese and other ingredients. Stir the cream cheese until the mixture is well combined. Thinly slice the cucumber lengthwise using a vegetable peeler.

Toast the bread on one side under the broiler. Turn and toast very lightly on the second side. Spread an equal amount of the cream cheese mixture over each piece of bread, on the lightly toasted side. Trim the cucumber to fit and arrange slices in one layer over the bread. Garnish with alfalfa sprouts, if using.

Sandwiches

These flavor-packed "fish-wiches" might remind you of burgers, but they are so much more. And they're less messy and faster to prepare than burgers. Serve these sandwiches with some gourmet potato chips, coleslaw or crudités on the side to make a complete meal.

SEE PHOTO INSERT

Roasted Garlic and Balsamic Salmon on a Bun

PREP: 25 minutes | **COOK:** 10 minutes | **YIELD:** 4 servings

3 tbsp (45 mL) each maple syrup and balsamic vinegar
1 tbsp (15 mL) finely chopped fresh rosemary leaves
½ tsp (2 mL) each salt and pepper
3 cloves garlic, peeled
⅓ cup (75 mL) mayonnaise (light or regular)
4 skinless salmon fillets, fresh or frozen
4 kaiser rolls, toasted
Arugula or other lettuce
Sliced tomatoes

Preheat the grill to medium-high. Combine the maple syrup, balsamic vinegar, rosemary, salt and pepper. Reserve this mixture.

Place the garlic cloves in the center of a piece of heavy-duty foil. Drizzle with 1 tbsp (15 mL) each of the reserved maple mixture and water. Fold the foil to surround the garlic and seal tightly. Place this packet on the grill and cook, turning often, for 20 minutes. Cool.

Remove the garlic from the foil. Mash the cloves and any juices to make a paste. Blend 1 tsp (5 mL) of the reserved maple mixture and the mashed garlic into the mayonnaise. Reserve.

Brush the fish all over with the remaining maple mixture. Lightly grease the grate and grill the fish, turning once, for 5 to 10 minutes if using fresh fish (10 to 15 minutes if using frozen) or until cooked but still slightly pink in the center. Spread the mayonnaise mixture over the toasted rolls; top with arugula, tomato and a piece of salmon.

A diner-style classic, these humble, hot, open-faced sandwiches and a cup of soup make a fast, filling supper that is sure to remind you of the good old days. In fact, as I was researching this book, I discovered that this retro basic has an enthusiastic cult following among those who covet the past.

There are actually chat rooms on a number of websites devoted to tracking down the best old-fashioned road food. Members of these sites debate the ultimate recipe for this modest little sandwich (at astonishingly great length!). While some people say a proper tuna melt has to have processed American cheese and others can't bear to eat one without tomato, my ideal tuna melt is quite plain and made with real Cheddar cheese. Whichever toppings you choose to use, do try to have a tuna melt every once in awhile to keep this sandwich tradition alive! You can use my recipe as a guide to create your own version of this classic sandwich.

Classic Tuna Melts

PREP: 5 minutes | **COOK:** 5 minutes | **YIELD:** 4 servings

1 can (6 oz/170 g) water-packed tuna
¼ cup (50 mL) mayonnaise
1 tbsp (15 mL) green hamburger relish
2 green onions, chopped
¼ tsp (1 mL) pepper
4 slices whole wheat bread
4 slices Cheddar cheese

Preheat the broiler to high. Drain the tuna and transfer it to a small bowl; flake with a fork. Add the mayonnaise, relish, half of the green onion and the pepper. Blend with the fork until the tuna is well blended with the other ingredients.

Lay the bread on a baking sheet and toast under the broiler until golden. Remove from the oven and reduce the temperature to 400°F (200°C). Turn the bread over. Spread the tuna mixture thickly and evenly over each slice of bread. Sprinkle evenly with remaining green onions. Drape a slice of cheese over each piece of bread.

Cook the sandwiches in the oven for 5 minutes or until the cheese is softened and the filling is heated through. Increase the oven temperature to broil (you don't have to preheat) and broil the sandwiches briefly, for about 30 seconds, or until cheese bubbles.

Variation

For Curried Tuna Melts, substitute mango chutney for the relish and add ½ tsp (2 mL) mild curry paste (or ¼ tsp/1 mL curry powder) to the mayonnaise mixture.

Wake up your taste buds with this bold new take on tuna salad. Thai green curry paste adds a hot spiciness that the apple tempers nicely. Seriously, if you think tuna is ho-hum, you need to try this sandwich. It's the perfect supper for a warm summer night when another grilled burger just won't satisfy your craving for flavor.

Thai Tuna Salad Pitas

PREP: 10 minutes | **COOK:** none | **YIELD:** 4 servings

¼ cup (50 mL) mayonnaise (light or regular)

2 tsp (10 mL) Thai green curry paste

1 celery stalk, chopped

2 tbsp (30 mL) chopped fresh parsley (optional)

1 can (6 oz/170 g) water- or broth-packed light tuna

1 green apple, cored and finely chopped

Salt

2 pitas

Leaf lettuce

Sliced tomato

Stir the mayonnaise with the green curry paste, celery and parsley (if using) until evenly combined. Drain the tuna and transfer it to a bowl; flake using a fork. Add to the mayonnaise mixture and blend well. Stir in the apple.

Season the tuna mixture with salt to taste. Cut the pitas in half and divide this mixture evenly between the pockets in each piece of bread. Add an equal amount of lettuce (whole leaves or torn) and tomato.

Egg salad sandwiches have long been a homey standby and a lunch counter must; however, the classic version is usually nothing more than chopped egg, mayonnaise and a few seasonings spread between two pieces of bread. This version takes that classic concoction to a new level by adding a gentle curry flavor to the dressing. Then the seasoned egg mixture is wrapped in a tortilla instead of using bread. Lime zest adds a nice bright note that cuts the richness of the egg and makes each bite taste fresh and fabulous!

Secure the bottom of the wrap shut by wrapping it with paper towel or some waxed paper.

Curried Egg Salad Wraps

PREP: 5 minutes | **COOK:** none | **YIELD:** 4 servings

4 hard-cooked eggs
¼ cup (50 mL) mayonnaise
½ tsp (2 mL) Indian curry paste
¼ tsp (1 mL) each salt and pepper
¼ tsp (1 mL) grated lime zest
1 green onion, finely chopped
4 whole wheat tortillas
Leaf lettuce

Chop the eggs coarsely and place in a bowl. Add the mayonnaise, curry paste, salt, pepper, lime zest and green onion. Blend until well combined.

Lay the tortillas out on a clean work surface. Place an equal amount of egg mixture in the middle of each tortilla. Top each mound of egg salad with a leaf of lettuce.

Fold up the bottom of each tortilla and then roll from one of the sides so that the egg mixture is encased by the flatbread and only the top remains open.

Sandwiches

This easy sandwich combines two popular North American foods—chicken salad and tacos—into one hand-held hot supper. Kids and teens are sure to give you a resounding "Yes!" when you tell them what's for supper. Although skinless, boneless chicken breasts can be used instead of thighs, I think I've mentioned I prefer the darker meat because it is juicier.

Grilled Caesar Chicken Tacos

PREP: 15 minutes | **COOK:** 12 to 15 minutes | **YIELD:** 4 servings

1 tbsp (15 mL) each olive oil and lime juice
1 tsp (5 mL) chili powder
¼ tsp (1 mL) each salt and pepper
6 skinless, boneless chicken thighs, about ¾ lb (375 g)
½ cup (125 mL) thick, creamy Caesar-salad style dressing
8 soft taco shells
½ cup (125 mL) shredded Cheddar cheese
Shredded lettuce
Chopped tomatoes
Sliced green onions

Preheat the grill to medium-high. Whisk the olive oil with the lime juice, chili powder, salt and pepper. Divide the mixture roughly in half. Brush half of the mixture over the chicken and let stand for 10 minutes.

Grease the grate lightly. Grill the chicken, turning as needed, for 12 to 15 minutes or until cooked through. Brush all over with remaining oil mixture. Remove the chicken from the grate and reserve until cool enough to handle. Using two forks, shred the chicken into long strips.

Spread an equal amount of the Caesar dressing on each taco shell. Divide the shredded chicken and the cheese evenly between each taco. Garnish with lettuce, tomatoes and green onions. Allow 2 tacos for each person.

Featuring many of the flavors that make tacos and nachos family favorite weeknight dinner choices, these hot sandwiches are considerably less messy to eat than either of those dishes. And the whole wheat tortillas are a healthier, lower-fat choice than fried chips or shells.

To cook all the quesadillas at once, spread in a single layer on a baking sheet. Cook in a preheated 375°F (190°C) oven for 8 to 10 minutes.

The chicken mixture could also be used as a Mexican-inspired Sloppy Joe topping for buns or toast.

Nacho Chicken Quesadillas

PREP: 10 minutes | **COOK:** 10 minutes | **YIELD:** 4 servings

- 1 tbsp (15 mL) vegetable oil
- ½ lb (250 g) ground chicken
- 1 small clove garlic, minced
- ½ tsp (2 mL) dried oregano leaves
- ¼ tsp (1 mL) each salt and pepper
- 3 green onions, finely chopped
- ½ cup (125 mL) finely chopped red pepper
- ¼ cup (50 mL) each barbecue sauce and salsa
- 8 6-inch (18 cm) whole wheat or plain flour tortillas
- 1 cup (250 mL) shredded Nacho-blend or Monterey Jack cheese

Heat the oil in a skillet set over medium-high heat. Crumble in the chicken. Stir in the garlic, oregano, salt and pepper. Cook the chicken, breaking up any clumps with a spoon, until browned, about 5 minutes. Stir in the green onions, red pepper, barbecue sauce and salsa. Cook this mixture until heated through. Reserve.

Lay the tortillas out on a clean work surface. Divide the chicken mixture and cheese equally among the tortillas, spreading over one half of each tortilla. Fold over to make half-circles. (Quesadillas can be assembled to this point, covered tightly and refrigerated for up to 8 hours.)

Warm a clean skillet over medium heat. Working with two quesadillas at a time, cook for 2 to 3 minutes per side or until golden and cheese is melted. Slice into wedges and serve.

173

Having a few appealing ways to reinvent leftovers hidden up your sleeve can be a real lifesaver for busy people. In fact, now that I have a few recipes like this one to fall back on, I actually plan to prepare "leftovers" a couple of times a week. Leftover cooked chicken, vegetables or potatoes can be used in recipes later in the week when you don't feel like cooking a whole meal from scratch. So consider preparing extra chicken one night to use in these cheesy burritos.

Purists can make these rolled and baked sandwiches with corn flour tortillas to add flavor and fiber; however, I prefer wheat flour tortillas since they don't become as chewy when heated in the oven.

Chicken and Mushroom Burritos

PREP: 10 minutes | **COOK:** 30 minutes | **YIELD:** 4 servings

1 tbsp (15 mL) butter
1 cup (250 mL) chopped onion
2 cloves garlic, minced
6 oz (180 g) button mushrooms, sliced
2 tbsp (30 mL) all-purpose flour
¾ tsp (4 mL) ground cumin
1 cup (250 mL) milk
2 cups (500 mL) shredded, cooked chicken
2 cups (500 mL) shredded Monterey Jack or mozzarella cheese
2 tbsp (30 mL) chopped fresh parsley
1 tsp (5 mL) each salt and pepper
8 large flour tortillas
½ cup (125 mL) mild salsa

Preheat the oven to 350°F (180°C). Melt the butter in a medium, nonstick skillet set over medium-high heat. Add the onion and garlic and cook until softened, about 5 minutes. Brown the mushrooms. Sprinkle in the flour and the cumin. Cook, stirring, for 1 minute.

Gradually stir in the milk and bring to a boil. Reduce the heat and simmer until mixture is thickened. Stir in the chicken and 1½ cups (375 mL) of the cheese. Add the parsley, salt and pepper and remove from the heat.

Place an equal amount of the chicken mixture in the center of each tortilla. Fold up the bottom of each tortilla, then fold in the sides and then the top to make enclosed packets. Arrange the burritos, seam side down, in a 13- by 9-inch (3 L) casserole. Spoon some salsa on top of each burrito. Sprinkle the remaining cheese over the salsa. Bake for 20 minutes or until the cheese is melted.

Caribbean roti are crêpe-like flatbreads filled with spiced stews and other saucy mixtures. These are messy to eat, hearty sandwiches that are strongly influenced by Indian flavors and cooking styles. As a result, curry spices are often the main flavors used in roti. In Jamaica, where roti enjoys the most popularity, goat is the most common meat base for the curry mixtures used to fill these soft, pliable flatbreads.

For this roti I was inspired by the traditional West Indian roti concept but adapted the ingredients to suit my own palate. Instead of a strong-flavored meat like goat, I use salmon paired with Cheddar cheese to make a saucy curried cheese-and-fish mixture. Many people who have tried this roti loved it at first bite! You can find roti breads in West Indian stores; they freeze well so stock up when you find them.

Cheesy Salmon Roti

PREP: 5 minutes | **COOK:** 12 minutes | **YIELD:** 4 servings

2 tsp (10 mL) butter
1 small onion, peeled and thinly sliced
¼ tsp (1 mL) each salt and pepper
1 tsp (5 mL) mild Indian curry paste
1 tsp (5 mL) all-purpose flour
1 tsp (5 mL) minced ginger
1 tbsp (15 mL) tomato paste
1 cup (250 mL) milk
2 boneless salmon fillets, chopped into bite-size pieces
¾ cup (175 mL) shredded Cheddar cheese
2 tbsp (30 mL) chopped fresh coriander leaves or green onions
4 large roti or very large tortillas

Melt the butter in a nonstick skillet set over medium heat. Add the onion and cook, stirring often, for 5 minutes. Add the salt, pepper and curry paste and cook for 2 to 3 minutes longer. Stir in the flour and cook, stirring, for 1 minute.

Stir in the ginger and tomato paste; gradually add the milk, stirring well, until combined. Add the salmon chunks and simmer, stirring gently, for 2 to 3 minutes or until salmon is cooked but still coral-colored in the center.

Spoon an equal amount of the salmon mixture onto each roti. Sprinkle each roti evenly with an equal amount of cheese and coriander. Fold in the sides of roti and then completely roll up from the bottom to encase the filling.

In this variation of an English-style toasted prawn and cheese sandwich, the filled naan is cooked in either a hinged grill or skillet until golden and lightly toasted. Although it takes only moments to make this simple, hot sandwich, it looks and tastes like a gourmet treat!

Naan is a leavened East Indian bread, made with white flour. The dough is hand stretched and then baked in a tandoor oven until pillowy, soft and golden. Traditionally this bread is eaten warm and used as an edible, hand-held tool to sop up saucy curries; however, increasingly often naan is being used as the bookends for yummy sandwich fillings. Many grocery stores now sell naan bread in their bakery sections. If you are unable to find it in your area, choose a soft, thin focaccia-style bread or Greek-style pocketless pita as a substitute.

SEE PHOTO INSERT

Toasty Shrimp Naanwiches

PREP: 5 minutes | **COOK:** 5 minutes | **YIELD:** 4 servings

½ lb (250 g) frozen cooked shrimp, thawed, tails and shells removed
3 tbsp (45 mL) mayonnaise (light or regular)
1 small clove garlic, minced
1 green onion, finely chopped
4 naan bread, halved crosswise
4 slices havarti cheese
2 tbsp (30 mL) melted butter

Pat the shrimp dry on paper towels and then chop coarsely if large. Blend with the mayonnaise, garlic and green onion. Lay two large naan portions out on a clean work surface; spread the shrimp mixture evenly over one slice. Top with the cheese slices and remaining naan bread.

Brush the butter evenly over the outside of the naan. Preheat a panini maker, hinged grill or a large skillet or griddle to medium. Add the sandwich and cook for 4 to 5 minutes or until the bread is golden on each side and the cheese is melted. If cooking in a skillet or on another flat surface, turn each sandwich halfway through cooking.

Variation

Stir ½ tsp (2 mL) of finely grated lemon zest into the mayonnaise mixture to add a fresh zip of flavor.

Soup

Not just for Thermos lunches anymore, statistics reveal that we love soup as a dinnertime main course. When you examine the origins of the word *soup*, this isn't surprising. *Soup* is derived from a Germanic root word that was also the origin of the English words *sup* and *supper* (although all these words first had to travel from their Germanic origins through Late Latin and then Old French before making their appearance in Middle English). So you can see that this fluid mixture has been on our daily menus for a very long time! In fact, we've probably been eating soup ever since we started cooking.

Every culture has its own signature roster of soups with names that range from bisque to borscht and from potage to chowder; call them what you will, soups can be a hearty and fulfilling meal. While there are many wonderful, brothy soups that are best served as introductory courses, this chapter focuses on the heartier soups that are more appropriate for main courses. From the familiar, comforting basics such as Hearty Cream of Mushroom Soup and Bistro French Onion Soup, to the more adventurous Pancetta and Chestnut Soup and St. Lawrence Oyster and Apple Soup, this chapter offers 20 delicious, slurpable ideas that can be served as dinnertime centerpieces.

Soups and Accompaniments

Although there are nights when a bowl of soup and a few crackers are all the food you need for a wonderfully satisfying meal, other times a sandwich can be the ideal addition that satisfies your hunger entirely.

For just such occasions, I've created this mix-and-match chart that combines soups from this chapter with recipes from other chapters in *Dana's Top Ten Table* in appealing ways.

Soup	pg	pg	Sandwich or Burger
Slow Cooker Curried Lentil Soup with Spinach	187	174	Toasty Shrimp Naanwiches
Costa Rican Black Bean Soup	183	171	Nacho Chicken Quesadillas
Lemon Parsnip Soup	194	159	Apple Cheddar Sandwich
Roasted Chicken and Rice Soup	180	158	Baked Triangle Toast Sandwiches
Hearty Cream of Mushroom Soup	190	167	Classic Tuna Melts
Cheddar and Bacon Soup	185	13	Sweet and Spicy Maple Chicken Burgers
Cold Potato Soup with Lovage and Smoked Salmon	186	21	Nicoise Burgers
Thai Coconut Noodle Soup with Scallops	192	168	Thai Tuna Salad Pitas
Kitchen Cupboard Black Bean Soup	195	170	Grilled Caesar Chicken Tacos
Minestrone Soup	178	157	Genoa Grilled Cheese Sandwiches
Double Coriander and Carrot Soup	188	165	Cucumber and Cream Cheese Tartines

For me, French onion soup has a retro appeal that is hard to resist. When made well, it's a rich, full-flavored broth in which tender, sweet onions bask. Instead of covering French onion soup with a heavy, greasy layer of cheese, I prefer to make a Gruyère-topped crostini (a large cheese crouton) that you can either float on the top of the soup or stand up on one side of the bowl.

Regardless of how you position the cheese and bread, be sure to choose good-quality Gruyère cheese, one that has been aged for 10 to 12 months for the best results. Better quality Gruyère has a rich, nutty flavor and a medium fat content. This Swiss cheese complements the flavor of the onions and the broth without overwhelming their taste.

If making 8 portions, increase the cheese to 1⅓ cups (325 mL) and use 8 baguette slices.

SEE PHOTO INSERT

Bistro French Onion Soup

PREP: 10 minutes | **COOK:** 1 hour | **YIELD:** 6 to 8 servings

3 tbsp (45 mL) butter
2 Spanish or 3 medium cooking onions, peeled and sliced
2 cloves garlic, minced
1½ tsp (7 mL) dried thyme leaves
½ tsp (2 mL) each salt and pepper
1 tbsp (15 mL) granulated sugar
⅓ cup (75 mL) dry sherry
1 tsp (5 mL) Worcestershire sauce
6 cups (1.5 L) beef broth
6 baguette slices
1 cup (250 mL) shredded Gruyère or Swiss cheese
1 tbsp (15 mL) chopped fresh parsley (optional)

Melt the butter in a Dutch oven set over medium-low heat. Add the onions, garlic, thyme, salt and pepper. Cook, stirring often, for 20 minutes or until the onions are translucent and very soft. Increase the heat to medium-high and cook, stirring often, for 5 minutes or until the onions are just beginning to brown. Sprinkle in the sugar and continue to cook, stirring often, until the onions are very brown but not scorched.

Add the sherry and Worcestershire sauce. Stir to scrape up any cooked-on brown bits from the bottom of the pan. Add the broth and bring the soup to a boil. Reduce the heat to low and simmer for 15 minutes.

Preheat the broiler to high. Toast the baguette slices on a baking sheet until golden on each side. Sprinkle the cheese and parsley (if using) evenly over the toasts. Broil the cheese-topped bread until the cheese is bubbly and golden. Ladle an equal amount of soup into each of 6 bowls. Top with a cheese crouton and serve immediately.

Soup

This Italian-inspired soup is hearty and heartwarming. In Italian, the word *minestrone* means "big soup," since it is thick and stew-like; this version certainly lives up to that description. (*Minestrina,* on the other hand, means "little soup," which is a thinner, brothier concoction that wouldn't be appropriate for a main course).

In its most authentic form, minestrone is a vegetable-based soup that contains pasta and sometimes beans. My supremely hearty version contains both of these ingredients as well as leftover cooked meat. And, like the Italian original, it is topped with a generous amount of flavorful Parmesan cheese. Although this soup is already a rich and filling meal, I love to dip in slabs of crusty Italian bread that have been spread thickly with butter. Yum!

Minestrone Soup

PREP: 15 minutes | **COOK:** 45 minutes | **YIELD:** 4 to 6 servings

2 tbsp (15 mL) olive oil
2 onions, peeled and chopped
2 carrots, peeled and sliced
2 celery stalks, sliced
2 cloves garlic, minced
1 tbsp (15 mL) tomato paste
1 tsp (5 mL) dried thyme leaves
½ tsp (2 mL) dried oregano leaves
½ tsp (2 mL) pepper
1 bay leaf
1 cup (250 mL) diced, leftover cooked beef, pork or chicken
1 cup (250 mL) canned diced tomatoes, with juices
5 cups (1.25 L) chicken broth
1 cup (250 mL) cooked short pasta such as oricchiette
1 cup (250 mL) cooked lima beans or fava beans (thawed if frozen)
¼ cup (50 mL) chopped fresh parsley
Salt and pepper to taste
¼ cup (50 mL) shaved Parmesan cheese

Heat the oil in a Dutch oven set over medium heat. Add the onions, carrots, celery, garlic, tomato paste, thyme, oregano, pepper and bay leaf. Stir until well combined. Partially cover and cook the vegetable mixture, stirring frequently, for 10 minutes or until the vegetables are softened. Add the meat, tomatoes and chicken broth.

Increase the heat to high and bring the soup to a boil. Reduce the heat to low and simmer for 30 minutes or until the vegetables are tender. Stir in the pasta, beans and parsley. Cook until heated through. Taste and season with salt and pepper as needed. Ladle the soup into bowls and sprinkle each one with an equal amount of Parmesan cheese.

OVEN-DRIED TOMATO, ASIAGO AND PESTO PIZZA
page 125

CARAMELIZED ONION, FIG AND GORGONZOLA PIZZA
page 126

FAMILY-SIZE STROMBOLI

page 129

HONEY GARLIC BRAISED PORK CHOPS AND BOK CHOY
page 141

CHEESE-WRAPPED SAUSAGES WITH ONIONS AND APPLES
page 143

BRIE AND CRANAPPLE STUFFED PORK TENDERLOIN
page 151

BAKED TRIANGLE TOAST SANDWICHES
page 160

ROASTED GARLIC AND BALSAMIC SALMON ON A BUN

page 168

Chorizo, made with chunks of smoked pork, is truly one of the culinary gifts that Spain has shared with the world! Although the Mexican version, which is often used in dishes such as enchiladas, is also good, it is made with fresh pork and isn't as chewy as the Spanish original.

In this particular recipe, chorizo adds spiciness and richness, creating a complex and enjoyable lingering taste. If chorizo sausage isn't available, and all else fails, good ol' bacon will make a fine substitute.

Navy Bean and Tomato Soup with Chorizo

PREP: 15 minutes | **COOK:** 35 minutes | **YIELD:** 4 to 6 servings

1 tbsp (15 mL) vegetable oil

1 each carrot, celery stalk and onion, chopped

1 Spanish chorizo sausage, halved lengthwise and sliced into half-moons, or 3 slices of bacon, chopped

2 tbsp (30 mL) chopped fresh parsley

1 tsp (5 mL) dried thyme leaves

2 cloves of garlic, minced

¼ tsp (1 mL) each salt and pepper

1 bay leaf

1 can (14 oz/398 mL) diced tomatoes, with juice

4 cups (1 L) low-sodium chicken broth

1 can (14 oz/398 mL) navy or white pea beans, drained and rinsed

Heat the oil in a Dutch oven or large saucepan set over medium heat. Add the carrot, celery, onion, sausage, parsley, thyme, garlic, salt, pepper and bay leaf to the pan. Partially cover the pot and cook, stirring often, for 10 minutes or until the onion is very soft and the sausage is beginning to brown. Increase the heat to high and cook until the sausage is brown, about 2 minutes.

Stir in the tomatoes with their juice, scraping up the cooked-on browned bits from the bottom of the pan. Using the edge of the spoon, break up the tomatoes into smaller pieces. Add the broth and bring the soup to a boil. Reduce the heat and simmer for 15 minutes. Stir in the beans and simmer the soup for another 5 minutes. Remove the bay leaf.

Make once, eat twice: Double the ingredients and freeze the extra soup for another day.

Soup

If you love the rich, full taste of a bowl of steaming, homemade chicken soup but don't have the time to make it from scratch, this recipe offers a wonderful alternative that delivers fabulous flavor and comfort, too. Not only can this soup be completed and served in under an hour from start to finish, but the wonderful aroma in the house while it is simmering will draw everyone into the kitchen. In fact, you likely won't even have to call them to the table!

Although you can use leftover rice or cook some fresh especially for this recipe, the rice that is sold in pouches already cooked can be used, too. You can also add additional fiber and a slightly nutty flavor by using brown rice.

Roasted Chicken and Rice Soup

PREP: 20 minutes | **COOK:** 45 minutes | **YIELD:** 6 servings

1 rotisserie-roasted deli chicken
1 onion, peeled and sliced
8 cups (2 L) low-sodium or homemade chicken broth
2 tsp (10 mL) tomato paste
¼ tsp (1 mL) dried rosemary leaves
1 bay leaf
½ cup (125 mL) each finely diced carrot and celery
1 cup (125 mL) cooked rice

Remove and discard the skin from the chicken. Pull the meat from the bone and reserve on a clean plate, covered. Place the bones and onion in a soup pot. Add the broth, tomato paste, rosemary and bay leaf to the soup pot. Bring to a boil over high heat. Reduce the heat to medium-low and simmer for 30 minutes.

Strain the broth through a fine mesh sieve into a clean pot. Discard the bones and onion. Add the carrots and celery to the strained broth. Bring to a boil and cook for 15 minutes or until the vegetables are fork tender. Tear the reserved chicken into bite-size pieces. Add the meat and the rice to the soup. Heat for 2 minutes or until piping hot. Ladle into bowls and serve.

Called *Tom-Yum Goong* on many Thai menus, this lemongrass-scented soup is famously hot, sour and spicy. It's one of my favorite cold weather indulgences since its taste always transports me to the tropics and a bowl never fails to warm me through and through!

If you have trouble finding ingredients such as lemongrass and kaffir lime leaves in the produce section, check the freezer area of the grocery store. Many markets sell these items in frozen packages and, truly, I've found that the flavor of frozen kaffir lime leaves and lemongrass is actually much better than the dried or bottled varieties.

Tom Yum Soup with Shrimp

PREP: 10 minutes | **COOK:** 30 minutes | **YIELD:** 4 servings

1 tbsp (15 mL) vegetable oil
1 onion, peeled and coarsely chopped
1 tbsp (15 mL) minced ginger
1 tsp (5 mL) Asian chili sauce or sambal olek
2 lemongrass stalks, chopped
3 kaffir lime leaves (optional)
4 cups (1 L) low-sodium chicken broth
1 cup (250 mL) tomato juice
1 tsp (5 mL) fish sauce
½ cup (125 mL) very thinly sliced red peppers
4 extra-large shrimp or 12 medium-size shrimp, peeled and cleaned
1 pkg (14 oz/400 g) cooked udon noodles
½ tsp (2 mL) toasted sesame oil
½ cup (125 mL) fresh coriander leaves
½ cup (125 mL) mung bean sprouts, well rinsed
Chopped peanuts (optional)
Lime wedges

Heat the vegetable oil in a large pot or Dutch oven set over medium heat. Add the onion, ginger, chili sauce, lemongrass and lime leaves to the pot. Partially cover and cook, stirring often, for 10 minutes or until the onion is softened.

Add the broth and tomato juice; bring to a boil over high heat. Reduce the heat to low and simmer for 20 minutes. Remove the onion, lemongrass and lime leaves using a slotted spoon. Stir in the fish sauce.

Add the red peppers and cook for 1 minute. Add the shrimp and simmer for 2 to 4 minutes or until the shrimp become opaque. Add the udon noodles and sesame oil; stir well to separate the noodles. (If the noodles are difficult to separate, use two chopsticks or forks to gently break them apart.) Ladle an equal amount of soup into 4 large bowls. Top each bowl with an equal amount of coriander leaves and bean sprouts. Sprinkle with peanuts (if using); serve with lime wedges.

Cook once, eat twice: Double the broth ingredients and freeze. Add the red pepper, shrimp and noodles once the broth is boiling.

Soup

The appeal of foods from the Far East is complex. On the simplest level, we enjoy the flavors of Asian cuisine; but we also appreciate these foods for the healthful benefits so many of them offer. These are just a couple of the reasons why Asian flavors have become an established part of our home cooking in the last 20 years.

For nights when you're looking for something "fast and easy" and "light and healthful," this soup is ideal. You can substitute shrimp or scallops for the chicken if you like. And if you have chicken broth on hand, you can use that instead of the consommé.

Asian Ginger Chicken Soup

PREP: 10 minutes | **COOK:** 25 minutes | **YIELD:** 2 servings

- **4 cups (1 L) canned consommé**
- **2 tbsp (30 mL) soy sauce**
- **20 thin slices fresh, unpeeled gingerroot**
- **1 clove garlic, thinly sliced**
- **1 skinless, boneless chicken breast, about 8 oz (250 g)**
- **½ cup (125 mL) very finely diced red pepper**
- **3 green onions, thinly sliced**
- **1 cup (250 mL) cooked capellini or angel hair noodles**

Combine the consommé, soy sauce, ginger and garlic in a saucepan; bring to a boil. Reduce the heat to low and simmer for 5 minutes. Remove the saucepan from the heat. Cover the pan and let stand for 10 minutes. Strain the broth; discard the ginger and garlic. Return broth to saucepan.

Bring the strained consommé mixture to a boil. Slice the chicken breast lengthwise into 3 pieces. Thinly slice each piece crosswise to make bite-size strips. Add the chicken to the consommé mixture and simmer for 2 to 3 minutes or until chicken is cooked through. Add the red pepper and cook for 2 minutes. Stir in the green onions and the noodles; cook for 1 minute longer.

Variation

Substitute 1 cup (250 mL) cooked brown or white rice for the noodles.

MAKE AHEAD: Prepare this soup up to the point of adding the red pepper, green onions and noodles. When ready to serve, bring the soup to a boil and proceed as directed.

Unlike the thick black bean soups eaten in many parts of Mexico and served in most North American restaurants, this soup is brothy and light bodied with a clean, fresh finish. The egg makes this soup substantial enough for dinner and makes it fun to serve and to eat, too. I've used sweet, white onions, which have exactly the clean taste and crunchy texture this soup needs; however, yellow cooking onions can be used, too.

I first tried this lovely soup in La Fortuna, a town near the Arenal Volcano in the Pacific Rainforest area of Costa Rica. Priscilla, a Costa Rican acquaintance of mine who lives in San Jose, Costa Rica, tells me this soup is quite popular throughout the country and that Costa Rican families eat it all the time.

Costa Rican Black Bean Soup

PREP: 10 minutes | **COOK:** 20 minutes | **YIELD:** 4 servings

1 tbsp (15 mL) vegetable oil
¼ cup (50 mL) finely diced white onion
¼ tsp (1 mL) ground cumin
1 can (19 oz/540 mL) black beans, drained and rinsed
6 cups (1.5 L) chicken broth
1 clove garlic, minced
½ cup (125 mL) roughly chopped fresh coriander leaves
4 hard-cooked eggs, peeled, but left whole

Heat the oil in a large saucepan set over medium-high heat. Add the onion and cumin and cook, stirring often, for 5 minutes or until the onion is softened. Stir in the beans, broth and garlic. Bring to a boil; reduce the heat to medium-low and simmer for 10 minutes.

Stir in the coriander and add the eggs; simmer the soup gently for 3 minutes. Turn the eggs occasionally. Ladle an equal amount of soup into 4 bowls, ensuring that each serving contains an egg.

In Greece, the word avgolemono refers both to a soup and to a sauce. Although both of these popular dishes have similar characteristics (each is a creamy, egg-thickened mixture that has a balancing tartness), the soup is thinner than the sauce. The soup version of avgolemono contains rice, which adds body and fullness to the broth.

Although light and frothy, this soup is quite rich and therefore filling so can easily be served as a main course. I recommend pairing avgolemono with mixed salad greens dressed in a tart vinaigrette that will cut the richness of the egg.

Boiling the soup after adding the eggs will ruin the texture of this soup—the protein in the eggs will congeal.

Because bottled lemon juice can have a metallic taste when used in quantity, it's important to use fresh lemon juice in this delicately flavored soup.

Avgolemono

PREP: 5 minutes | **COOK:** 20 minutes | **YIELD:** 4 servings

   6 cups (1.5 L) low-sodium chicken broth
   ⅓ cup (75 mL) long-grain white rice
   8 egg yolks
   5 tbsp (75 mL) fresh lemon juice
   Salt and pepper
   2 tbsp (30 mL) chopped fresh parsley

Bring the broth to a boil in a large saucepan. Stir in the rice and cook for 15 minutes or until the rice is tender.

Place the egg yolks and the lemon juice in a bowl and whisk until frothy. Whisking constantly, drizzle in about 1 cup (250 mL) of hot broth.

Reduce the heat under the soup to low. Stirring constantly, whisk the egg yolk and broth mixture into the saucepan. Cook, stirring constantly, just until soup thickens, about 5 minutes. Do not boil. Add salt and pepper to taste. Stir in parsley and serve.

Containing just enough cream to add a silky texture, this soup has a deep, satisfying flavor that is very comforting. You can use either white or orange Cheddar, but just be sure that whichever Cheddar you use is well aged so that the bacon doesn't outshine the flavor of the cheese.

I love this soup with a piece of crusty bread and a chicory salad dressed with a cider vinegar or mustard-based dressing.

For a change, try Asian or regular pears as a garnish instead of apple.

SEE PHOTO INSERT

Cheddar and Bacon Soup

PREP: 10 minutes | **COOK:** 30 to 40 minutes | **YIELD:** 4 servings

1 tbsp (15 mL) vegetable oil
2 strips bacon
½ cup (125 mL) finely chopped peeled onion
1 tsp (5 mL) dried thyme leaves
½ tsp (2 mL) pepper
4 cups (1 L) low-sodium chicken broth
1 tbsp (15 mL) cornstarch
½ cup (125 mL) 35% whipping cream
3 cups (750 mL) shredded aged Cheddar cheese
½ tsp (2 mL) hot pepper sauce (approx)
1 Granny Smith apple, cored and julienned

Heat the oil in a deep saucepan set over medium heat. Add the bacon and cook until crisp. Transfer the bacon to a paper towel-lined plate and blot well. Reserve.

Add the onion, thyme and pepper to the pan; cook for 5 to 7 minutes or until the onion is softened. Whisk 1 cup (250 mL) of the chicken broth with the cornstarch until smooth. Stir the cornstarch mixture and the remaining chicken broth into the saucepan; bring to a boil. Simmer over low heat for 10 minutes or until slightly thickened. Stir in the cream.

Stirring constantly, gradually add handfuls of the cheese to the soup. Only add additional cheese to the pan once the first addition is fully incorporated into soup. Cook the soup for 5 minutes, stirring until the texture is silky, but do not allow the mixture to boil.

Strain the soup through a fine mesh sieve. Discard the onion and herbs. Stir in hot pepper sauce to taste. Ladle the finished soup into 4 soup bowls. Garnish each bowl with crumbled reserved bacon and apple.

This soup is perfect for a light, summertime meal. It's very similar to the classic French chilled potato soup called vichyssoise but I've updated and enhanced it with smoked salmon to make it more substantial for a main course.

Lovage is an herb that has a celery-like flavor. In fact, the French call it *celeri batard,* which translates as "false celery." Lovage grows very well in North American gardens and can be purchased in many gourmet green grocers; however, if you can't find lovage easily, substitute celery leaves for the lovage called for in this recipe. The taste will be very similar.

Cold Potato Soup with Lovage and Smoked Salmon

PREP: 10 minutes | **COOK:** 40 minutes | **YIELD:** 6 servings

3 tbsp (45 mL) butter
1 cup (250 mL) thinly sliced leeks, white part only
¼ cup (50 mL) chopped celery
2 tbsp (30 mL) chopped fresh lovage leaves
¼ tsp (1 mL) each salt and white pepper
3 cups peeled and diced russet potatoes, about 2 large
5 cups (1.25 L) chicken or vegetable broth
1 tsp (5 mL) lemon juice (approx)
1 cup (250 mL) 35% whipping cream
4 oz (125 g) thinly sliced smoked salmon
Lovage leaves

Melt the butter in a large saucepan set over medium heat. Add the leeks, celery, lovage, salt and pepper. Partially cover the pan and cook, stirring occasionally, for 10 minutes or until the celery is softened. Add the potatoes, broth and half the lemon juice. Bring to a boil. Reduce the heat and simmer for 30 minutes.

Remove this mixture from the heat and purée it in batches, in a blender. (Alternatively, purée the soup in the cooking pot using an immersion blender or over a bowl using a food mill.) Strain the soup into a clean bowl. Discard all the solid ingredients. Cover and refrigerate the soup until well chilled. Stir in the cream. Adjust the flavor by adding more lemon juice, salt and pepper to taste.

Slice the salmon into long strips, each about 1½ inches (4 cm) wide. Shape each piece of salmon into a rosette by first rolling it into a fat log. Then, holding one end of the log between pinched fingers, gently ease open the other rolled end to make a rosebud-shaped garnish. (You'll need to roll the salmon strip tightly but not so tight that you can't open it into a rosette.) Reserve the rosettes. Ladle the cold soup into 6 chilled bowls. Garnish with a salmon rosette and lovage leaves.

Dana's **TOP TEN TABLE**

This slow cooker soup is a great introduction to Indian-style cooking. Indian curry paste is generally smoother tasting and easier to add to recipes than dry curry powder so I recommend that you purchase paste if you are just starting an Indian pantry.

When shopping for lentils, choose brown or green ones, or even Egyptian red lentils for this particular dish. They cook down to a lovely soft consistency that will create a satisfying thick soup. The more expensive du Puy lentils favored by French chefs still have their seed coat on so they stay quite firm even after slow cooking, and that is not what you want here.

Chop the onion and carrot in the food processor for even easier preparation.

Slow Cooker Curried Lentil Soup with Spinach

PREP: 10 minutes | **COOK:** 6 hours | **YIELD:** 8 servings

1 tbsp (15 mL) vegetable oil

1 onion, peeled and finely chopped

1 carrot, peeled and finely chopped

2 cloves garlic, minced

1 tbsp (15 mL) mild Indian curry paste

1 tsp (5 mL) each ground cumin and pepper

¾ tsp (3 mL) each ground allspice and coriander seed

2 tbsp (30 mL) tomato paste

1½ cups (375 mL) dried brown or green lentils, sorted and rinsed

6 cups (1.5 L) vegetable broth

⅓ cup (75 mL) lemon juice

3 cups (750 mL) lightly packed fresh baby spinach

Lemon juice

Plain yogurt (optional)

Heat the oil in a large skillet set over medium heat. Add the onion and carrot to the pan and cook until the vegetables are lightly browned. Stir in the garlic, curry paste, cumin, pepper, allspice, coriander and tomato paste. Cook for 2 minutes, stirring. Transfer the sautéed ingredients to the slow cooker.

Add the lentils, vegetable broth and lemon juice to the slow cooker. Stir to combine. Cook, on high heat for 6 hours or on low heat for 10 hours, until the lentils are tender. Turn off the slow cooker. Remove 2 cups (500 mL) of the soup and purée in the blender. Stir the puréed soup back into the remaining soup along with the spinach. Let stand, covered, for 5 minutes.

Adjust seasonings and add extra lemon juice to taste. Garnish each serving with a dollop of yogurt (if using).

This soup is probably one of the most attractive color combinations I've ever created. The lovely, soft orange of the carrot mixture and the verdant green of the coriander drizzle are truly striking. The flavor is balanced and only slightly sweet so eating a filling portion of this soup is very easy.

Adding sour cream to the carrot soup makes the soup silkier and slightly smoother; however, this soup is also very good when made as a dairy-free version.

Although this soup can be made ahead and frozen very successfully, the coriander drizzle should be prepared just before serving to preserve the fresh flavor and vivid color. To drizzle the coriander mixture into the soup you can use a spoon, or, for the best looking presentation, a squeeze bottle. Use any leftover coriander swirl as a marinade for fish; or combine one part white wine vinegar with 3 parts coriander swirl to make a delicious salad dressing.

SEE PHOTO INSERT

Double Coriander and Carrot Soup

PREP: 20 minutes | **COOK:** 45 minutes | **YIELD:** 4 to 6 servings

2 tbsp (30 mL) vegetable oil

2 lb (1 kg) carrots, peeled and sliced

1 large onion, peeled and chopped

½ tsp (2 mL) ground coriander

¼ tsp (1 mL) each salt and pepper

1 bay leaf

4 cups (1 L) vegetable or low-sodium chicken broth

1 tsp (5 mL) cider or red wine vinegar (approx)

½ cup (125 mL) sour cream (optional)

Thinly sliced red onion, for garnish

CORIANDER SWIRL:

2 cups (500 mL) loosely packed coriander leaves

½ cup (125 mL) extra virgin olive oil

¼ cup (50 mL) lemon juice

¼ tsp (1 mL) each salt and pepper

1 clove garlic, minced

Heat the vegetable oil in a Dutch oven set over medium heat. Add the carrots, onion, ground coriander, salt, pepper and bay leaf. Partially cover the pan and cook, stirring often, for 10 minutes or until the onions are softened.

Add the broth and bring to a boil. Reduce the heat and simmer the soup for 30 minutes or until the carrots are very soft. Remove and discard the bay leaf. Working in batches, purée the carrot mixture and transfer it to a clean saucepan. Taste and add up to 1 tsp (5 mL) of the cider vinegar as needed to balance the flavors.

Heat the soup over medium heat until hot throughout but not boiling. Whisk in the sour cream (if using).

Meanwhile, to make the coriander swirl, combine the coriander leaves, extra virgin olive oil, lemon juice, salt, pepper and garlic in a blender or mini chopper.

Ladle the soup into bowls. Drizzle a little of the coriander mixture over top of each bowl to make an attractive design; serve leftover swirl on the side as a condiment. Sprinkle each bowl of soup with a few slices of red onion.

Although all chowders are soups, not all soups are chowders. Generally speaking, chowders differ from soup in that they are chunky and quite thick.

The cozy feeling I get when eating this soup reminds me of sitting in front of a roaring fire on a cold night. This particular chowder can be made very quickly using common pantry ingredients. If fat and calories are not a particular concern, do make it with the optional cream since it adds silkiness and heft to the mixture. Even without the cream this chowder is still far better than any of its canned cousins.

Easy Clam Chowder

PREP: 10 minutes | **COOK:** 30 minutes | **YIELD:** 4 to 6 servings

1 tbsp (15 mL) vegetable oil
2 strips of bacon, chopped
1 onion, peeled and chopped
1 clove garlic, minced
3 cups (750 mL) peeled, cubed potatoes
1 can (7 oz/198 g) baby clams, with juices
1 cup (250 mL) bottled clam juice or chicken broth
2 cups (500 mL) milk
½ cup (125 mL) light cream (optional)
Salt and pepper
2 tbsp (30 mL) chopped fresh parsley

Heat the oil in a saucepan set over medium heat. Add the bacon and cook, stirring, for 3 to 5 minutes or until browned. Drain off all but 1 tbsp (15 mL) of the fat.

Reduce the heat to low and add the onion. Cook, stirring often, for 5 minutes. Add the garlic and potatoes. Drain the clams and reserve the juices. Add reserved clam juices, additional 1 cup (250 mL) of clam juice and milk to the pan. Bring to a boil. Reduce the heat to medium-low and simmer for 20 minutes or until the potatoes are fork tender.

Stir in cream (if using) and the drained clams. Taste the soup and add salt and pepper to taste. Heat the soup until steaming hot but not boiling. Stir in parsley.

Cream of mushroom soup is a homey favorite that moms of yore have served by the gallon. When served with crusty rolls and a crisp lettuce salad or vinaigrette-dressed coleslaw, this soup can easily be the main course for a fast, easy supper. Although it is perfectly delicious when made with button mushrooms, shiitake or cremini mushrooms add nice color and deepen the flavor—a plus for mushroom lovers.

Even though the lemon zest is an optional ingredient, I recommend adding it since its gentle tartness nicely balances the creaminess of the soup base.

Hearty Cream of Mushroom Soup

PREP: 10 minutes | **COOK:** 20 to 25 minutes | **YIELD:** 4 servings

1 tbsp (5 mL) vegetable oil

1 small onion, peeled and chopped

6 cups (1.5 L) sliced button, shiitake or brown mushrooms

2 tsp (10 mL) finely chopped fresh thyme or 1 tsp (5 mL) dried thyme leaves

¼ tsp (1 mL) finely grated lemon zest (optional)

¼ tsp (1 mL) each salt and pepper

2 tbsp (30 mL) butter

3 tbsp (45 mL) all-purpose flour

2 cups (500 mL) each chicken or vegetable broth and milk

In a deep saucepan set over medium heat, heat the oil. Add the onion and cook, stirring occasionally, for 5 minutes. Increase the heat to high and add the mushrooms. Cook, stirring often, for 5 minutes or until the vegetables are browned. Stir in the thyme, lemon zest (if using), salt and pepper; cook for 30 seconds and remove from the heat. Transfer the vegetable mixture from the cooking pot to a bowl.

Return the pan to the stovetop but reduce the heat to medium-low. Melt the butter and sprinkle in the flour. Blend until well combined and flour is lightly browned. Add a splash of broth and whisk this mixture until smooth. Add the remaining broth and milk; whisk until blended. Increase the heat and, stirring, bring the soup to a boil.

Cook, stirring continuously, for 5 minutes or until the mixture is slightly thickened. Stir in the mushroom mixture and any accumulated juices in the bowl. Cook, stirring, for 8 to 10 minutes longer or until the soup is thickened. Taste and adjust seasoning if necessary. Let stand for 5 minutes before serving.

Cook once, eat twice: Make a double recipe and freeze half of the finished soup for a family supper or in individual portions for grab-and-go meals.

This soup is inspired by the excellent home cooks of Canada's Gaspé region, where apple orchards, dairy farms and plenty of fresh oysters are easy to find. This rich soup has a complex and exciting flavor but is simple to make. One of the shortcuts I often take is to buy already shucked oysters that are sold in plastic containers at my local fish store. Not only does this shortcut make it easier to prepare this soup when I'm hungry or rushed, but it means I'm not paying for a bunch of heavy shells that will need to be disposed of later.

You can substitute ¼ cup (50 mL) apple juice for the calvados, pommeaux or cider.

St. Lawrence Oyster and Apple Soup

PREP: 15 minutes | **COOK:** 10 minutes | **YIELD:** 4 servings

2 tbsp (30 mL) butter
1 small onion, peeled and finely chopped
1 small apple, peeled, cored and finely chopped
½ cup (125 mL) finely chopped celery
½ tsp (2 mL) salt
¼ tsp (1 mL) each ground nutmeg, cayenne and dry mustard
1 bay leaf
½ cup (125 mL) calvados, pommeaux or dry apple cider
2 cups (500 mL) fresh shucked oysters and their juices
1½ cups (375 mL) each milk and 35% whipping cream
Apple slices

Melt the butter in a large saucepan or Dutch oven set over medium heat. Add the onion, apple, celery, salt, nutmeg, cayenne, dry mustard and bay leaf. Cook, stirring often, for 5 to 7 minutes or until the onion is softened. Stir in calvados and stir for 1 minute or until the alcohol evaporates.

Add the oysters and their juices and cook just until the edges of the oysters begin to curl, about 2 minutes.

Pour in the milk and cream and heat the soup until steaming (but not boiling). Taste and adjust the seasoning if necessary. (Soup can be made to this point, cooled, covered and refrigerated for up to 1 day. If making ahead, reheat without boiling.) Ladle into 4 soup bowls and garnish each serving with a slice of apple.

Soup

A meal in a bowl, this hearty soup tastes like gourmet take-out but is so fast to make that you won't even have to wait for delivery.

Sea scallops are my favorite choice for this soup because they are so silky and smooth. Bay scallops will also work just fine in this recipe. Whichever type of scallops you use, be sure to pick off and discard the little knob-shaped muscle that is on the side of each scallop. Although this piece is edible, its function is to attach the scallop to the shell and, once cooked, can become tough. If using frozen scallops, place them in a colander and run cold water over them briefly until thawed.

Thai Coconut Noodle Soup with Scallops

PREP: 20 minutes | **COOK:** 30 minutes | **YIELD:** 4 to 6 servings

6 oz (175 g) whole wheat spaghettini or soba noodles
1 tsp (5 mL) sesame oil
3 cups (750 mL) light coconut milk
2½ cups (625 mL) vegetable or chicken broth
2 tbsp (30 mL) fish sauce
2 tbsp (30 mL) minced ginger
2 tbsp (30 mL) lime juice
1 tbsp (15 mL) mild Indian curry paste
2 tsp (10 mL) grated lime zest
1½ tsp (7 mL) hot pepper sauce (approx)
1 lb (500 g) scallops
½ red pepper, thinly sliced
¼ cup (50 mL) lightly packed fresh coriander leaves

Cook the noodles in boiling salted water for 10 minutes. Drain well. Toss the hot noodles with sesame oil and reserve.

Combine the coconut milk, broth, fish sauce, ginger, lime juice, curry paste and lime zest in a large saucepan set over high heat; bring to a boil. Reduce the heat and simmer the mixture for 15 minutes. Strain and discard all the solid ingredients. Taste the liquid and add hot pepper sauce to taste. Return the soup base to the pan.

Meanwhile, remove and discard the knob-shaped connective muscle on the sides of the scallops. Add the scallops and red pepper to the broth. Simmer for 3 minutes or until scallops are opaque and the peppers are slightly tender. Just before serving, stir in reserved the noodles and the coriander leaves.

Dana's TOP TEN TABLE

During the years that I was a food editor at *Gardening Life* magazine, I had an opportunity to learn about all kinds of exciting produce. One of my favorite stories to write was about the Grimo Nut farm in Niagara–on-the-Lake near the Canada-US border. The Grimo family grows chestnuts and dries them so that they can be stored and used anytime. I developed this lovely soup after that visit and although it may sound gourmet, it's actually a very easy recipe to make. The flavors are deep and earthy but the light, silky texture of the finished soup prevents it from being heavy.

I've made this soup with both rehydrated chestnuts from the Grimo farm as well as the kind that are sold cooked in vacuum-sealed bags at large and specialty grocery stores. Both versions produce a wonderful tasting soup. Unfortunately, the chestnuts sold in cans and jars don't taste nearly as good, so if you can't use fresh chestnuts or one of the other two varieties, I recommend you wait until the appropriate chestnuts are available.

Pancetta is Italian bacon that is cured with salt and spices but not smoked. If you can't find it, substitute a very mildly smoked bacon instead.

Recipe doubles easily.

Pancetta and Chestnut Soup

PREP: 10 minutes | **COOK:** 45 minutes | **YIELD:** 2 to 3 servings

    1 tbsp (15 mL) butter
    2 shallots, peeled and finely chopped
    ¼ cup (50 mL) each chopped celery and carrot
    2 cloves garlic, minced
    2 tsp (10 mL) chopped fresh thyme
    1 bay leaf
    ¼ cup (50 mL) chopped sweet pancetta
    ½ tsp (2 mL) ground pepper
    2 tbsp (30 mL) dry sherry
    4 cups (1 L) chicken broth
    2 cups (500 mL) chopped chestnuts
    ⅓ cup (75 mL) 35% whipping cream
GARNISH:
    2 slices sweet pancetta
    3 thinly sliced cooked chestnuts

Melt the butter in a deep saucepan set over medium heat. Add the shallots, celery, carrot, garlic, thyme and bay leaf. Partially cover and cook, stirring often, for 5 to 7 minutes or until the vegetables are very soft. Increase the heat to medium-high and add the pancetta and pepper. Cook stirring, for 3 minutes or until browned. Add the sherry and stir to scrape up any cooked-on bits.

Stir in the broth and chestnuts and bring to a boil. Reduce the heat to medium-low and simmer the broth mixture for 30 minutes. Remove the bay leaf and purée the soup in batches in the blender, until very smooth. Strain if necessary. Stir in cream. Taste and adjust seasoning if needed. Reheat without boiling.

GARNISH: Place pancetta in a skillet set over medium-high heat. Cook, turning as needed, until crisp. Blot on paper towel and slice into long strips. Toss with sliced chestnuts to combine. Ladle soup into small bowls and garnish with a little of the pancetta mixture.

Parsnips are one of the most under-used yet commonly available vegetables. They were introduced to North America in the 1600s but have never gained the popularity of other root veggies such as carrots and turnips. I think the reason many people dislike this vegetable is because they have been served dishes made with parsnips that were picked too early in the season. Parsnips need to be picked after the first frost since it is this shock of cold that converts their natural starches to sugar and makes them palatable. This recipe uses a gentle, moist cooking method that further coaxes out the natural sweetness of this long thin, ivory-colored vegetable, making this soup sure to please.

The flavors in this soup are inspired by the recipe repertoire of my husband, chef Martin Kouprie. He first made a similar version of this soup at his Toronto restaurant Pangaea. I love it since it is thick and satisfying but cream-free and low calorie. It makes an excellent change from the ordinary. Try a bowl with a rustic breadstick and a legume-based salad for a homey, healthful dinner.

Lemon Parsnip Soup

PREP: 15 minutes | **COOK:** 40 minutes | **YIELD:** 6 to 8 servings

1 tbsp (15 mL) butter or vegetable oil
1 onion, peeled and chopped
2 tbsp (30 mL) chopped fresh thyme
1 tsp (5 mL) finely grated lemon zest
½ tsp (2 mL) salt (approx)
½ tsp (2 mL) pepper (approx)
6 cups (1.5 L) peeled, chopped parsnips
10 cups (2.5 L) chicken or vegetable broth
1 tbsp (15 mL) lemon juice
Thyme sprigs
Lemon slices

Heat the butter in a large saucepan set over medium heat. Add the onion, thyme, lemon zest, salt and pepper. Cook, stirring often, for 5 minutes. Add the parsnips, cover the pan and reduce the heat to medium-low. Simmer, stirring occasionally, for 10 minutes or until the parsnips start becoming tender. Stir in the broth and bring the mixture to a boil. Cook, stirring often, for 20 to 25 minutes or until the parsnips are very soft.

Transfer the parsnip mixture to a blender or food processor in batches. Purée until smooth; return each batch of purée to the pot. Stir in the lemon juice and bring to a boil. Taste and adjust seasonings if necessary. Serve soup garnished with thyme sprigs and lemon slices.

When made with frozen or rinsed canned black beans, this soup can be prepared in about 15 minutes, which makes it a perfect recipe for a busy weeknight meal. If you find you really like black bean soup and you've got more time to cook, you might also like to try the Costa Rican Black Bean Soup on page 183.

Black bean skins don't break down completely in a blender or food processor. If you want a finer texture, use a food mill for the puréed portion of this soup.

Kitchen Cupboard Black Bean Soup

PREP: 10 minutes | **COOK:** 15 minutes | **YIELD:** 4 servings

- 1 tbsp (15 mL) vegetable oil
- 1 onion, peeled and chopped
- 2 cloves garlic, minced
- 1 tsp (5 mL) each chili powder, dried oregano leaves and ground cumin
- 1 can (28 oz/796 mL) diced canned tomatoes, with juices
- 2 cans (19 oz/540 mL each) black beans, drained and rinsed
- 1½ cups (375 mL) chicken or vegetable broth
- 1 cup (250 mL) corn kernels
- ¼ cup (50 mL) chopped fresh coriander
- 1 tbsp (15 mL) lime juice
- Salt and pepper (optional)
- Sour cream (optional)

Heat the oil in a deep saucepan set over medium heat. Add the onion, garlic, chili powder, oregano and cumin. Cook, stirring occasionally, for 5 minutes. Add the tomatoes with their juices, black beans and broth. Bring to a boil and cook, stirring often, for 5 minutes.

Purée 2 or 3 cups (500 to 750 mL) of the soup using a blender, food processor or food mill and return to the pan. Stir in the corn, coriander and lime juice. Taste and adjust seasoning by adding salt and pepper if necessary. Garnish each bowl with a dollop of sour cream (if using).

Soup

This velvety smooth soup, bursting with vitamin A, tastes so rich and wonderful that it's hard to imagine it is so easy to make. Teaming coconut, curry and lime with the sweet potato tempers this vegetable's natural sweetness and creates a rounded, complex but pleasing flavor that can't be duplicated by a canned soup.

When shopping for sweet potatoes, read the signs in the produce section carefully. Often sweet potatoes are labeled "yams" mistakenly. The good news is that true yams are hard to find unless you go to a Latino market. Botanically, sweet potatoes belong to the morning glory family and come in pale-skinned and red-skinned varieties. Both of the common varieties have a pale orange flesh that becomes quite a vivid orange when cooked. Yams, which come from a different family of plants and are used in West Indian and Latino cooking, are usually off-white or yellow under their skin.

Sweet Potato Coconut Soup

PREP: 5 minutes | **COOK:** 25 minutes | **YIELD:** 3 to 4 servings

1 tbsp (15 mL) vegetable oil
1 small onion, peeled and chopped
½ tsp (2 mL) mild Indian curry paste
1 lb (500 g) peeled sweet potato, about 1 large
1 clove garlic, chopped
3 cups (750 mL) chicken or vegetable broth
1 cup (250 mL) coconut milk or light coconut milk
1 tsp (5 mL) lime zest, finely chopped
2 tsp (10 mL) lime juice (from zested lime)
2 tbsp (30 mL) chopped fresh coriander
½ tsp (2 mL) pepper
Salt
6 to 8 peeled, deveined, cooked shrimp (optional)

Heat the oil in a medium pot set over medium heat. Add the onion and curry paste and cook, stirring often, for 5 minutes. Meanwhile, chop the sweet potato into small pieces. Add the sweet potato and garlic to the pot and cook, stirring often, for 10 minutes or until potato is slightly softened. Stir in the chicken broth and bring the mixture to a boil. Reduce the heat to medium-low and simmer, covered, for 10 to 15 minutes or until potato is soft.

Transfer the soup in batches to a blender or food processor and purée until smooth. Return the soup to the pan and stir in the coconut milk. Using a zester or a hand grater, remove the zest from the lime and chop finely. Add 1 tsp (5 mL) of the zest to the soup. Juice the lime and add 2 tsp (10 mL) of the juice to the soup. Stir in the coriander, pepper and salt to taste. Stir in the shrimp (if using) and cook for 2 to 3 minutes or until heated through.

Cook once, eat twice: Double the soup ingredients and divide the batch in half before adding the shrimp. Freeze one half, but add the shrimp only after reheating.

Steak

It's easy to understand why steaks have been on our top 10 dinnertime entrée list for more than 20 years. Busy people who like to eat well know that beef steaks are the ultimate gourmet convenience food since a delectable, tender cut of steak can be cooked and ready to serve in less than 15 minutes. Steaks usually need very little preparation to taste good, another reason they're an attractive mealtime choice.

One of the trickiest tasks for new cooks is learning the different names for various steak cuts. This learning curve is lengthened by the fact that the names for many steaks change not just from country to country but regionally. The good news is that if you describe the cooking method you plan to use to a capable butcher, they should be able to recommend an appropriate cut. So don't hesitate to ask for assistance if you don't see exactly what you're looking for on display.

When buying steaks, choose meat that is moist but not wet and that has a thin ribbon of fat around the edge and many small, white veins of fat distributed throughout the lean. These qualities ensure that the meat will be juicy and flavorful when cooked. Food scientists assure us that the marbled fat in the lean will render during cooking so this fat is not a big dietary concern. As far as the ribbon fat is concerned, trim it away after cooking to avoid consuming extra saturated fat.

This chapter, like the others in this book, features recipes inspired by diner culture, such as Swiss Steaks with Onions and Mushrooms, as well as culinary adventures like Martini Steaks and Rib-eye Steaks with Stilton and Port.

Although made traditionally from minced and not whole steak, this entrée, by virtue of its name, belongs in the steak chapter.

As our awareness about the ill effects of dietary fat has grown, more and more home cooks have switched from regular to lean ground beef. The change isn't a problem for dishes such as chili or Sloppy Joes; however, for patties like these ones, the grade of beef you choose is vitally important.

To enjoy maximum flavor and have the best texture, regular ground beef is really the best choice for this retro diner classic. I recommend splurging once in a while and making this entrée and then serving it with buttery mashed potatoes. The mental health benefit is sure to be at least as important as any edge you might get from making this meal with lean ground beef or sirloin.

Smothered Salisbury Steaks

PREP: 10 minutes | **COOK:** 20 minutes | **YIELD:** 6 servings

2 tbsp (30 mL) vegetable oil
1 onion, peeled and minced
1 egg, beaten
1 tbsp (15 mL) Worcestershire sauce
½ tsp (2 mL) each dry mustard, salt and pepper
1 clove garlic, minced
1½ lb (750 g) regular ground beef (see note at left)

SAUCE:
1 onion, peeled and sliced
2 cups (500 mL) beef broth, divided
1½ cups (375 mL) thickly sliced mushrooms
2 tbsp (30 mL) ketchup
1 tbsp (15 mL) cornstarch

Preheat oven to 200°F (95°C). Heat half the oil in a large skillet set over medium heat. Add the minced onion and cook, stirring often, for 5 minutes. Cool slightly. Combine the cooked onion, egg, Worcestershire sauce, mustard, salt, pepper and garlic in a large bowl. Stir until well blended. Crumble in the meat and stir gently until combined evenly. Divide the meat mixture into 6 equal-size patties. Using the tail end of a butter knife, score the top of each patty to make three horizontal, equally spaced impressions.

Heat the remaining oil in the skillet used to cook the onions. Increase the heat to medium-high and add the patties, lined side up. Cook each Salisbury steak for 10 minutes, turning 3 or 4 times or until cooked through. Transfer to a baking sheet and keep warm in the oven.

SAUCE: Drain off all but 1 tbsp (15 mL) of the fat in the skillet. Set the skillet over medium heat. Add the onion and ¼ cup (50 mL) of the beef broth; cook for 2 minutes, stirring and scraping up any cooked-on bits from the bottom of the pan. Stir in the mushrooms and increase the heat to medium-high. Cook, stirring often, for 3 minutes.

Stir the ketchup into the remaining beef broth. Whisk in the cornstarch until smooth. Pour into the mushroom mixture and bring to a boil. Reduce the heat to low and simmer, stirring, for 3 to 5 minutes or until the sauce is thickened and glossy. Taste the sauce and add additional salt and pepper if needed. Serve the warm Salisbury steaks smothered with gravy.

In England, this meal made from round or chuck steak is called "Smothered Steak." Truthfully, this moniker much better describes this meal since the meat truly is served smothered in a tomatoey gravy that contains toothsome pieces of mushroom and onion.

Swiss steak always reminds me of my grandmother; it was one of the meals she and I would make when my mom was working late. Then, when my parents would get home we'd all gather round the table, dig in and share the details of our day. Our favorite way to eat Swiss steak was with mashed potatoes and a crisp green salad dressed with oil and enough vinegar to cut the richness of the gravy. To me, this humble entrée always tastes like home!

Pounding meat with the side of a sturdy plate is a professional chef's technique—*sturdy* is the key word here. You can get much more pressure on the steak when you use the edge of a plate rather than a meat mallet. You don't want to use your everyday dishes for this, or your best china. You'll need a fairly thick, heavy plate, like the kind often used in cafeterias.

Swiss Steaks with Onions and Mushrooms

PREP: 15 minutes | **COOK:** 30 to 40 minutes | **YIELD:** 4 to 6 servings

¼ cup (50 mL) all-purpose flour
¼ tsp (2 mL) each salt and pepper
1½ lb (750 g) round steak, trimmed
2 tbsp (30 mL) vegetable oil
SAUCE:
1 tbsp (15 mL) vegetable oil
½ onion, thinly sliced
1 cup (250 mL) canned diced tomatoes, drained
1¼ cups (300 mL) chicken or beef broth
1 tsp (5 mL) dried thyme leaves
½ tsp (2 mL) each salt and pepper
2 cups (500 mL) sliced button mushrooms

Blend the flour with the salt and pepper in a shallow bowl. Cut the meat into palm-size pieces. Coat the meat on both sides in the flour mixture. Pound the meat with a metal tenderizing mallet or the edge of a sturdy plate. Pound it until the meat has almost doubled in size and begins to look lacy.

Heat the oil in a deep skillet or Dutch oven, set over medium-high heat. Brown the beef, working in batches, for about 1 minute per side. Remove portions as they become browned, and reserve.

SAUCE: Add the oil to the skillet used for browning the meat. Add the onion and cook, stirring often, over medium heat, for 5 minutes. Stir any of the remaining flour mixture into the onion. Stir the tomatoes, broth, thyme, salt, pepper and mushrooms into the skillet until well combined.

Add the browned meat and any accumulated juices back to the pan and bring the sauce to a boil. Reduce the heat to low. Cover the pan and cook for 30 to 40 minutes or until the beef is very tender.

Inspired by the diner-style steak dinners that were often "Blue Plate Specials" in the fifties and sixties, this economical steak entrée is well complemented by a classic condiment such as HP or A1 steak sauce. This is another classically retro entrée that just begs to be served with mashed potatoes and then followed by a slice of fruit or cream pie! Or, pile the steak, peppers and onions on a soft bun and serve this entrée as a sandwich. Either way, it will be a satisfying, homey meal that can be prepared in about half an hour.

Minute Steaks with Green Peppers and Onions

PREP: 10 minutes | **COOK:** 20 minutes | **YIELD:** 4 servings

2 tbsp (30 mL) vegetable oil (approx)
1 large onion, peeled and sliced
1 green pepper, sliced thinly
1 clove garlic, minced
2 tbsp (30 mL) vinaigrette-style salad dressing such as Italian
¾ cup (175 mL) dry bread crumbs
¾ tsp (4 mL) each salt, pepper and paprika
1½ lb (750 g) very thinly sliced minute or fast-fry steak
2 eggs, beaten

Heat half the oil in a nonstick skillet set over medium heat. Add the onions and cook, stirring often, for 5 minutes. Increase the heat to medium-high and add the green pepper. Stir-fry for 3 to 5 minutes or until the onions are very soft. Add the garlic and dressing and cook, stirring, for 1 minute. Transfer the cooked vegetables to a platter. Cover and keep warm.

Add the remaining oil to the skillet. Toss the bread crumbs with the salt, pepper and paprika until evenly combined. Spread this mixture out on a dinner plate. Pat each piece of steak dry with paper towel and dip into the egg. Coat each side in the crumb mixture and place in the skillet. Cook the prepared meat in batches for 2 minutes per side or until golden. Wipe the pan out with a piece of paper towel between batches and add extra oil as needed. Serve steaks topped with pepper mixture.

Although they seem as common as meatloaf and fried chicken, fajitas have only been a popular dinnertime choice for about three decades.

The Mexican word *fajita* translates to "little belt," which is fitting since the most authentic fajita recipes use skirt steak. This cut of meat comes from the diaphragm area where, if they wore them, a cow's belt would sit. Also sold as flank steak, skirt steak is a flavorful, lean, well-developed muscle that can be very difficult to chew if not marinated and cut properly. To make the fibers easy to chew, it is essential that the skirt steak be cut thinly across the grain.

My version of this classic Mexican recipe gives busy people the option of marinating the meat for as little as 15 minutes; however, the end result will be more delicious if marinated for a day or even two in advance.

Classic Fajitas

PREP: 25 minutes | **MARINATE:** 15 minutes
COOK: 10 minutes | **YIELD:** 4 servings

3 tbsp (45 mL) vegetable oil
2 tbsp (30 mL) lime juice
1 tbsp (15 mL) chili powder
2 cloves garlic, minced
½ tsp (2 mL) each ground cumin and dried oregano leaves
½ tsp (2 mL) hot pepper sauce
½ tsp (2 mL) each salt and pepper
1 skirt or flank steak, about 1 lb (500 g)
1 each red and green pepper, sliced
1 onion, peeled and thickly sliced
4 large wheat flour tortillas, warmed
Sour cream
Salsa
Guacamole
Shredded Cheddar cheese

Blend 1 tablespoon (15 mL) of the oil with the lime juice, chili powder, garlic, cumin, oregano, hot pepper sauce, salt and pepper in a large bowl. Cut the steak into long, thin strips and add to the marinade; turn to coat the meat all over. Let stand for at least 15 minutes or for up to 48 hours.

Heat a large cast iron or other skillet over medium-high heat. Add the remaining oil and the peppers and the onion. Stir-fry the vegetables for 3 to 5 minutes or until browned. Remove from the pan and reserve. Add the marinated meat and stir-fry for 3 minutes. Add the reserved vegetables and cook for 2 minutes or until all the meat and vegetables are well browned.

Place an equal amount of this mixture in the center of each tortilla and garnish with your choice of sour cream, salsa, guacamole and cheese. Roll up and serve immediately.

The first documented gastropub, The Eagle, opened in Clerkenwell, London, in 1991. Since then this restaurant concept, which features a relaxed atmosphere, excellent food and comprehensive beer and wine menus, has flourished. In fact, the interest in eating gourmet comfort food in England is so great that grocery stores in the UK now sell frozen lines of gastropub-style meals.

In North America, gastropubs are virtually unknown; however, the practice of bistros and casual restaurants updating classic comfort food recipes by adding upscale, posh ingredients or new flavors is common. This recipe for a steak pie is the sort of dish you might find on the menu at these restaurants. Using beef tenderloin tips not only adds a gourmet touch, it also greatly reduces the cooking time for the stew that makes up the base of this savory pie.

Gastropub Steak and Leek Pies

PREP: 20 minutes | **COOK:** 30 minutes | **YIELD:** 4 servings

1 tbsp (15 mL) butter
2 leeks, white part only, washed and sliced
½ tsp (2 mL) dried thyme leaves
1½ lb (750 g) beef tenderloin tips or cubed beef tenderloin
¼ cup (50 mL) all-purpose flour
¼ tsp (1 mL) each salt and pepper
1 tbsp (15 mL) vegetable oil
¼ cup (50 mL) red wine (optional)
1 cup (250 mL) beef or chicken broth
3 tbsp (45 mL) steak sauce
2 cloves garlic, minced
½ pkg (12 oz/350 g) frozen puff pastry, thawed
1 egg white, beaten

Preheat the oven to 425°F (220°C). Melt the butter in a deep skillet or Dutch oven set over medium heat. Add the leeks and thyme and cook for 5 minutes, stirring often, or until softened. Transfer the leek mixture to a plate. Reserve.

Cut the meat into bite-size pieces. Blend the flour with the salt and pepper in a large bowl. Add the meat and toss to combine. Increase the temperature under the skillet to medium-high. Heat the oil in the pan and add the meat in batches. Brown all over. Add each browned batch of meat to the leeks before browning the next batch of meat. Reserve.

Stir the red wine into the pan (if using), scraping up any cooked-on bits. Cook until the wine has reduced, about 45 seconds. Sprinkle any flour remaining in bowl into the pan and whisk in the broth until smooth. Add the steak sauce, garlic, and reserved leek and steak mixture. Bring to a boil. Remove from the heat.

Divide mixture between 4 buttered 1-cup (250 mL) ovenproof ramekins. Roll pastry out thinly and cut into 4 squares. Stretch each square to cover the dish and drape over the sides. Brush with egg and make several vent holes in the top. Bake the pies for 20 minutes or until pastry is golden. Use a knife to lift edge of pastry to see if it is cooked on the bottom. If underdone, drape loosely with a piece of foil to prevent the top from over browning. Bake for an additional 5 minutes or until cooked through.

Cook once, eat twice: Double the meat mixture ingredients and divide the second batch between 4 foil containers. Don't cover the pie with pastry before freezing. Instead, cover tightly with plastic wrap and freeze. Thaw and heat meat mixture in the oven. When warm, top with pastry and proceed as directed.

TOASTY SHRIMP NAANWICHES
page 176

BISTRO FRENCH ONION SOUP
page 179

CHEDDAR AND BACON SOUP

page 187

DOUBLE CORIANDER AND CARROT SOUP
page 190

RIB-EYE STEAKS WITH STILTON AND PORT
page 205

MUSHROOM LOVER'S CARPETBAGGER STEAKS
page 210

GRILLED ARGENTINE STEAKS WITH CHIMICHURRI SAUCE
page 213

**BOMBAY STEAK AND SWEET PEPPER KABOBS
WITH MINTED CHATNI SAUCE**

page 215

I have a feeling that the butcher who works at the food store I frequent cringes when he sees me coming. He and I have become locked in a heated battle about how to tie a rib-eye steak. To make them easy to handle, he trusses the rib-eye steaks very tightly. They look great raw, but once these pricey steaks hit the hot grill or skillet, the meat expands and strains against the string, which causes the steaks to curl and cook unevenly. So, if you find your rib-eye steaks curling, don't blame the meat or your cooking skills; instead, next time you shop ask the butcher to tie your rib-eyes more loosely or re-truss them yourself when you get home.

This full-flavored dinner features a combination of rich and flavorful beef, red wine and blue cheese, which makes it a real hit with many adults. Serve it with either a glass of the wine you used to make the sauce or another full-flavored red wine such as a zinfandel or amarone (my fav!).

SEE PHOTO INSERT

Rib-eye Steaks with Stilton and Port

PREP: 5 minutes | **COOK:** 9 to 13 minutes | **YIELD:** 4 servings

4 rib-eye steaks, each ¾ inch thick
1 tbsp (15 mL) each butter and olive or other vegetable oil
1 tsp (5 mL) each salt and pepper
¼ cup (50 mL) coarsely crumbled Stilton, Roquefort or other blue-veined cheese

SAUCE:
1 tbsp (15 mL) minced shallot or onion
1 rosemary sprig (optional)
½ cup (125 mL) port

Bring the steaks to room temperature for 15 minutes. Heat the butter and oil in a heavy skillet set over medium-high heat. Sprinkle the steak evenly with salt and pepper.

Place the steaks in the pan and cook for 4 to 6 minutes. Turn the steaks; reduce the heat to medium and cook for about 3 to 4 minutes for rare or 5 to 6 minutes for medium doneness. Remove the steaks from the pan and rest on a heated platter for about 5 minutes.

SAUCE: Add the onion and rosemary (if using) to the hot pan. Cook, stirring often, for 1 minute. Stir in the port. Boil for about a minute or until reduced. Remove and discard the rosemary sprig (if used).

To serve, drizzle the pan juices over the steaks and top each one with an equal amount of cheese.

If you were to cut a prime rib roast into steaks, the result would be rib steaks. This means that rib steaks are juicy, tender and well larded with flavorful fat. Most steak lovers are quite familiar with this piece of meat being cooked as a steak since rib-eye steaks are basically the same cut of meat. However, one preparation is cooked with the bone attached and one without. Leaving the bone on means that a rib steak is even juicier and more flavorful than a rib-eye.

The preparation for this steak recipe is wonderfully simple since, quite truly, this cut of meat needs very few additions to make it a special meal.

Go for the seventies steak house experience by serving these pepper-encrusted steaks with a baked potato with all the toppings and creamed spinach; or, update the presentation by serving the steaks with a side dish of mushroom risotto and steamed green beans or broccoli.

Peppercorn Rib Steaks

PREP: 10 minutes | **COOK:** 6 minutes | **YIELD:** 4 servings

½ cup (125 mL) steak sauce, such as A1 or HP
2 tsp (10 mL) each brown sugar and tomato paste
½ tsp (2 mL) lemon juice
½ tsp (2 mL) butter
2 bone-on rib steaks, about 2 lb (1 kg)
¼ cup (50 mL) cracked peppercorns
1 tsp (5 mL) salt

Preheat the grill to high. Blend the steak sauce with the brown sugar, tomato paste, lemon juice and butter until well combined. Spread evenly over both sides of each steak. Sprinkle the steaks evenly with cracked peppercorns and salt.

Place the steaks on the greased grate and cook for 2 minutes. Rotate each steak a half-turn and cook for 2 minutes longer. Flip the steak and repeat the above steps. Reduce the heat to medium-high and grill for 2 minutes for medium-rare or for up to 5 minutes for medium-well doneness.

Remove the steaks from the grate and let rest for 5 minutes before carving into portions and serving.

Because T-bone steaks are cut from a tender part of the cow, there truly is no need to marinate them. Instead, anything added to such premium cuts of meat is merely to enhance flavor.

In this recipe, a mopping sauce is used to baste the steak as it quickly cooks. Featuring butter, smoky chipotle peppers, lime and fresh coriander, the end result is a sensational, juicy steak that is thickly coated in southwestern flavors. All this steak needs to complement it is some corn on the cob or baked beans.

T-Bone Steaks with Chipotle Butter Mopping Sauce

PREP: 10 minutes | **COOK:** 10 to 16 minutes | **YIELD:** 2 to 3 servings

- 1 T-bone steak, about 1½ lb (750 g)
- ¼ cup (50 mL) melted butter
- 1 tbsp (15 mL) minced chipotle peppers or 1 tsp (5 mL) chipotle chili powder
- 2 tsp (10 mL) honey
- ½ tsp (2 mL) ground cumin
- ½ tsp (2 mL) finely grated lime zest
- 1 clove garlic, minced
- 2 tbsp (30 mL) chopped fresh coriander
- ½ tsp (2 mL) each salt and pepper

Bring the steak to room temperature for 15 minutes. Blend the butter, chipotle peppers, honey, cumin, lime zest and garlic together until well combined. Stir in the coriander. Divide this mixture in half and set each portion aside.

Preheat an indoor or outdoor grill to medium-high. Cut notches in the fat that surrounds the steak. Sprinkle evenly with salt and pepper and brush all over with one half of the reserved mopping sauce.

Place the steak on the grate and grill for 5 to 7 minutes per side for medium–rare or 7 to 8 minutes per side for medium doneness. Before serving, slather the steak all over with the second half of the mopping sauce using a clean brush. Rest for about 5 minutes on a heated platter before carving into portions.

It really doesn't matter if you shake or stir the marinade for this recipe; either way, the end result will taste remarkably like the famous drink but without the tipsy effects!

Beef tenderloin steaks are the perfect choice for this dish since they are already very tender and have a more delicate flavor than steaks cut from more developed muscles. Because they are so tender, the steaks require only a short marinating time, infusing the meat with flavor that enhances but doesn't overwhelm the wonderful taste of this excellent cut of beef.

For best results, use deli olives, which have a firm texture and better flavor than the canned or jarred varieties sold in the grocery store.

Martini Steaks

PREP: 10 minutes | **MARINATE:** 30 minutes
COOK: 10 to 12 minutes | **YIELD:** 4 servings

4 beef tenderloin steaks, about 6 oz (180 g) each
¼ cup (50 mL) dry vermouth
2 tbsp (30 mL) olive oil
1 clove garlic, minced
1 tsp (15 mL) finely grated lemon zest
¼ cup (50 mL) thinly sliced green olives
2 tbsp (30 mL) finely chopped fresh parsley
1 tbsp (15 mL) finely chopped red pepper
1 tsp (5 mL) gin
½ tsp (2 mL) each salt and pepper

Trim the steaks and place in a shallow dish. Blend the vermouth with the olive oil, garlic and lemon zest. Measure out 1 tbsp (15 mL) of the marinade and reserve in a small bowl. Pour remaining mixture over the steaks and turn to coat evenly. Let stand for 30 minutes at room temperature or overnight in the refrigerator. Meanwhile, combine the reserved marinade mixture with the olives, parsley, red pepper and gin; stir well.

Preheat an indoor or outdoor grill to medium-high. Sprinkle the steaks evenly with salt and pepper. Place on the hot grate and cook for 5 to 6 minutes. Turn and cook for 5 to 6 minutes longer or until cooked to medium doneness. Remove from heat and let rest for 3 to 5 minutes. Top each steak with an equal amount of the olive mixture and serve.

The traditional steak house version of surf 'n' turf usually features a juicy, thick-cut fillet steak served with a steamed lobster tail and garlic butter. In this updated version, the steak is a more flavorful strip loin and the seafood is shrimp, which has become the most popular seafood choice in North America.

I've also added an inventive twist to two classic American foods, just enough to make this meal exciting and appealing to people who may not be adventurous enough to try exotic or new flavors but who want a special meal that is out of the ordinary. Instead of butter, I've created a creamy sauce that has the distinct tang of horseradish, evoking both a traditional roast beef dinner and the ubiquitous cocktail sauce often associated with shrimp cocktail.

Surf 'n' Turf
with Creamy Horseradish Sauce

PREP: 10 minutes | **COOK:** 20 minutes | **YIELD:** 4 large servings

8 large shrimp, peeled and deveined
2 tbsp (30 mL) vegetable oil
4 strip loin or New York strip steaks, each about 8 oz (500 g)
¾ tsp (4 mL) each salt and pepper
¾ cup (175 mL) 35% whipping cream
3 tbsp (45 mL) each ketchup and drained, bottled horseradish
¼ tsp (1 mL) finely grated lemon zest
1 tbsp (15 mL) chopped fresh parsley
½ tsp (2 mL) lemon juice
Salt

Preheat an indoor or outdoor grill to medium-high. Cut the shrimp down the length of their backs with a sharp knife to butterfly. Toss the shrimp with enough oil to coat. Brush the remaining oil evenly over the steaks. Sprinkle steaks and shrimp with salt and pepper.

Bring the cream almost to a boil in a saucepan set over medium-high heat. Add the ketchup and horseradish and stir well. Stir in the lemon zest and cook, stirring, for about 2 minutes or until reduced and thickened enough to coat the back of a spoon. Remove from the heat and stir in the parsley and lemon juice. Taste and add salt if necessary. Keep warm.

Place the steaks onto the grate. Grill the steaks for 5 to 7 minutes per side or until medium-rare. Remove the meat from the grate and rest on a warm platter for 5 minutes. Meanwhile, place the shrimp on the grate with the cut side spread open and touching the grate. Cook for 2 to 3 minutes. Turn and grill on each side for about 1 minute or until the shrimp become opaque. Top each steak with two shrimp and drizzle some sauce on the plate around the meat.

This variation on a popular Australian steak dish is named for its shape and resemblance to a stuffed purse. In its original form, a pocket is cut into the side of a thick steak which is then packed until brimming with fresh oysters and seasonings. My version requires less effort to prepare since there is no oyster shucking. Instead, the stuffing mixture is a toothsome blend of canned smoked oysters and sautéed button mushrooms combined with buttery-tasting garlic bread crumbs.

The cut of beef used for carpetbagger steak should be a lean sirloin. The meat should be cooked to no more than medium-doneness so that it remains juicy and tender.

SEE PHOTO INSERT

Mushroom Lover's Carpetbagger Steaks

PREP: 15 minutes | **COOK:** 30 minutes | **YIELD:** 4 to 6 servings

FILLING:
- 1 tbsp (15 mL) each butter and vegetable oil
- 1 small onion, peeled and thinly sliced
- 8 oz (250 g) button mushrooms, coarsely chopped
- ½ tsp (2 mL) each salt and pepper
- 1 tbsp (15 mL) oyster sauce
- 1 tsp (5 mL) Worcestershire sauce
- 1 clove garlic, minced
- 1 can (3 oz/85 g) smoked oysters, drained
- 2 tbsp (30 mL) toasted fresh bread crumbs
- 1 tbsp (15 mL) chopped fresh parsley

STEAK:
- ⅓ cup (75 mL) red wine or beef broth
- 1 2-inch (5 cm) thick sirloin steak, about 2 lb (1 kg)
- 2 tbsp (30 mL) vegetable oil
- ¾ tsp (4 mL) each salt and pepper

FILLING: Heat the butter and oil in a large skillet set over medium-high heat. Add the onion and sauté, stirring often, for 5 minutes. Add the mushrooms and cook, stirring every minute or so, for 4 to 5 minutes or until golden all over. Reduce the heat to medium and stir in the salt, pepper, oyster sauce, Worcestershire sauce and garlic. Stir in the smoked oysters. Cook for 1 minute, stirring. Sprinkle with bread crumbs and parsley. Scrape into a bowl and cool to room temperature.

STEAK: Return the empty skillet to the stovetop and set over medium heat. Add the red wine to the pan, scraping up the browned bits with a spoon. Reserve.

Preheat the grill to medium-high. Using a sharp knife, cut a slit in the side of the steak to make a 2-inch (5 cm) wide pocket deep enough to contain the warm mushroom mixture. Secure the pockets closed with toothpicks or poultry pins. Brush the meat all over with oil and sprinkle evenly with salt and pepper.

Place the steak on the greased grate of the hot grill and cook for 3 minutes. Rotate the steak a quarter turn; baste with reserved juices and cook for 5 minutes longer, basting often. Turn and cook for 7 to 8 minutes, or until steak is cooked to medium-rare. Continue to cook 2 to 3 minutes longer for medium, basting often. Transfer the meat to a cutting board and let rest for 5 minutes. Slice thickly to serve.

Because kiwifruit contains an enzyme that quickly breaks down the connective tissues that can make sirloin steaks chewy, using a kiwi-based marinade is the perfect way to enhance the tenderness of these full-flavored steaks. (Other fruits that contain similar enzymes include pineapple, papaya and figs.) Be sure you don't leave the steak in the marinade for longer than called for—it may become over-tenderized and develop an unappealing, mushy texture.

Grilled Peppercorn Sirloin for Two

PREP: 10 minutes | **MARINATE:** 6 hours
COOK: 12 minutes | **YIELD:** 2 servings

1 large ripe kiwifruit
1 tbsp (15 mL) each cider vinegar and apple juice
½ tsp (2 mL) granulated sugar
¼ tsp (1 mL) each salt and pepper
¼ tsp (1 mL) hot pepper sauce
1 small clove garlic, peeled
3 tbsp (45 mL) olive oil
1 12-oz (375 g) sirloin steak, about 1½ inches (4 cm) thick
1 tbsp (15 mL) coarsely ground mixed peppercorns
½ tsp (2 mL) salt

Peel the kiwi and cut into chunks. Place the fruit in a blender or mini chopper. Add the cider vinegar, apple juice, sugar, salt, pepper, hot pepper sauce and garlic. Blend until smooth. With the motor running, drizzle in the olive oil. Cover and refrigerate for up to 2 days.

Trim the excess fat from the steak and discard. Place the steak in a shallow bowl or zip-top bag. Add the marinade and turn to coat the meat. Refrigerate for at least 6 hours but no longer than 24 hours.

Preheat grill to high. Remove meat from marinade. Discard marinade. Sprinkle meat evenly with pepper and salt. Grease the grate.

Grill the steak for 3 minutes. Rotate the steak a quarter-turn and cook for 3 minutes longer. Turn the steak over and cook for 3 minutes. Rotate the steak a quarter-turn and cook for 3 minutes longer for medium-rare doneness. Increase the cooking time as necessary for medium or greater doneness. Rest the steak on a cutting board for 5 minutes before slicing into two portions.

This recipe features one of the leanest steak cuts, which is great if you have to watch how much fat you consume. In fact, beef tenderloin steaks (also called tournedos) are so lean, they are sometimes wrapped in bacon prior to cooking to keep the meat from drying out. Rather than bacon to add moisture and flavor, I've used a mushroom relish here, which makes this steak dinner truly memorable. This warm, mushroom-based condiment has a tangy edge that cuts the richness of the beefsteak nicely but it isn't pickled like the bottled relishes used to top hamburgers and hot dogs.

Tenderloin Steaks with Fresh Mushroom Relish

PREP: 15 minutes | **COOK:** 20 minutes | **YIELD:** 4 servings

4 beef tenderloin steaks/tournedos
½ tsp (2 mL) each salt and pepper (approx)
2 tbsp (30 mL) each butter and vegetable oil
2 cups (500 mL) sliced cremini or other mushrooms
½ cup (125 mL) sweet onion, finely chopped
1 tbsp (15 mL) red wine vinegar
2 Roma (or plum) tomatoes, seeded and chopped
1 clove garlic, minced
¼ cup (50 mL) finely chopped fresh basil

Bring the steaks to room temperature for at least 15 minutes. Sprinkle evenly with salt and pepper. Heat half of the butter and half of the oil in a large heavy skillet set over medium-high heat. Add the steaks and cook for 5 minutes. Turn the steaks and reduce the heat to medium. Cook for 5 to 7 minutes or until cooked to medium-rare to medium doneness. Transfer the meat to a warm platter and keep warm.

Meanwhile, add the remaining butter and oil to the pan. Add the mushrooms and onion and sauté for 5 minutes or until browned. Stir in the red wine vinegar. Add the tomatoes and garlic. Remove the pan from the heat and stir in the basil. Taste and season with salt and pepper if necessary. Divide the relish evenly among 4 dinner plates. Top each relish portion with a steak. Serve immediately.

Argentina has the highest per capita meat consumption in the world and beef is usually Argentinians' protein of choice. As a result, there are many exciting steak dishes to be found in Argentine cuisine. One of the most popular and really terrific ones is chimichurri steak. Chimichurri is an Argentine basting and dipping sauce for grilled meats. In fact, it is as common in Argentina as ketchup is in North America. Fresh, tangy and utterly terrific-tasting, chimichurri is appearing more and more often on steak-house and fine-dining menus on this continent.

The most popular cuts of beef to be served with chimichurri sauce in Argentina are *Bife de Chorozo,* a steak cut off the rib that is a lot like a porterhouse, and *Bife de Costilla,* equivalent to our T-bone steak. Both of these cuts work very well in this recipe but my favorite is a rib steak, which is a well-marbled, flavorful cut that can stand up to the astringency of the sauce.

SEE PHOTO INSERT

Grilled Argentine Steaks with Chimichurri Sauce

PREP: 5 minutes | **MARINATE:** 15 minutes
COOK: 11 to 17 minutes | **YIELD:** 4 servings

SAUCE:
   3 tbsp (45 mL) red wine vinegar
   2 tbsp (30 mL) water
   4 cloves garlic, minced
   ¾ tsp (4 mL) salt
   ½ tsp (2 mL) dried hot red pepper flakes
   ½ tsp (2 mL) coarsely ground black pepper
   1 small bay leaf
   ¼ cup (50 mL) olive oil
   ½ cup (125 mL) finely chopped fresh parsley

STEAK:
   1 rib, T-bone or porterhouse steak, about 2 lb (1 kg)
   1 tsp (5 mL) salt

SAUCE: Stir the red wine vinegar with the water, garlic, salt, red pepper flakes, black pepper and bay leaf until salt is dissolved. Whisk in the oil and stir in the parsley. Divide this mixture in half.

STEAK: Brush the half of the sauce without the bay leaf evenly over the steak. Reserve the remaining sauce. Let the steak marinate for 15 minutes.

Preheat an outdoor grill to high. Use a sharp knife to cut notches in the thicker pieces of fat that surround the outside of the steak. Sprinkle the meat evenly with salt.

Grease the grate; place the steak on the grate. Reduce the heat to medium and cook, covered, for 6 to 7 minutes. Turn the steak and grill for 5 to 10 minutes longer or until medium-rare. Remove the steak and rest, loosely tented with foil, for 5 minutes. Cut meat into portions. Discard the bay leaf and stir the reserved sauce. Serve sauce alongside the steak, for dipping.

The classic flavors of Greek cooking include tangy dairy products such as yogurt and feta cheese as well as herbs such as marjoram and mint. Although the best-quality Greek feta cheese is made with sheep's or goat's milk, many of the commercial varieties sold in grocery stores are made from cow's milk. Whatever the source of the milk, feta is always a white, crumbly, rindless cheese, sold in a pool of salty whey that helps keep the cheese moist. Before adding feta to this or any other recipe, remove it from the whey.

While most home cooks often cook with mint, marjoram may not be as familiar. Marjoram is related to mint and is slightly milder than oregano but very similar in flavor. Besides flavoring many Greek foods, marjoram plays a large role in many Greek rituals, symbolizing happiness in both this life and the afterlife.

These lemony-flavored ribbons of thinly sliced steak are an ideal topper for a bed of shredded iceberg or romaine lettuce. Garnish with a few gaeta or kalamata olives for a fresh warm-weather dinner. Or, serve these steak skewers with garlic roasted potatoes and a cucumber salad or sautéed zucchini chunks for a hot supper.

Grecian Beef Ribbon Skewers with Yogurt and Feta Sauce

PREP: 15 minutes | **MARINATE:** 30 minutes
COOK: 5 minutes | **YIELD:** 6 servings

1½ lb (750 g) sirloin steak, trimmed
¼ cup (50 mL) lemon juice
2 tbsp (30 mL) honey
3 cloves garlic, minced
1½ tsp (7 mL) dried marjoram or oregano leaves
1 tbsp (15 mL) chopped fresh mint or ½ tsp (2 mL) dried mint leaves
Salt (optional)
SAUCE:
½ cup (125 mL) plain yogurt
⅓ cup (75 mL) crumbled feta cheese
1 tsp (5 mL) lemon juice
1 tsp (5 mL) chopped fresh mint leaves
1 small clove garlic, minced
½ tsp (2 mL) each black pepper and hot pepper flakes

Slice the steak across the grain into long, thin strips. Whisk the lemon juice with the honey, garlic, marjoram and mint. Toss the beef strips with this marinade mixture and let stand at room temperature for 30 minutes. Meanwhile, soak 24 wooden skewers in cold water for several minutes.

SAUCE: Stir the yogurt with the feta, lemon juice, mint, garlic, black pepper and hot pepper flakes until combined. Let stand for 15 minutes.

Preheat a broiler to high. Thread the beef strips onto the soaked skewers and place on a broiler pan or rack set over a rimmed baking sheet. Season with salt (if using). Broil (or grill) the beef, turning once, for about 5 minutes or until it reaches medium doneness. Serve with the dipping sauce.

Most of the chutneys sold in jars are cooked varieties based on recipes created by colonial Britons who wanted to recreate Indian foods when they returned to England. Although these chutneys have become popular even at Indian restaurants, the genuine hallmark of Indian cooking is the fresh condiment called chatni. The word *chatni* means "strong spices." Chatnis are more perishable than long-simmered chutneys; in fact, chatnis only last a day or two (at most) in the refrigerator.

When making chatni, the initial step is usually to grind herbs and spices such as ginger, chilies, mint, coriander and garlic. To such mixtures, sour ingredients such as tamarind, lime or lemon juice, yogurt, and occasionally fresh fruit purées are added. These fresh condiments add piquancy to traditional Indian meals, especially rice, lentils and grilled meats like these kabobs, which are only mildly spiced with curry.

SEE PHOTO INSERT

Bombay Steak and Sweet Pepper Kabobs with Minted Chatni Sauce

PREP: 30 minutes | **MARINATE:** 1 hour
COOK: 10 minutes | **YIELD:** 8 servings

2 tbsp (30 mL) vegetable oil
2 tbsp (30 mL) mild Indian curry paste
3 cloves garlic, minced
1 lb (500 g) boneless beef tenderloin or tenderloin tips
1 each red, green and yellow pepper
½ tsp (2 mL) each salt and pepper
½ cup (125 mL) plain yogurt
2 tbsp (30 mL) mango chutney
1 tsp (5 mL) ground cumin
Dash hot pepper sauce
10 fresh mint leaves

Stir the vegetable oil with the curry paste and half the garlic. Divide this mixture in half. Cut the beef into 1-inch (2.5 cm) cubes. Place the beef cubes and half the curry mixture in a large bowl or plastic bag; toss to coat meat with the curry mixture. Cover tightly and marinate in the refrigerator for at least 1 hour.

Remove the stems, seeds and white membranes from the peppers and cut into chunks. Toss the peppers with the remaining curry mixture and reserve.

Preheat the grill to medium-high. Thread equal amounts of cubed beef and peppers alternately onto metal or wooden skewers. (If using wooden skewers, soak them in water for a few minutes while the grill heats up.) Brush all over with any remaining marinade. Sprinkle the kabobs evenly with salt and pepper.

Grease the grate. Grill the kabobs, turning as they brown, on the greased grate for about 10 minutes or until the meat is medium-rare and distinct char marks are visible on each side. Let the kabobs rest for 5 minutes. Meanwhile, combine the remaining garlic, yogurt, chutney, cumin, hot pepper sauce and mint in a mini chopper, blender or food processor and blend until smooth. Serve the kabobs with chatni sauce on the side.

Inspired by the classic Korean barbecue dish called *bulgogi*, this savory steak recipe has broad appeal. In fact, one of the reasons bulgogi is known by so many Westerners is that this dish is often what Koreans serve to non-Koreans as a first taste of their cuisine.

Traditional mealtime accompaniments for this savory-sweet steak entrée are grilled onions and green peppers and steamed rice. Thinly sliced steak made in this style is also sometimes served with whole lettuce leaves that are used as the casing to wrap the steak, peppers and onions so that this meal can be eaten out of hand like tacos.

Korean Marinated Sirloin Steaks

PREP: 10 minutes | **MARINATE:** 45 minutes
COOK: 12 to 14 minutes | **YIELD:** 4 servings

- 1 thick sirloin steak, about 2 lb (1 kg)
- ½ cup (125 mL) soy sauce
- ¼ cup (50 mL) granulated sugar
- 3 tbsp (45 mL) sake, mirin or sweet sherry
- 2 tbsp (30 mL) sesame oil
- 6 cloves garlic, minced
- ¾ tsp (4 mL) black pepper
- ½ tsp (2 mL) toasted sesame seeds
- 1 green onion, thinly sliced

Trim the fat from the steak and place in a shallow baking dish or into a zip-top bag. Whisk the soy sauce with the sugar, sake, sesame oil and garlic. Pour the marinade over the steak and turn to coat. Cover tightly and refrigerate for at least 45 minutes or for up to 2 days.

Preheat an outdoor or indoor grill to medium-high. Remove the steak from the marinade and sprinkle all over with pepper. Place the steak on a lightly greased grate and grill for 6 minutes per side for medium-rare. Transfer to a cutting board; tent with foil and rest for 5 minutes. Slice thickly and sprinkle with sesame seeds and green onion.

Make once, eat twice: Freeze the steak in the marinade; thaw and grill as directed.

Pomegranate has soared to popularity as a flavoring for both sweet and savory foods over the last few years. One of the reasons for this is that these seed-filled fruits have been identified as a food that is rich in flavinoids—plant compounds that research is showing can produce a variety of antiviral, anti-carcinogenic, anti-inflammatory, antihistamine and cholesterol-lowering effects.

Another reason for the pomegranate's popularity is that this tart-sweet flavored fruit is wonderfully food friendly. Pomegranate molasses, which is available in most large grocery stores or at Middle Eastern and Persian stores, is a thick, syrupy reduction of pomegranate juice that has a rich, tart flavor. In this flank steak recipe the tart pomegranate and orange flavors penetrate and tenderize this muscular cut of meat without making it sweet.

Pomegranate Orange Steaks

PREP: 10 minutes | **MARINATE:** overnight
COOK: 12 to 15 minutes | **YIELD:** 4 servings

¼ cup (50 mL) thawed orange juice concentrate
3 tbsp (45 mL) pomegranate molasses
1 tbsp (15 mL) balsamic vinegar
2 tsp (10 mL) finely grated orange zest
2 cloves garlic, minced
½ tsp (2 mL) each salt, pepper and granulated sugar
½ tsp (2 mL) each ground cumin and paprika (preferably smoked)
⅓ cup (75 mL) olive oil
1 tbsp (15 mL) finely chopped fresh mint or rosemary leaves
1½ lb (750 g) flank or skirt steak

Blend the orange juice concentrate with the pomegranate molasses and balsamic vinegar. Stir in the orange zest, garlic, salt, pepper, sugar, cumin and paprika. Whisking, drizzle in the oil until well combined. Stir in the mint. Divide the marinade in half.

Place one half of the marinade in a microwaveable bowl and microwave at High for 2 minutes, stirring occasionally, or until glossy and slightly thickened. Reserve. Meanwhile, pour the remaining marinade over the steak; cover tightly and marinate in the refrigerator overnight.

Preheat the grill or broiler to high. Remove the steak from the marinade, shaking off the excess. Set the steak on the grate or broiling pan. Brush all over with reserved, boiled marinade. Grill, turning once and brushing with remaining marinade, for 12 to 15 minutes or until cooked to no more than medium doneness. Let rest for 5 minutes. Slice thinly across the grain and serve.

Sweet, crisp, plump snap pea pods filled with tender baby peas have long been a favorite vegetable of mine. That said, stringing snap peas so that they are edible is a task that always deterred me from making them on weeknights. Fortunately it's easier now to enjoy the health and culinary benefits of this delicious vegetable since bagged, pre-washed and pre-strung snap peas are now available in most supermarkets.

Vaguely inspired by the Chinese beef and snow pea stir-fries most fast-food Chinese restaurants feature on their menus, this sesame-flavored beef mixture goes well with rice or chow mien noodles.

Sesame Snap Pea and Steak Tangle

PREP: 15 minutes | **COOK:** 20 minutes | **YIELD:** 2 to 3 servings

STEAK:

   2 tbsp (30 mL) each hoisin and barbecue sauce

   1 tbsp (15 mL) vegetable oil

   1 strip loin steak, about 12 oz (375 g)

   ½ tsp (2 mL) each salt and pepper

VEGETABLES:

   1 bag (8 oz/227 g) trimmed snap peas

   2 tbsp (30 mL) toasted sesame oil

   1 cup (250 mL) very thinly sliced, halved and peeled red onion

   2 cloves garlic, minced

   ½ tsp (2 mL) salt and pepper

   2 tsp (10 mL) granulated sugar

   1 tbsp (15 mL) rice vinegar

   2 tbsp (20 mL) vegetable oil

   1½ tsp (7 mL) toasted sesame seeds

STEAK: Preheat an indoor grill to high or an outdoor grill to medium-high. Blend the hoisin and barbecue sauces with the vegetable oil; transfer to a shallow pan. Add the steak and turn to coat. Remove steak from the pan and sprinkle evenly with salt and pepper.

Lightly grease the grate. Grill the steak, turning once, for 7 to 8 minutes per side or until medium doneness. Let rest for 5 minutes.

VEGETABLES: Blanch the snap peas in boiling, salted water for 2 minutes or until bright green. Drain and plunge into ice water. Drain well in a paper towel-lined colander. Reserve in a large bowl.

Heat the sesame oil in a deep skillet or wok set over medium-high heat. Add the onion and stir-fry for 1 to 2 minutes or until softened but still slightly crisp. Stir in the garlic, salt and pepper. Add the onion mixture to the reserved snap peas; toss to combine. Stir the sugar with the vinegar until almost completely dissolved. Stir in the oil and drizzle mixture over vegetables. Toss to coat.

Thinly slice the steak across the width and add to the bowl with the vegetables. Sprinkle with sesame seeds and toss to combine.

Canadian whisky adds depth and a buttery flavor to this grilled steak, while orange juice and ginger provide a subtle fruity spiciness. Although the combination of steak and whisky sounds rather manly, rough and rugged, the finished dish is actually quite crowd-pleasing.

I call for Canadian whisky in this recipe as a show of patriotism and because the flavor of most Canadian whiskies is clean and rich without being too sweet. Although you can use other rye-based spirits in this dish very successfully, avoid using bourbon (which is too sweet for what you want here) or single-malt spirits (they can overwhelm the taste of the meat).

Whisky-marinated Flank Steaks

PREP: 5 minutes | **MARINATE:** 4 hours
COOK: 14 minutes | **YIELD:** 4 to 6 servings

½ cup (125 mL) Canadian whisky (see note at left)
¼ cup (50 mL) orange juice
2 tbsp (30 mL) brown sugar
1 tbsp (15 mL) vegetable oil
2 tsp (10 mL) pure vanilla extract
2 tsp (10 mL) ground ginger
3 cloves garlic, minced
¼ tsp (1 mL) hot pepper sauce
2 lb (1 kg) flank steak, about ¾ inch (1.5 cm) thick
½ tsp (2 mL) each salt and pepper

Stir the whisky with the orange juice, brown sugar, oil, vanilla, ginger, garlic and hot pepper sauce. Pour over steak; cover and marinate for at least 4 hours or up to 48 hours.

Brush marinade from the steak and reserve. Bring the meat to room temperature for 30 minutes. Meanwhile, preheat grill to medium-high and transfer the marinade to a small saucepan. Place saucepan over high heat and bring to a boil. Reduce heat to medium and simmer marinade until reduced by about half. Reserve.

Sprinkle steak evenly with salt and pepper. Place steak on lightly greased grate and brush liberally with reduced marinade. Cook, covered, for 7 minutes. Turn and brush with marinade. Grill for 5 to 7 minutes or until cooked to no more than medium doneness. Cool to room temperature. Slice thinly across the grain and serve.

Index